Orgasmic Bodies

Orgasmic Bodies

The Orgasm in Contemporary Western Culture

Hannah Frith
Principal Lecturer in Psychology, University of Brighton, UK

© Hannah Frith 2015

First published 2015 by
PALGRAVE MACMILLAN

Palgrave Macmillan in the UK is an imprint of Macmillan Publishers Limited, registered in England, company number 785998, of Houndmills, Basingstoke, Hampshire RG21 6XS.

Palgrave Macmillan in the US is a division of St Martin's Press LLC, 175 Fifth Avenue, New York, NY 10010.

Palgrave Macmillan is the global academic imprint of the above companies and has companies and representatives throughout the world.

Palgrave® and Macmillan® are registered trademarks in the United States, the United Kingdom, Europe and other countries.

ISBN 978-1-137-30436-0   ISBN 978-1-137-30437-7 (eBook)
DOI 10.1057/9781137304377

A catalogue record for this book is available from the British Library.

A catalog record for this book is available from the Library of Congress.

With love to Nancy, Melanie, Susan and Roger

Contents

Acknowledgements

Thanks to all those who have listened to me puzzling about orgasm, including my generous colleagues in the Department of Applied Social Science at the University of Brighton – especially Jayne and Orly. Special thanks to Kate, Thelma, Craig, Cristina, Sarah, Charles, Nicola, Mark, boozy book club and stitching folks for all your love and support. Some of the ideas in this book have been published in a different format and with a different focus as 'Sexercising to orgasm: Embodied pedagogy and sexual labour in women's magazines' in *Sexualities* (Forthcoming); 'Visualising the 'real' and the 'fake': emotion work and the representation of orgasm in pornography and everyday sexual interactions', *Journal of Gender Studies* (Forthcoming), and 'Ejaculatory timing and masculine identities: The politics of ab/normalising sexual performance', in J. Louth (ed.) *Edges of Identity: The Production of Neoliberal Subjectivities* (2015) Chester: University of Chester Press.

1
What Is an Orgasm and Why Does it Matter?

Explaining what exactly an orgasm is seems to become more elusive even as science tries to specify it more precisely. Indeed, some would argue that orgasm is a mystical and magical thing which should not be subject to too much scrutiny in case this mysteriousness is unravelled and spoiled. But what exactly orgasm is, is perhaps a less interesting question than why it matters. Scientific work on orgasm focuses on trying to establish definitively what an orgasm is, specifying the biological pathways through which physical sensation is perceived as pleasurable, and the mechanisms through which this 'response' is triggered. But the more interesting question – at least for social scientists – is why orgasm is seen as having such significance, to be worthy of such attention. Orgasm, and female orgasm in particular, has been dogged by scientific and social controversy – from disagreements about whether orgasm originates in the vagina or the clitoris (or any other part of the body), whether or how it serves any evolutionary function, whether it is a necessary part of women's sexual satisfaction, and whether it is a site of women's oppression, liberation or both. Orgasms are also big business – for pharmaceutical companies desperate to find the 'pink' Viagra™ to 'help' women orgasm more easily or more frequently, for those who profit from visual representations of orgasm in everything from shampoo adverts to hard core pornography, for sex workers who are paid to elicit orgasms from clients, and for those who trade in creams, gels, toys, self-help books, and therapeutic services designed to enhance orgasmic pleasure. This cacophony of cultural chatter about female orgasm draws attention both to its problematisation and its symbolic significance in relation to a range of competing professional and commercial interests. This book, then, explores the *meaning* of orgasm. Noisy debates about female orgasm, accompanied by intense scrutiny, monitoring, measurement, and disciplining of female bodies, are not paralleled by similar careful and considered attention to men's orgasm. Here there is relative silence. This is not to suggest that men's sexuality or bodies are not subject to the clinical (and other) gaze – the recent commercial success of pharmaceutical treatments for 'erectile dysfunction' and the reshaping of the aging body as 'forever sexual' would suggest otherwise. But the bodily location, presence, or availability of men's orgasm has not been considered controversial or even particularly interesting. This suggests that the meaning of orgasm is heavily gendered, and that the 'doing' of orgasm has a bearing on the 'doing' of masculinity and femininity. The place of orgasm in heterosex (sexual practices – especially penis-in-vagina intercourse – between men and women) is subject to intense surveillance and offers a focus for this book. Evidence of an 'orgasm gap', where men experience orgasm more frequently and reliably than women, is often the focus of social and scientific scrutiny in ways which reaffirm heterosexuality as an institution and reproduce the unequal gendered power relationships on which this rests. Treating orgasm as primarily an embodied sociocultural 'event' (rather than a biological response) – something which is experienced in and through the body but which becomes knowable only through its socially embedded meaning – this book uses orgasm as a useful springboard for examining the relationships between gender, the body, sexuality, science and consumption.

Orgasmic origins

One way of exploring the social construction of the orgasm, and unsettling its status as a biological/medical 'fact', is to understand how the meaning of orgasm has changed over time. Laqueur's (1986, 2009) invaluable historical analysis of the use of the term 'orgasm' is illuminating. For centuries, he argues, orgasm was an allegory of the cosmos and creation, an event of cosmic significance signalling the origin of the soul and its entry into the body during conception. But, between the early 18th and late 19th century orgasm transformed into being understood as 'simply a feeling' (1986: 1), something that a body might or might not experience. According to Laqueur, these changes were not the result of new scientific discoveries, but were closely tied to cultural shifts in the status of biology as a science and the social, economic and political roles of women. He identifies a number of key points at which the meaning of orgasm shifted. In 1556, Realdo Columbus claimed to have discovered the clitoris, which marked a 'decisive shift from orgasm being understood as pleasure which overwhelms the whole body to a pleasure fixed primarily on an organ' (Laqueur, 2009: 429). In 1716 masturbation became seen as a sinful practice resulting in a variety of physical, mental and societal ills. This signalled a shift away from understanding orgasm as linked to the cosmos and generation, and towards orgasm being constructed as a feeling which is intimately connected to the inner world of the individual. In 1899 the word 'orgasm' was first applied to the distinct pleasure associated with the culmination of sexual excitement, and by 1918 climax became synonymous with orgasm. Finally, in 1905 when Freud gave the transferral from clitoral to vaginal orgasms an essential role in women's psychosexual development, orgasm became central to distinguishing between psychological health and pathology.

As Laqueur demonstrates, the story of 'orgasm' as a distinct phenomenon has a long history. Collectively these changes have constructed orgasm as a distinct event located in specific areas of the body, as the culmination of sexual activity but as separate from reproduction, as linked to the inner world or subjectivity of the individual, as indicative for psychological ill/health, and as essentially different for men and women. These ideas set the stage for the contemporary discursive context in which gendered sexual subjectivities are produced and negotiated. In this book I explore how orgasm is constructed, negotiated and managed in relation to a range of 'modern' phenomena – including the rationalisation and medicalisation of sexuality (Jackson and Scott, 1997; Tiefer, 1995, 1996), the increased importance of expert systems and knowledges in the pedogogisation of life (Bernstein, 2001), the rise of postfeminism and the sexualisation of culture (Gill, 2009), and the infusion of neoliberal discourse into the most personal and private spheres of life (Tyler, 2004).

Orgasm, discourse and heterosex

By focusing on the meaning of orgasm in heterosex, this book contributes to the growing scholarship on critical heterosexualities which seeks to explore the diversity of meanings, social arrangements, and hierarchies within heterosexuality (Hockey et al., 2007; Richardson, 1996). The concept of compulsory heterosexuality (see also Rich, 1980), initially developed by lesbian feminists and gay liberationists in the late 1960s and early 1970s, identified heterosexuality as a social institution, rather than a freely chosen (or biologically determined) sexual orientation or preference. Heterosexuality became recognised as a highly structured social arrangement maintained through norms, rules and rituals which guide the behaviour of large numbers of people (Ingraham, 2002), and which reflect distinct power relations between men and women, and between heterosexuals and homosexuals (and any non-straight identities that fall between). While initial analyses focused on the consequences of heteronormativity (the privileging of heterosexuality throughout social life) for the pathologisation of non-heterosexualities (Seidman, 2009), a parallel strand of work has been keen to unpack heterosexuality as a site for the reproduction of women's subordination and the privileging of male sexuality (Rich, 1980; Vance, 1984; Dworkin, 1987; Kitzinger and Wilkinson, 1993). Heteronormativity creates a structural pattern of gendered binaries and sexual hierarchies *among heterosexuals*, according to those who fall closest to a normative standard.

Conceptualising heterosexuality as a social institution draws attention to the consequences of heteronormativity across a broad range of social spheres, but how individuals 'do' heterosex, what they do in bed (or elsewhere), constitutes a central mechanism for the reproduction of heterosexuality. Situated with a critical feminist framework (Tiefer, 1995), this book argues that heterosex – including orgasm – is not a 'natural' act, but is a product of the social discourses through which sex is constituted, defined, experienced and made sense of. Consistent with poststructuralist theories of language (e.g., Gavey 1989; Weedon 1987), I take as my starting point the idea that language constitutes meaning through discourses which enable and constrain people's choices for how to be and act in the world.This includes what counts as 'sex', with whom one 'should' have sex and under what circumstances, as well as the meanings attributed to, and the experience of, sex. Using orgasm as a lens, this book identifies the norms, rules and rituals of orgasm in heterosex, as these are communicated through popular culture, biomedical and sexological discourse, and through the talk of women and men. This reflects an understanding that institutional (bio)medical, scientific and mediatised discourses and practices are mutually constitutive rather than oppositional (Polsky, 2002), and that these might shape, and be shaped by, 'lay' understandings of orgasm as evidenced in the talk of men and women. This allows an understanding of how subjectivities are negotiated in and through biomedicine, science, media and everyday experience. In particular, the book focuses on the ways in which discourses through which orgasm is given meaning reproduce heterosexuality and gendered hierarchies. Heterosexuality rests on the assumption that men and women have essentially different, but complementary, bodies, desires, motivations and ways of being in the world which mean that they 'naturally' belong together in a heterosexual union. Heterosex is a key practice through which boys/men negotiate their place in relation to hegemonic masculinity and girls/women negotiate femininity. Feminists have identified the 'coital imperative' – the privileging of penis-in-vagina intercourse as 'real sex' – as central to the reproduction of gendered subjectivities and the privileging of male sexuality (Richardson, 1996; Tiefer, 1995; Gavey, 1992; Hite, 1976; Holland, Ramazanoglu, Sharpe and Thomson, 1998; Roberts, Kippax, Waldby and Crawford, 1995). Hollway's (1984) classic work articulating three powerful discourses of heterosexuality – the 'male sexual drive' discourse, the 'have/hold' discourse, and the permissive discourse – has provided an influential springboard for exploring heterosex. The 'male sexual drive' discourse constructs men as driven by a biological need for sex which is urgent and (once aroused) unstoppable. Men are depicted as sexually active and agentic, taking responsibility for initiating and seeking sex while women are passive and responsive, either acquiescing or resisting men's demands for sex. In contrast, the 'have/hold' discourse, which is typically associated more with women, situates sex within the broader context of monogamy, intimacy, partnership and family life. Here sex is constructed as essential to emotional connectedness and the maintenance of relationships. In this sexual division men are often positioned as 'wanting sex' while women are positioned as motivated by a desire for a relationship. The 'permissive' discourse offers an 'anything goes' approach to sex in which freedom of sexual expression is taken as a right for both men and women as long as it is consensual and without harm. This analysis provides a useful foundation for exploring the construction of orgasm and its role in heterosex. To help us to get an insight into the meaning of orgasm, we will look first at three discursive frames: the biomedical frame, the behavioural frame and the spiritual/experiential frame. These approaches frame the production of knowledge about orgasm in different ways, draw on different mechanisms of legitimation, and have different consequences for action. I sketch them here, giving a rough characterisation of each. I explore how each of these frames relate to key themes which will be picked up throughout the book – before identifying some contemporary shifts in heterosexual relations which are further elaborated throughout the book. These different approaches offer us varied ways of answering the question: 'what is an orgasm?'

The biomedical frame

> Orgasm is a sensation of intense pleasure creating an altered consciousness state accompanied by pelvic striated circumvaginal musculature and uterine/anal contractions and myotonia that resolves sexually-induced vasocongestion and induces well-being/contentment. (Meston et al., 2004a: 66)

Within the biomedical frame, orgasm is primarily constructed as a bodily response, an event which is accompanied by a series of physiological changes which can be discovered, documented and described using scientific rationality and methods. Sex and sexuality are inextricably linked to biomedical understandings of the body in contemporary Western cultures in which sexuality has become increasingly medicalised and amenable to surveillance, intervention and management. The aim of this approach is to isolate and locate the exact physiological triggers and correlates of orgasm. Researchers are concerned to document the biological pathways to orgasm by studying the physiological changes that occur prior, during and after orgasm. They seek to document the role of the central nervous system and the sensory pathways activated during sexual arousal and orgasm, the neurochemistry of orgasm and how orgasm might be affected by drugs and medications, the different areas of the brain involved in orgasm and the connections between the genitals and the brain, and the role of hormones in regulating sexual behaviour (see Komisaruk, Beyer-Flores and Whipple, 2006 for an overview).

Masters and Johnson, although far from the first investigators to scientifically study sexuality – including orgasm – are perhaps the most well known and the most credited with transforming the study of human sexuality. As such, they provide a useful exemplar to illustrate the biomedical approach. The aim of their research was to document the physiology of sexual behaviour by observing masturbation and partnered sexual activities within the laboratory. Volunteers were wired up to the latest technological devices to measure the physiological changes that occurred before, during and after orgasm. From 1957 until 1965, they recorded extensive data on the anatomy and physiology of human sexual response by observing of over 600 men and women in what they conservatively estimated to be over '10,000 complete cycles of sexual response' (Masters and Johnson, 1966: 15). One of their most significant contributions was not simply documenting physiological changes (such as uterine contractions, lubrication, increased blood flow to the vagina, penile erection, contractions in the anus, etc.), they also brought these observations together to describe what they claimed was a universal pattern of sexual responses – the Human Sexual Response Cycle (HSRC). A sequence of four essential stages, characterised by observable and measurable physiological changes was identified: 'excitement', 'plateau', 'orgasm' and 'resolution'. This placed orgasm as an essential part of normal sexual response, and the pinnacle of sexual responsiveness. They documented the precise nature of the physiological changes that occurred during orgasm – both those that are externally observable on the body, and those which are internal and less visible. In addition, building on their invention of a universal sexual response cycle, they developed new therapeutic techniques for treating sexual difficulties and 'dysfunctions'. In contrast to the psychodynamic approaches which proceded them, Masters and Johnson positioned sexuality as central to health and well-being and saw sexual difficulties as arising primarily from poor sex education, a sexually restrictive upbringing or conservative social norms rather than from intrapsychic conflicts. They revolutionised therapeutic approaches to sexual problems by advocating a treatment programme based largely on psycho-education and behavioural techniques which was brief, solution-focused and directive, designed to bring wayward sexual responses more into line with the normative model they had developed (Masters and Johnson, 1970).

There are a number of key aspects of the biomedical approach, as illustrated by Masters and Johnson's research, to which I wish to draw particular attention, since these capture some of the key tensions which are addressed in the book. This includes: the construction of orgasm as an essential and 'peak' aspect of normal (as opposed to dysfunctional) sexual response; the role of technologies of visualisation in scientific expertise; the similarity of male and female sexual response; and the construction of body and embodiment in relation to orgasm.

Firstly, the model gives scientific legitimacy to the idea that orgasm is the 'peak' of sexual experience, and that sexual response follows a normative pattern in which orgasm is a key component. Not only does orgasm form one of the key stages in the model, it is also positioned as the 'ultimate point' in the cycle, and psychologically as the 'subjective perception of a peak of physical reaction' (Masters and Johnson, 1966: 127). Although revised, largely influenced by the work of Helen Kaplan (1977, 1995), to include an initial stage of 'desire', the HSRC model retains its privileged status as bearing the standard of sexual functioning despite intensive methodological and conceptual critique (Basson, 2000; Tiefer, 1991). This resilient model continues to form the basis of the 'diagnosis' and 'treatment' of sexual dysfunction outlined in the Diagnostic and Statistical Manual (DSM) of the American Psychiatric Association (APA). By providing a universal normative framework of human sexual response, the model offers a standard against which *abnormal* or *dysfunctional* sexual response can be identified. Failing to 'achieve' the sexual peak of orgasm falls short of normal sexual functioning since orgasm is an expected part of the sexual response cycle. The absence of orgasm is cause for concern and may trigger an intervention to 'correct' this dysfunction.

Secondly, Masters and Johnson's work made distinctive use of technologies, often developed specifically for the research, with which to meticulously document, observe and visualise physiological changes during sexual excitement:

> The techniques of defining and describing the gross physical changes which develop during the human male's and female's sexual response cycles have been primarily those of direct observation and physical measurement [...] supported by many accepted techniques of physiological measurement and the frequent use of color cinematographic recording in all phases of the sexual response cycle. (Masters and Johnson, 1966: 4)

Although these cinematic colour recordings are not shown in their book, diagrams, photographs and visualising techniques (such as readings of blood pressure, heart rate etc.) are included. In *The Birth of the Clinic* (1973) Foucault explored the historical development of modern medicine in which body became an object of knowledge whose interior processes can be mapped, calculated and systematised with the emergence of the clinical *gaze*. The work of Masters and Johnson is a good example of the way in which the clinical gaze, aided by technological advancements, attempts to map the interiority of the body and often to map these onto visible changes on the exterior of the body. Sexual arousal – a subjective state marked by physiological changes within the body – becomes visible and knowable through the identification of external signs allowing arousal to be 'read off' from the body. Precise bodily measurements – for example that 'erective response may increase nipple length by 0.5–1.0 cm' (Masters and Johnson, 1966: 28), serve to position expert knowledge about the body, and its sexual responses are as definitive and as superior to lay or subjective knowledge. As well as producing 'expert' knowledge, this visualisation (through description, diagrams, images, etc.) reveals the interior of the body to the gaze of scientists and clinicians and allows new connections to be drawn between interior processes and external bodily signs. The proliferation of new technologies, such as PET and FMRI scans, which produce 3-dimensional 'maps' of active regions of the brain, has enabled new mechanisms for the scientific surveillance of the orgasmic body. Using such technologies, Masters and Johnson hoped to make definitive claims about the nature of orgasm by identifying objective signs of orgasm which would eliminate the need for 'unreliable' sexual reporting. Yet 50 or more years on, this objective, definitive physiological marker of orgasm remains curiously elusive. Our sense of our 'bodily insides' is largely governed by the imagery and discourses of the biological sciences, and these practices structure our bodily experience (Birke, 1999).

Thirdly, a key feature of the HSRC is the assertion of the basic similarity of sexual response for males and females, and the standardisation of a series of stages or phases of physiological change that define 'normal' sexuality. As Masters and Johnson note:

> the parallels in reaction to effective sexual stimulation emphasise the physiologic similarities in male and female responses rather than the differences. Aside from obvious anatomic variants, men and women are homogeneous in their physiological responses to sexual stimuli. (1966: 285)

Gender ideologies infuse the biomedical approaches, in particular the assumption of both gender differences and similarities in sexual physiology and functioning, and the particular emphasis placed on female orgasm and women's bodies as sites for scrutiny and intervention. Although Masters and Johnson emphasised the universality of human sexual response, and the similarities in the physiological changes experienced by both men and women, they also argued that there were three different sexual response patterns identified for women (compared to only one for males) and devoted 100 pages to describing this response compared to only 39 pages for describing the male response. Moreover, the model has been heavily criticised for better describing male sexual response, and for failing to adequately capture female sexuality (Basson, 2000; Tiefer, 1991).

Finally, although this approach is concerned with the body in detail, it is not especially concerned with the experience of *embodiment*. The body is an object to be studied, dissected, measured and known. This frame adopts a scientific approach to identify the 'truth' about orgasm which is located in bodily systems (nerves, hormones, etc.) and the task of science is to identify, observe, measure and document the operation of these systems in producing orgasm. There is little concern with the subjective experience of orgasm aside from whether or not this experience coincides with the objective observations of scientists. Yet, for social constructionists, bodily experience is constituted and structured through biomedical discourses and practices. The tension between the objective knowledge about the body and the subjective experience of embodiment is one which permeates scientific debates about the nature of orgasm.

In summary, the biomedical frame signals the transformation of a 'private' experience into an object of legitimate scientific enquiry governed by the generation of expert knowledge. It positions orgasm as a physiological event located within the body – primarily the genitals – and a mechanical response triggered by appropriate stimulation. Orgasm is accorded a special place in the sexual response cycle as a peak experience. This approach provides a framework within which sexuality is made meaningful, but it tells us little about the *meaning* or *experience* of sexual behaviours and practices for the individuals involved. It might tell us something about how messages are sent from parts of the body to the brain, but it fails to tell us anything about how the person interprets and recognises these sensations and the interpretative work which goes into recognising this as 'orgasm'.

The behavioural frame

Like the biomedical frame, this approach treats orgasm as a self-evident 'thing' – an event – which can be counted and objectively measured. Orgasm either happens or it does not. This approach asks questions about who is most likely to experience orgasm, in what kinds of relationships, and during what kinds of sexual practices. Researchers within the behavioural frame are interested in trying to identify patterns in the occurrence or frequency of orgasm by examining a range of social and psychological variables such as relationship status, religiosity, education, gender, race/ethnicity, experiences of childhood sexual abuse, and relationship conflict or satisfaction. Moreover, this research explores the relationship between orgasm, psychological well-being, sexual satisfaction and physical health. For the most part, these patterns are identified through the use of quantitative sexual surveys in which people self-report their sexual practices and behaviours.

Orgasm has received rather mixed attention in large-scale national (and international) surveys of sexual behaviour. Kinsey and colleagues' ground-breaking sexual surveys of the 1940s and 1950s asked a host of questions about the orgasmic experience of Americans, including sources of first orgasm, age of first orgasm, frequency of orgasm during marital coitus, prevalence of multiple orgasm, and nocturnal orgasm (Kinsey et al., 1948/1998, 1953). In contrast, a survey of sexual behaviour in Britain in the 1990s asked only one *hypothetical* question about the 'importance' of orgasm since this was considered 'less intrusive' (Johnson et al., 1994: 255). National surveys and questionnaire measures of orgasmic experience are typically limited to questions about the occurrence or non-occurrence of orgasm, or to crude measures of orgasmic frequency. Despite the apparent simplicity of these questions, clear figures about orgasmic frequency and prevalence are hard to obtain due to methodological differences in the way that orgasms and sexual practices are defined and measured in different studies. Despite this variation, one of the key findings in this body of literature, and one which is reiterated in popular culture, is the existence of an 'orgasm gap' between men and women:

- 31.1% of women compared to 5.2% of men did not have an orgasm during their last heterosexual encounter according to findings from the *Australian Study of Health and Relationships* which involved computer assisted telephone interviews with 10,000 men and 9,000 women aged 16–59 (Richters, de Visser, Rissel and Smith, 2006).
- 75% of men, but only 29% of women, report that they always have orgasms with their partner. Nevertheless, around 40% of both men and women say they are extremely pleased physically and emotionally with their sex life according to the US *National Health and Social Life Survey* (Laumann, Gagnon, Michael and Michaels, 1994).
- 92% of men and 56% of women experienced orgasm in their last sexual intercourse in a Finnish national survey (Haavio-Mannila and Kontula, 1997).

This 'orgasm gap' is also reflected in surveys looking at the prevalence of sexual problems, where women are more likely to report problems with achieving orgasm than are men:

- Inability to orgasm was reported by 14.5% of women in Britain's *National Survey of Sexual Attitudes and Lifestyle* (Natsal) which surveyed over 11,000 men and women aged 16–44, and was the second most frequently reported sexual problem after lack of desire (Mercer, Fenton, Johnson et al., 2003).
- The *Global Study of Sexual Attitudes and Behaviors* (GSSAB), an international survey among adults aged 40–80 from 29 countries found that inability to reach orgasm was one of the two most common sexual problems reported by between 18% and 41% of women across the world regions (Laumann et al., 2005).

The behavioural frame, then, is concerned with identifying socially structured patterns in the frequency of orgasm across a population. In addition to the gendered 'orgasm gap', social researchers and sexologists have been interested in documenting the relationship between orgasmic occurrence/frequency or the prevalence of orgasmic dysfunctions and a wide range of psychological and social factors including age (Janus and Janus, 1993; Wilkins and Warnock, 2009), education (Laumann, Paik and Rosen, 1999; Haavio-Mannila and Kontula, 1997), social class (Fahs and Swank, 2011), and personality (Harris et al., 2008 – see Meston et al., 2004b and Mah and Binik, 2001 for overviews). These questionnaire-based, self-report studies often suffer from a range of conceptual and methodological issues, which prevents clear comparisons between studies leading to contested claims about the frequency of orgasm across different conditions and populations, and the prevalence of orgasmic dysfunctions. Again, there are some key aspects of the behavioural approach to which I wish to draw attention: the acceptance of orgasm as the 'norm'; the construction of orgasmic absence as a female problem; the construction of orgasm as a distinct event which is either present or absent; and a lack of attention to embodiment.

Firstly, by uncritically adopting orgasm as the 'natural' and most desirable endpoint to sexual interaction, this approach treats whether or not a person experiences orgasm, or the number of orgasms a person has, as inherently meaningful. Moreover, the behavioural frame (like the biomedical frame) constructs normative standards of sexual behaviour by offering ways of measuring how closely individuals meet the orgasmic ideal. Counting the frequency or consistency with which individuals experience orgasm, enables the identification of gaps and absences which are taken as indicative of problematic or dysfunctional sexual responses.

Secondly, the centrality of orgasm during intercourse as a defining act of heterosex, together with sexological reports that many women do not orgasm during intercourse, serves to construct an 'epidemic' of female sexual dysfunction which must be accounted for by scientific research and 'fixed' by pharmaceutical or therapeutic interventions. Take as an illustration, Harris et al. (2008: 1177) who start with the observation that 'As many as 20–30% of women report an inability to orgasm during sexual intercourse', before going on to identify women who are 'at risk' from having or developing this 'problem'. If orgasm is a normative part of the human sexual response cycle (as established by Masters and Johnson, 1966), the existence of an 'orgasm gap' serves to position women as having a problem with orgasm. The finding that women do not orgasm 'as frequently' or 'as consistently' as men is constructed as problematic since the implicit 'norm' is that orgasm will always accompany sexual behaviour. While these findings may be advantageous to those who wish to profit from the construction of a rising tide of orgasmic dysfunction, these figures depict women as malfunctioning in droves and female orgasm as somewhat elusive. There is good reason to treat these facts with caution. It is usual, for example, for questionnaires to privilege penis-in-vagina sex by asking women to report on their experience of orgasm *during intercourse only*. Researchers have criticised this approach for misrepresenting the prevalence of sexual dysfunction and reinforcing the cultural myth that the female orgasm is more elusive, mysterious or difficult to achieve.

Thirdly, although the behavioural frame has an interest in orgasm, for the most part the nature of orgasm itself is left unquestioned. The biomedical frame aims to identify the exact nature of orgasm, to establish objectively and definitively what an orgasm is, and what physiological markers indicate orgasm. In contrast, orgasm is treated as an end product of sex, and a conveniently measurable variable marked by its presence or absence, which is meaningful because of what it implies about sexual satisfaction or success. In other words, orgasm is treated as an indicator of happiness, satisfaction or adequate sexual functioning without much concern for what an orgasm actually is. Orgasm just is. As a distinct event, people are assumed to be able to report on the presence or absence of orgasm in a straightforward way. Notwithstanding some concerns about the accuracy with which people report the frequency of orgasm – for example, Laumann et al., 1994 suggest that women may over-report orgasm due to cultural pressures – people are assumed to be able to reliably report on whether they have, or have not, had an orgasm. Orgasm is treated as a subjective experience that is inherently knowable and recognisable, but the behavioural approach offers expertise in measuring this experience, and placing individual experience in the context of broader social patterns.

Finally, although this approach assumes that orgasm is a bodily event, it has little interest in exploring the corporeal nature of this experience. This approach is more concerned with identifying the variables which are more or less likely to result in an orgasm. This includes documenting the number and variety of sex acts which take place in a sexual encounter, or which body parts are brought into contact with each other (e.g., whether a penis is inserted into a vagina, an anus or a mouth), and the impact of this on orgasmic frequency. This approach shows little interest in the body as either a mechanically functioning biological organism or as something which is felt or experienced beyond capturing the presence or absence of orgasm. Unlike the biomedical frame which located orgasm *within* the individual, an event which happens within the body of the individual in response (typically) to 'external stimuli' from a sexual partner, the behavioural frame places these activities within the broader context of the individual (personality, age, experience), the relationship (levels of conflict, satisfaction, communication) and wider society (indicators of social equality, traditional or liberal gender norms). Interest in the social aspects of orgasm typically takes the form of variables which are assumed to affect an individual's ability to orgasm and account for social patterning of orgasmic experience.

So, while this research addresses the *frequency* with which orgasm occurs, it does not really address the *meaning* that this has for individuals beyond whether it is considered 'important' or is linked to ratings of sexual satisfaction. Like the biomedical frame though, it does provide a framework through which orgasm is made meaningful. In particular, the presence or absence, the frequency or consistency and the number of orgasms is treated as saying something significant about sexual functioning, happiness, satisfaction or success.

The experiential frame

The *experiential frame* provides an alternative understanding of orgasm to the biomedical and behavioural approaches since it is explicitly concerned with the lived experience of orgasm. The experiential frame attempts to move beyond simply whether or not orgasm has occurred, to explore what orgasm feels like. Although not prevalent in academic research – with the exception of a body of qualitative, mostly feminist, research – it is ubiquitous in popular discourse. This approach focuses both on the embodied pleasures and sensations of orgasm, and on the emotional and relational significance of orgasm. Criticising biomedical definitions of orgasm as reductionist, limiting orgasm to a physical response to sexual stimuli located in the genitals, Lousada and Angel (2011) offer a more expansive model which distinguishes three key dimensions of orgasmic experience: the *intra*personal, the *inter*personal and the *trans*personal.

The *intrapersonal* dimension refers to components of the person's individual experience including both physiological (including genital) sensations and affective, cognitive or spiritual elements. In her famous study of women's sexuality Shere Hite (1976) reported that some women described an 'emotional orgasm', characterised by an intense emotional peak, feelings of closeness, yearning or exaltation. This distinction between the physical and emotional experience of orgasm has become reified in studies of sexual satisfaction such that even large-scale national surveys distinguish between the two. Posing the question 'Do all orgasms feel alike?' psychologists Mah and Binik (2002) built on subjective reports of orgasmic experience by developing a two-dimensional model of orgasmic experience comprising of a sensory dimension (capturing physical sensations such as building sensations, flooding sensations, shooting sensations, throbbing sensations, flushing sensations and general spasms) and a cognitive-affective dimension (capturing psychological and emotional experiences including pleasurable satisfaction, relaxation, emotional intimacy, and ecstasy). The US *National Health and Social Life Survey* asks participants to rate how physically and how emotionally satisfied they are with their sex life (Laumann et al., 1994). Finally, reflecting ongoing controversies about the physical location of female orgasm, differences in the *experience* of 'clitoral' versus 'vaginal' orgasms are often reported with women often describing vaginal orgasms as the 'real thing', 'deeper' or more pleasurable than clitoral orgasms (Lavie-Ajayi and Joffe, 2009: 103). Men's orgasmic experience has received little attention since it is often assumed that ejaculation and orgasm are synonymous. However, others stress that orgasm should not be confused with the sensations of *overspilling* or *bursting*, terms often used to describe ejaculation since orgasm is linked to a 'more comprehensive and deeper emotional reaction or bodily explosion' (Lorentzen, 2007: 72).

The *interpersonal* dimension refers to components of a shared, partner experience including intimacy and the inter-subjective experience of being one rather than separate. The cultural fascination with locating orgasm within the bodies of individuals, serves to obscure what is often characterised as the 'special' significance of experiencing orgasm with another, as part of a sexual *inter*action. Simultaneous orgasm through intercourse, in particular, is positioned as the pinnacle of sexual intimacy. This approach shares in common with the biomedical and behavioural frames, an understanding of orgasm as the peak sexual experience, but adds a focus on inter-subjectivity. Alice, interviewed by Potts (2000a) illustrates this:

> it's when I feel that I've achieved a kind of bond I think, when you have kind of intercourse and...you're kind of reaching that other person's soul that you're not able to achieve at any other moment...When you look into their eyes you feel as if you're looking into their soul and it's a bond [...]. (2000a: 62)

Orgasm is seen as a route to increased intimacy with sexual partners. Although there may be little difference in the physical sensations in masturbation compared to partnered sex, the emotional intimacy offered by partnered sex means that the 'experience of orgasm attained through solitary masturbation may be qualitatively different from that of orgasm attained with a partner' (Mah and Binik, 2002: 111). Orgasm-through-intercourse in particular, is constructed as a privileged site of physical and emotional connectedness, offering 'ultimate intimacy' (Gavey, McPhillips and Braun, 1999) or intense closeness through the 'merging of souls' (Potts, 2000a: 63). Relationships lacking this experience are sometimes experienced as inferior, less satisfying or lacking intimacy (Potts, 2000b; Revicki et al., 2008).

Finally, the *transpersonal* dimension refers to components of the experience that transcend the personal level of awareness, including a broad spectrum of emotional and spiritual experiences (such as out-of-body or other types of peak experiences) which are rarely recognised by mainstream research. In a nationwide survey of over 3000 people on sexuality and spirituality in the US, 58% of participants over 60 responded positively to the question 'Have you ever experienced God in a moment of sexual ecstasy?' (Ogden, 2001). One 74-year-old male participant described sex as:

> culminating in spiritual orgasm simultaneously where for a sacred moment the bodies blend as one, and the face of creation is seen. (n.p.)

Similarly, in an interview study which solicited respondents who had 'nonordinary, mystical, or transcendent experience during sex with a partner', Wade (2000) found that reports of momentary loss of self, time and space during orgasm is so familiar that people seem to identify this sensation as 'ordinary'. However, participants described experiences of altered states which were distinct from orgasm including out of body experiences, a feeling of oneness with animals or nature, and connectedness to higher-order beings. Although given little attention in scientific studies of sex, this approach holds popular appeal with books on 'tantric sex' being widely available. Even a cursory search of a bookshop reveals titles such as *Red Hot Tantra: Erotic Secrets of Red Tantra for Intimate Soul-to-Soul Sex and Ecstatic, Enlightened Orgasms* (Ramsdale and Gentry, 2004), *Tantric Orgasm for Women* (Richardson, 2004) and *Urban Tantra: Sacred Sex for the Twenty-first Century* (Carrellas, 2007). These texts interweave sexuality and spirituality while promising that:

> By harnessing the power of the ancient Taoist tradition of sexual wisdom, you and your partner can learn to use physical and

psychological techniques to experience the bliss of a whole body sexual experience with orgasm after orgasm. Male and female sexual energies have unique qualities, which the traditional western approach often neglects. 'The Multi-Orgasmic Couple' shows how you can fully explore your sexual energy and potential, creating the ultimate blissful harmony between partners. (Chia et al., 2001, back cover)

'Selling' tantric and/or spiritual approaches to sex, these books promise sexual enlightenment as a route to self-awareness, personal development, spiritual growth and self-actualisation.

Orgasm is depicted as a natural potential of every individual and as necessary for psychic and holistic health and well-being (Lousada and Angel, 2011). Within this frame orgasm is seen as both a pleasurable embodied experience, and as a conduit for self-awareness, greater intimacy with others, and transcendence. Orgasm is positioned as:

> *the* moment when a person is *most fully present* in her or his body; or the moment when the body meets the soul; or a *holistic* experience which melds body, mind, emotions and spirit; or the ultimate liberation of (usually) two persons – their *union* (the completion of woman by man and vice versa). (Potts, 2000: 59, emphasis in original)

As such, orgasm is imbued with mystical and magical properties. In this frame, then, the subjective experience of orgasm is paramount – offering an important corrective to biomedical and behavioural accounts of orgasm. The body is not a mechanical machine, but a source of 'pure' sensory experience that is linked to spiritual awareness. The body itself is not of interest, the body is a route to, or a mechanism for, enlightenment and intimacy. This uncritical turn to the body or to subjective experience, as if these were unmediated by social and cultural forces, is problematic.

Contemporary shifts

A number of interrelated shifts in the social organisation of sexuality and relationships are pertinent to our discussion of the meaning of orgasm in contemporary Western culture. These include: the shift towards expert knowledge and the pedogisation of culture, the shift towards a neoliberal rationality and the emergence of a postfeminist sexuality, and the transformation of intimacy.

The transformation of intimacy

A number of social and economic changes that have occurred since the turn of the century have created new ideals for intimate relationships. These include: the unshackling of sex from procreation; the increasing secularisation of society; the rise of pre- and extra-marital sex; divorce law reform; changes in the public role of women (not least the right to vote); and two world wars. Amid this turmoil, new ideals for intimacy and sexuality emerged to meet new sociopolitical and economic demands and shifting patterns of heterosexual relationships and gender relations. Encapsulated in the idea of the 'companionate marriage' this was characterised by an emphasis on greater 'teamwork', 'sharing' or equality between husband and wife (Finch and Summerfield, 1991), and a shift from seeing marriage as an institution to marriage as a relationship. With this came a shift in sexual norms. While Victorian sex advice depicted sex as something dangerous and to be endured rather than enjoyed, the turn of the century saw the reconfiguring of sex as a desirable and pleasurable act, essential for the stability of the marriage (Clark, 1991; Connell and Hunt, 2006; Finch and Summerfield, 1991; Richards and Elliott, 1991). The 'sexual revolution' of the 1960s and 1970s marked a key turning point in the legitimacy of sexual expression as 'healthy' and necessary. 'Modern' sexual relationships were characterised by the prioritising of sexual pleasure and satisfaction *equally* for both men and women, the liberalisation of sexual attitudes, and an emphasis on sexual variety and experimentation. In describing the impact of 20th century social changes on intimate lives, Giddens (1991) outlines what he calls 'the pure relationship' – one which is not formed on the basis of social and political requirements, but one which is 'entered into for its own sake, for what can be derived by each person from a sustained association with another; and which is continued only in so far as it is thought by both parties to deliver enough satisfaction for each individual to stay within it' (Giddens, 1992: 58). Sexuality has a new form and a new role within the pure relationship. Sexuality is 'plastic' – more flexible, creative, less constrained and more completely separated from procreation. Indeed, according to Giddens, sexuality becomes 'doubly constituted as a medium of self realisation and as a prime means, as well as an expression, of intimacy' (Giddens, 1991: 164). While Giddens is optimistic about the transformative potential of the 'transactional negotiation of personal ties by equals' (1992: 3), feminists have criticised this utopian view, arguing that there are few indicators of increased equality in heterosexual relationships (Jamieson, 1999). Nonetheless, some agree that contemporary discourse espouses the view that a good relationship will be equal and intimate and that equality is necessary for intimacy. Thus, contemporary heterosexual relationships can be said to be characterised by an ethic of reciprocity (Jagose, 2010).

Neoliberalism and postfeminism

Neoliberalism, with its emphasis on free market supremacy, competitive freedom, privatisation, deregulation and efficiency, has emerged in the post-war years to dominate the economic, political and social policies and practices of the West. Of particular interest to social scientists is the emergence of a new neoliberal subject to meet the demands of late-capitalist consumer culture and to replace the apparently eroding structural bases of identity and belonging. This neoliberal subject is a highly individuated, entrepreneurial and self-responsible consumer, engaged in a self-actualising project of the self (Brown, 2003). The entry of neoliberalism into the intimate sphere has heralded a re-conceptualisation of sex and the construction of a new sexual actor. Rather than an irrepressible force of nature, sex is recast as 'work' and subject to managerial discourse which positions it as something which can be worked on, improved, made efficient, developed, invested in, and capitalised upon (Gill, 2009; Jackson and Scott, 1997; Tyler, 2004). Sexual pleasure is refashioned as a rational goal which can be pursued through the accumulation of knowledge and skill, and sexual practices and lifestyles as the outcome of deliberate and purposeful individual choices made in the pursuit of sexual self-actualisation (often defined as orgasmic sex – see Chapter 2). Neoliberal sexual subjects are characterised as entrepreneurial actors who are rational, calculating and self-regulating, and who are engaged in sexual encounters based on contractual exchange. This provokes a new consideration of risk, responsibility and ethics since sexual failings become fixed in individual accountability rather than structural inequalities. Although neoliberal rhetoric is 'ostensibly democratic, respectful, nonjudgemental, and non-coercive' (Adam, 2005: 341), the responsibility for sexual safety is unevenly distributed with the less powerful or socially marginalised having a greater burden of responsibility (Gotell, 2008).

In a series of articles Gill (2007, 2009) has consistently demonstrated that neoliberal and postfeminist discourses weave together in the production of a new female sexual subject. Postfeminism is characterised by discourses of choice, freedom, agency, empowerment and an agentic 'up for it' sexuality (see also Gill, 2009). Rather than being passive or responsive to male sexuality, modern women are actively desiring sexual subjects who dress 'sexily', depilate, wear make-up, use hair products, and watch porn – not to gain men's favour or attention, but as an *active choice to please themselves*. Gill (2009) outlines a number of key features of this postfeminist sensibility:

- A shift from sexual objectification which positions women as passive objects of a male gaze, towards sexual subjectification which positions women as active subjects empowered by the certainty of their sexual appeal.
- An emphasis on individual choice, personal empowerment and autonomy.
- An intensification of self-surveillance, monitoring and discipline and the dominance of discourses of self-transformation.
- A shift towards power being exercised through self-policing and regulation, moving women towards goals which are experienced as authentically desired rather than externally imposed.
- The replacing of innocence and virtue as the foundations of female sexuality towards the accumulation of sexual knowledge and skills.
- The acquisition of a 'sexy' body as the cornerstone of femininity – replacing attributes such as care, motherhood and nurturance.
- A repackaging of feminist goals for female empowerment and autonomy into an individualised understanding of equality, alongside a repudiation of feminism itself as unnecessary, obsolete and redundant.

The neoliberal imperative to 'work' at sex falls heavily on the postfeminist woman who is expected to 'take control' of her intimate life by studying and learning what pleases men, working on her body, taking responsibility for the emotional management of relationships, and becoming a 'sexual adventurer' who overcomes repression to actively pursue sexual enlightenment (see also Gill, 2009). Yet, despite the emphasis on choice, women are expected to work towards very traditional 'goals' – a secure, monogamous heterosexual relationship which delivers emotional and physical fulfilment. Feminist scholarship, in looking at the ways in which postfeminist discourse shapes women's sexual subjectivities and practices, has consistently demonstrated how the apparently gender-neutral framing of neoliberal discourse persistently ignores gender power relations in positioning women as making unconstrained, autonomous, sexual choices (e.g., Burkett and Hamilton, 2012; Bay-Cheng, Livingston and Fava, 2011). In short, *compulsory (sexual) agency* has been identified as a key disciplinary feature of contemporary postfeminist, neoliberal subjectivity. In focusing on orgasm, in this book we consider how neoliberal discourses position orgasm as the pinnacle of sexual experience and the differing responsibilities and obligations it produces for both men and women.

These shifts – particularly the ethic of reciprocity and the postfeminist sensibility – inform our exploration of orgasm throughout this book as we examine the construction of orgasm through the biomedical, behavioural and experiential frames. Chapter 2 examines the construction of an 'orgasmic imperative' which positions orgasm as the most healthy, functional, pleasurable and expected outcome of sexual activity. We examine how this orgasmic imperative is both interrupted and reinforced by the construction of women's orgasms as complex and elusive, and men's as certain (Chapter 3). The ways in which men and women are expected to mould their bodies to the 'orgasmic imperative' by delivering orgasms in a timely way is explored in Chapter 4. This notion of working on the body is picked up in Chapter 5, which focuses on the neoliberal drive towards sexual improvement. Chapter 6 explores the notion of uncertainty in discussions about distinguishing real from fake orgasms, and how to determine bodily sensations is the focus of Chapter 7. Finally, Chapter 8 considers some of the omissions in the existing literature (and this book) including an understanding of how orgasm relates to the intersections of privilege and disadvantage, the lack of attention to male embodiment, and the need to study orgasmic meaning-making in local, interactional contexts.

2
The Orgasmic Imperative

> Putting pressure on myself to orgasm feels strange. For something that's supposed to happen spontaneously, supposedly, it feels like there's a lot of thought put into this and a lot of anxiety around it, like this is some kind of benchmark of not only the sex, but who this person is as a lover, or how I am as a lover, or how I am as a woman. It just is supposed to be an index of how liberated you are, how in touch with your body or yourself you are.
>
> Fahs, 2011: 54

This chapter is concerned with the privileging of orgasm as a natural, inevitable and *necessary* part of sexual interactions – not only something which one could experience, but something which one *should* experience. This 'orgasmic imperative' (Potts, 2002) transforms orgasm from pleasurable option, into a requirement which individuals have an obligation or responsibility to deliver. The young woman quoted above, describes feeling a 'pressure' to produce an orgasm. Constructing orgasm as a distinct 'event' located in the body (Laqueur, 1986, 2009), produces an understanding of hetero-orgasm as structured by the dichotomous opposition of presence/absence (Potts, 2000a). An orgasm is a bodily event which either happens or it does not; it is either present or absent. The pressure to orgasm which this young woman describes draws our attention to a number of ways that the *presence* of orgasm takes on symbolic significance. Firstly, she describes orgasm as a 'kind of benchmark' for sex. The presence of orgasm is used as a yardstick by which the 'success' of sex and/or the relationship is measured. Secondly, the obligation to orgasm is described as signalling something about the 'kind of person' we are. The *presence* of orgasm comes to signify the competence of sexual actors (how I am as a lover), to represent a successful gendered performance (how I am as a woman), and to signal a particular relationship with the body (how 'in touch' with your body you are). Finally, this woman describes orgasm as indicative of 'how liberated you are' – the presence of female orgasm is emblematic of female empowerment and liberation. The shifting status of orgasm is wrapped up in changing gender power relations. It is not surprising, then, that the 'orgasmic imperative', the obligation to orgasm, plays out differently for men and women.

To explore the meaning of orgasmic presence and absence in contemporary heterosex, this chapter explores two key domains. Firstly, the ways in which the *presence* of orgasm is constructed as central to successful sexual relationships in marital advice books and lifestyle magazines[1]. Specifically we examine how the orgasmic imperative for women arises out of the merging of postfeminist discourse which fuses women's empowerment and agency with sexuality and neoliberal requirements for (sexual) self-improvement, and how these same neoliberal conditions fuse with hegemonic masculinity to create an imperative both to *have* an orgasm and to *give* an orgasm. Secondly, we interrogate the ways in which the *absence* of orgasm is pathologised in diagnostic and classificatory systems of sexual health. These two realms form separate but interrelated spheres of 'expertise' about sexual relating. Marital advice books and lifestyle magazines are pedagogical texts offering aspirational instruction in how to be 'the best' sexual subject one can, and are a place where scientific research is disseminated to mass audiences as part of this educative agenda. Classificatory systems and the scientific evidence based on which they rest claim to offer objective evidence of sexual normality/abnormality or adequate/inadequate sexual function. As such these systems offer normative standards against which our own sexual performance can be (and is) measured. Both can be seen as places where norms and ideals about sexual behaviour and subjectivities are circulated.

Orgasm = good sex = successful relationships

The contemporary obligation to orgasm must be understood in the context of shifting conceptualisations of intimacy in which 'good sex' comes to be positioned as the glue which holds relationships together. While men's orgasm/ejaculation has remained a constant (if unmarked) presence in the period since the turn of the century, the fate of female orgasm has fluctuated amid shifting articulations of gender relations. These shifts can be seen in the advice presented in marital sex manuals over this time. These manuals present a set of rules and etiquette for the management of sexual lives, and their pages reflect the shifting constructions of heterosexual relationships and gendered subjectivities which emerge to meet changing sociopolitical and economic demands. Although the content of these texts may not accurately reflect the actual sexual practices of men and women, they can be seen as representing sexual ideals – gendered norms for sexual behaviours, interactions and subjectivities which 'experts' impel individuals to adopt. With the exponential growth of marital sex advice manuals at the turn of the 20th century which defined sexual intercourse as a desirable and necessary act of pleasure in marriage (Clark, 1991; Connell and Hunt, 2006; Finch and Summerfield, 1991; Richards and Elliott, 1991), orgasm become positioned as vital to definitions of good sex (Neuhaus, 2000). But the centrality of orgasm – especially female orgasm – differed markedly in manuals published in the 1920s and 1930s to those published after the 1950s and generated differing orgasmic obligations for men and women (Neuhaus, 2000). The earlier manuals redefined sexual intercourse from being an unfortunate procreative necessity, to being a pleasurable activity, vital for the happiness of both partners and essential to marital success. Reflecting their changing social status, women were newly defined as having essential sexual needs in which orgasm was central to their good health and happiness. Yet, the manuals placed responsibility for awakening women's essentially dormant sexuality squarely on the husband. Advice was primarily targeted at men who were depicted as ignorant, bumbling lovers in need of expert guidance to correct their faulty sexual technique and instruct them in how to please their wives (Laipson, 1996; Neuhaus, 2000). Men were given greater responsibility for controlling or holding back their own pleasure *and* for eliciting their wife's orgasm. These deeply conflicting messages about male and female sexuality vividly illustrate 'a nation at work constructing a middle-class view of sexuality that acknowledged women's political gains while simultaneously reasserting male privilege' (Neuhaus, 2000: 454). Unlike male orgasm/ejaculation, the presence of which had been positioned as essential for (procreative) sex and remained so, women's orgasm shifted from being optional to being mandatory for ensuring the stability of the marital relationship. The *presence* of women's orgasm became positioned as evidence both of 'successful sex' and the effective deployment of male sexual skills. The presence of both men and women's orgasm marked the rise of a new 'erotico-ethical relation of parity and reciprocity' (Jagose, 2010: 526), or what Gordon (1971: 53) refers to as the 'cult of mutual orgasm'.

The period following the Second World War was also characterised by rapidly changing gender relations and although later manuals continued to emphasise the importance of 'good sex' for marital harmony, Neuhaus (2000) notes a number of important changes in the conceptualisation of female sexuality. Specifically, writers in the 1950s responded to the findings of Kinsey which highlighted the gendered 'orgasm gap' by downplaying the centrality of women's orgasm, problematising female sexuality and depicting women as essentially non-orgasmic. Men were characterised as buckling under the unequal responsibility for ensuring sexual success and beset by anxieties about their sexual self-worth and performance, while a woman's orgasmic incapacity was attributed to her own prudishness or neuroticism. Responsibility shifted to women for ensuring their own sexual responsiveness in order to maintain the relationship, and for caring for the fragile male ego. In other words, the *presence* of women's orgasm continued to confirm sexual compatibility and men's sexual expertise, but the *absence* of orgasm became attributed to women's deficiencies rather than men's poor technique.

This shift was exacerbated by the 'sexual revolution' of the 1960s and 1970s when the influential work of Masters and Johnson and the activism of feminists and gay liberationists marked a key turning point in the legitimacy of sexual expression as 'healthy' and necessary. 'Modern' sexual relationships were characterised by the prioritising of reciprocal sexual pleasure, the liberalisation of sexual attitudes, and an emphasis on sexual experimentation. Women's 'right' to pleasure – symbolised by orgasm – was adopted as a useful lever by some feminists with which to argue against sexual orthodoxies (e.g., Koedt, 1974). Reflecting on this period, Gerhard (2000) notes that claims to orgasmic equality and evidence of the centrality of the clitoris in female sexual pleasure, were mechanisms for arguing for the abandonment of intercourse as an instrument of patriarchal control, for problematising heterosexuality and de-pathologising lesbianism, for critiquing male 'expertise' about female sexuality, and for exploring the relationship between sexual practices and the institution of heterosexuality. She claims that the female orgasm came to signify the 'political power of women's self-determination' (2000: 450). This feminist rhetoric often made its way into sexual advice. In their analysis of British magazines, Lavie-Ajayi and Joffe (2009) note that during the first decade of publication (1972–1982) *Cosmopolitan* typically briefly rehearsed Freudian ideas about the difference between vaginal and clitoral orgasms before dismissing this with reference to the 'more scientific' evidence about the importance of the clitoris. This was often explicitly packaged in feminist rhetoric about the need to reject male-defined standards of sexuality and the magazine repeatedly reiterated that most women do not orgasm through intercourse alone but through clitoral stimulation. However, for many feminists this union between sexual freedom and women's liberation sat uncomfortably within a context of sexual oppression and violence. Some argued that the sexual revolution had created pressure for women to have sex and to orgasm (e.g., Densmore, 1973), and that women's interest in sex was presented as enhancing women's attractiveness and availability to men rather than offering sexual autonomy.

This brief sprint through changing constructions of heterosexuality since the 1900s illustrates the ways shifting sociopolitical landscapes and associated gender relations are mirrored in fluctuating norms about orgasm. The presence of female orgasm was central to these changing sexual relations and crystallised in an orgasmic imperative – the require-ment to orgasm. There are three things that I want to take into a discus-sion of contemporary articulations of the orgasmic imperative. Firstly, the positioning of orgasm as synonymous with 'good sex', as essential to healthy sexual expression, and as fundamental to maintaining harmo-nious, strong and satisfying relationships. Secondly, the aligning of mutual orgasm with an 'ethic of reciprocity' in heterosex, where sex is expected to be equally pleasurable for both men and women. Thirdly, the role of orgasm in signalling changing gender power relations and the trumpeting of orgasm as emblematic of women's sexual self-determination. While all of these threads feed into contemporary articulations of the orgasmic imperative, I pick up this latter idea to explore how feminist rhetoric is appropriated in lifestyle magazines which weld together sexual autonomy and female empowerment in a postfeminist sensibility which positions the *presence* of orgasm as the embodiment of women's liberation.

Postfeminism and the orgasmic imperative

> We know you already know how to please your man – and your-self – in bed. That's why we're taking it to the next level. This expert advice (and hot sex positions) will help you have your best.orgasm. ever. Want to have multiple orgasms? We've got you covered there, too. [Cosmopolitan 10]

Within the pages of contemporary lifestyle magazines like *Cosmopolitan*, women's 'right' to equality through sexual pleasure is unquestioned; women's 'right' to orgasm is treated as self-evident, an established gain of the sexual revolution and second wave feminism. As this article acknowledges 'We know you already know how to please you man – and yourself – in bed'. The goal of the magazine is to help women take it 'to the next level'. Mirroring the content of romantic novels (Abramson and Mechanic, 1983), orgasms are represented as a 'peak' experience and are often depicted hyperbolically as 'incredible', 'earth-shattering', a 'feel-good explosion', a 'full-body earthquake', 'mind-blowing', and 'bed-rattling'. Orgasm is represented as the expected, natural, and (relatively) easily attainable pinnacle of sexual fulfilment, and as the taken-for-granted goal of sexual interactions. The imperative is not only to have an orgasm, but to have a phenomenal orgasm – 'the best.orgasm. ever'. 'Great sex' is synonymous with orgasmic sex, and magazines focus on providing expert advice about how to achieve this orgasmic endpoint rather than defending its position as an essential and expected part of sex (Ménard and Kleinplatz, 2008).

Orgasm has a key, but under-acknowledged, role to play in what feminist media scholars have identified as the emergence of a new post-feminist sensibility; an 'up for it' female sexuality in which women are characterised as actively desiring sexual subjects who are adventurous, knowledgeable, empowered and who choose to engage in sexual activities and interactions to please *themselves* (Gill, 2007, 2009; Gill and Scharff, 2011; Tasker and Negra, 2007). In characterising post-feminist media culture, Gill (2007) draws attention to a number of key features: a shift from objectification to subjectification; an emphasis on self-surveillance, monitoring and discipline; a focus on individualism, choice and empowerment; and the dominance of discourses of self-transformation. Moreover, she argues that one of the distinctive features of this cultural moment is that it is a response to, and has a relationship with, feminism(s) (Gill, 2007). Women's magazines present a lightweight version of feminism by positioning themselves as explicitly 'for women' and concerned with women's rights. Fusing together female sexuality with power and agency, these magazines depict sex as bold and transgressive in itself, and women as liberated and empowered for engaging in sexual practices (Machin and Thornborrow, 2003). Orgasm comes to represent women's liberation from the apparently more repressive sexuality of earlier times (Lavie-Ajayi and Joffe, 2009). Postfeminism reworks and appropriates feminist debates about the role of orgasm in women's sexual repression/equality by presenting the (multi) orgasmic woman as the epitome of the liberated and empowered sexual subject, and the *presence* of orgasm as the continual embodied enactment of her social status.

In the pursuit of the 'best.orgasm.ever' women are persuaded to embody a new sexual subjectivity. Drawing on a discourse of self-transformation women are encouraged to conquer repression by changing negative, shameful or unconfident feelings about one's sexual self by becoming a 'sexual adventurer' (Gill, 2009: 357). Melding with the neoliberal drive towards self-improvement, readers are positioned as constantly seeking to develop their sexual knowledge, understanding and experience, and as investing in their sexual skills to achieve the ultimate orgasm. The magazines are on hand to offer instruction to these adventurous pleasure-seeking women who develop their sexual selves through orgasmic self-actualisation. Sexual innocence and virtue as the defining features of femininity are replaced by the requirement to develop a 'technology of sexiness' – a body of sexual knowledge, practice and expertise – which must be constantly monitored and improved to both embody femininity and secure sexual power (Gill, 2009). Readers are (with the exception of a few articles aimed at teaching non-orgasmic women to climax) addressed as already orgasmic, sexually motivated and curious to learn how to develop their orgasmic potential. The imperative to experience one 'ordinary' orgasm is no longer enough:

> With a little bit of know-how, you can experience more than one climax in a single sack session. In fact, from now on, you *should have* a new between-the-sheets mantra: No more one and done! (*Cosmopolitan* 7, emphasis added)

Advice is typically directed not merely towards having an orgasm, but rather towards how to experience more intense, more rapid or more 'specialist' orgasms – including multiple orgasms, G-spot orgasms, extended orgasms, blended orgasms, and simultaneous orgasms amongst others. Women are told that they *should* have more than one orgasm and that is a 'natural' capability of the female body: 'The average woman is built to come again and again [...] Meaning that once you've mastered that first peak, the climb to the next one is absolutely obtainable' (*Cosmopolitan* 7). Women are called upon to enthusiastically explore and experiment with different ways of achieving orgasm. Drawing on the words of sexual 'experts' and referring to the latest 'discoveries' in sexual science, the magazines present themselves as pioneers in women's sexual equality by translating this expertise for a lay audience. Readers are depicted as 'empowered' by their access to up-to-the minute sexual information. Importantly, this transformation into a multi-orgasmic sexual subject is presented as a choice that women make to please themselves, and the idea that this performed to meet the needs of male partners (or patriarchal norms) is explicitly rejected (Gill, 2009). Moreover, without destabilising penis-in-vagina intercourse as the defining act of heterosexuality, magazines emphasise that women should orchestrate different sexual positions with their male partners to achieve greater orgasmic pleasure (see Chapter 5). Different sexual positions are suggested which put women in control of their orgasmic experience:

> This erotic arrangement also allows for better command of pacing and depth of thrusts (it's easy to vary between deep and shallow), which *helps put you in control of your climax*, says Kenneth Ray Stubbs, PhD, author of *The Kama Sutra of Sexual Positions: The Tantric Art of Love*. (*Cosmopolitan* 42, emphasis added)

Representing yet another shift in the representation of female orgasm, I argue that contemporary sexual advice positions women as responsible for taking control of their sexuality and orgasm: 'You have to own your orgasm – you can't just rely on a man to get the job done' (*Cosmopolitan* 29). At the same time, men – and specifically the male penis – retain a central role (see also Lavie-Ajayi and Joffe, 2009). Feminist analyses which might position the *absence* of orgasm in the context of unequal gender power relations and institutionalised heterosexuality, are rejected in favour of more individualised explanations. In short, orgasmic absence is attributed to women's failures: 'Women wind up getting in the way of their own sexual satisfaction' (*Cosmopolitan* 29). Failure to be sufficiently knowledgeable about her own body, failure to educate male partners in how to touch them, or failure to adopt the right mental attitude, means that women are held responsible for their own (lack of) orgasm: 'We all know it's easy to get distracted during sex. Everything from "Is my stomach jiggling?" to "Wow, he should have that mole on his chest checked out" can make you lose frisky focus' (*Cosmopolitan* 29). The gloss of female empowerment and control barely conceals more conservative messages which reaffirm traditional gender power relations. Women are encouraged to work on their sexual confidence and free themselves from the last glimmers of sexual repression in order to transform themselves into 'up for it' sexual beings, yet they are simultaneously held responsible for maintaining relationships, protecting the masculinity of their male partners, and pleasing themselves in ways which also please men. For example, despite the prevalence of the orgasmic imperative women are occasionally warned about becoming too 'obsessed' with the goal of orgasm – not only because this may reduce the chances of actually achieving orgasm, but because it also risks emasculating their partner and threatening their relationship (Lavie-Ajayi and Joffe, 2009). These requirements are packaged as self-actualisation, but the language of empowerment is typically used to encourage women towards very traditional goals.

Nonetheless, the orgasmic imperative positions orgasm as not only a women's right, but their obligation. One orgasm is no longer enough to meet the requirements of this imperative – orgasmic experience must be continually improved upon such that orgasms are faster, more frequent, stronger, more intense, or longer-lasting. The aspirational sexual subject is multi-orgasmic, knowledgeable and sexually skilled and women are positioned, recognised and comparable in a hierarchy of sexual know-how in which some are able to 'master' the necessary skills and others are not: 'Though all females have the potential to be plural peakers, not all women are able to master it' (*Cosmopolitan* 21). Only the most adventurous and committed to self-improvement will conquer the climatic peaks of orgasmic superiority. Women are impelled towards orgasmic excellence not (solely) to please men, but because it 'demonstrates, simultaneously, their pleasure and their liberation' (Lavie-Ajayi and Joffe, 2009: 101). It is the *presence* of orgasm which signals the postfeminist woman, and she is given the responsibility for repeatedly bringing this orgasm into being to signal anew her self-determination. We turn now to considering the ways in which men's responsibilities have shifted in contemporary sex advice as neoliberal imperatives for sexual improvement fuse with hegemonic masculinity to produce an orgasmic imperative for men.

Hegemonic masculinity and the orgasmic imperative

for furniture-breaking orgasms your body needs further training. By delaying ejaculation and letting tension build to higher and higher peaks before the final explosion, you'll have an all-over-body sensation. (*Men's Health* 20)

If neoliberalism produces obligations for women to become 'sexual adventurers' who are continually 'up for it' (Gill, 2009), it requires men to become 'sexual champions' (Stibbe, 2004) who deliver a 'perfect intercourse performance' (McCarthy and Metz, 2008). Male (hetero)sexuality is central to constructions of hegemonic masculinity – or the 'culturally idealised form of masculine behaviour' (Connell, 1987: 83) which is presented as if it were natural, inevitable, and morally right that men behave in particular ways. Having sexual intercourse for the first time plays a compelling role in the transition from childhood to 'manhood' (see, for example, Holland et al., 1998; Richardson, 2010), and sex is key to the performance of masculine identities. Hegemonic masculinity is characterised by the 'male sex drive discourse' in which men are depicted as being naturally driven by sex, as constantly seeking and ever ready for sex, as actively initiating and 'doing' sex to women, and as in competition with other men (Hollway, 1984). Sexual gratification is characterised by conquest, competition, competence and variety. Critical work has focused on exposing heteronormative constructions of masculinity in which a penis which is erect for the purposes of vaginal penetration is the model of healthy and functional male sexuality (Tiefer, 1994). The coupling of masculinity to hardness, strength, endurance, control and activity is intimately tied to the function of the penis and the physical performance of sex, which is narrowly defined as inserting an erect penis into a bodily orifice ending with climax and ejaculation or delivering the 'perfect intercourse performance'. Neoliberal discourse means that is not enough for men just to be having sex; they must be having the 'best' or 'ultimate' sex (Rogers, 2005). Neoliberal imperatives to work towards the 'ultimate orgasm' also feature in sexual advice aimed at men – in the example above, orgasm is 'furniture-breaking', explosive and 'an all-over-body sensation'. But for the most part the language is less hyperbolic and typically the goal is described as a more 'intense orgasm' or an 'all-over-body' orgasm. Unlike female orgasm, the presence of men's orgasm has never really been in question. The goal presented in men's magazines is more sex; sex which is assumed to be orgasmic. Consequently, the imperative to orgasm has not had to be explicitly addressed since men's orgasms are assumed to be inevitably present, so much so that its absence is certainly seen as more problematic (see Frith, 2013). However, the orgasmic imperative to work towards an increasingly intense or pleasurable orgasmic experience fuses with hegemonic masculinity to produce obligations for men to 'give' orgasms to women or to 'make' women climax. Delivering a 'perfect intercourse performance' means delivering an orgasm which will 'blow her mind' (*Men's Health* 10), will give her 'wave after wave of multiple orgasms' (*Men's Health* 11), or 'an orgasm she won't forget' (*Men's Health* 13). The magazines advise men on how to improve their 'performance' by overcoming anxieties, building up their stamina and endurance, and by developing sexual knowledge and skills in being able to 'give' women orgasms (see Chapter 5). As Seidler (1997: 119) notes, 'heterosexual men's sexuality becomes focused upon giving women an orgasm, as if their virility is to be measured by whether a woman has come or not'. This construction of sex as masculinity-on-trial forms a significant part of the way men's magazines depict uncertainty/danger in sexual relationships, and the obligation for men to deliver orgasms is sometimes presented as a duty or burden (Rogers, 2005). To assuage this anxiety, men are encouraged to invest in acquiring orgasm-giving skills in order to (a) secure access to more sex, and (b) build their reputation as sensational lovers.

Men are expected to actively initiate and pursue all sexual opportunities, whereas women are expected to delay sexual activity until emotional intimacy has been established (Byers, 1996). Magazines and self-help books promote the idea that the greater quantity or frequency of sex, and the more sexual partners, the better, with much advice directed towards getting 'more sex' (Farvid and Braun, 2014; Krassas, Blauwkamp and Wesselink, 2003; Stibbe, 2004). 'Giving' women an orgasm is presented as a key route to accessing more sex. Magazines advise men to 'Follow this technique to give her great orgasms, and ensure she keeps coming back for more' (*Men's Health* 14) or that 'After such a mind-blowing orgasm, your lady will feel eternally sexy and very very grateful, meaning lots of blow jobs and sex for you in return' (*Men's Health* 11). This message is reflected in men's beliefs that women who are not sexually satisfied will not continue to have sex with them, as expressed by one participant in a focus group study looking at urban men's sexuality in the US:

> The attempt is always to make a woman scream ... to give as much an orgasm as you possibly could so that she'd come back. If you made them happy sexually they tend to come back. (Seal and Ehrhardt, 2003: 304)

The assumption is that any sex is good sex for men – that quantity is important. Although there is advice about improving their own orgasmic sensation, by far the majority of advice is geared towards helping her get 'the ride of her life' (*Men's Health* 16).

Sexual activity is a key path to masculine status and enhancing a man's reputation as a competent lover (Seal and Ehrhardt, 2003). The ability to 'make' a woman orgasm is taken as a tangible recognition of the man's skills and sexual labour:

> Gaining yourself a sexual reputation for the ages doesn't have to involve six hours of Tantric foreplay. Here's our step-by-step guide to giving her an orgasm in 15 minutes. (*Men's Health* 4)

This focus on producing a woman's orgasm is also taken as indicative of men's sexual competence in magazines aimed at women (Farvid and

Braun, 2006). Not only do men assume that women talk to each other about their sexual performance (Seal and Ehrhardt, 2003), other men are the audience, imagined or real, for one's sexual activities (Flood, 2008). Men negotiate their position in socio-sexual hierarchies by competing against other men on 'markers of manhood' including occupational achievement, wealth, power and status, physical prowess and sexual achievement (Kimmel, 1994: 129). There is emphasis in the magazines on becoming a better lover and gaining a good reputation, and standing out from the crowd by giving her an 'unforgettable' orgasm (*Men's Health* 48). Men's success at delivering this orgasm is fraught with difficulty, as sex itself is presented as complicated, women's bodies as mysterious, and their orgasms elusive or requiring hard work (see Chapter 3). Sex is presented as a competitive domain, and developing sexpertise and mastery of the mysterious female is key to competitive success (Schneider et al., 2008). The *presence* of women's orgasm is central to affirmation of men's masculinity, and its *absence* is a threat to masculinity.

If the *presence* of orgasm is key to the 'doing' of sexual success and the successful enactment of femininity and masculinity, then the *absence* of orgasm is troublesome and problematic. We turn now to the construction of orgasmic absence as a sexual dysfunction, paying particular attention to the Diagnostic and Statistical Manual of the American Psychiatric Association as a key place in which definitions of normative sexuality are institutionalised.

Pathologising orgasmic absence

> The results from the NHSLS indicate that sexual problems are widespread in society. [...] With the strong association between sexual dysfunction and impaired quality of life, this problem warrants recognition as a significant public health concern. (Laumann et al., 1999: 544)

One of the most frequently cited (and most controversial) figures on women's sexual difficulties is that 43% of women suffer from a sexual dysfunction. This figure comes from Laumann et al.'s (1999) *National Health and Sexual Lifestyle Survey* (NHSLS) conducted in the US. The definition of 'sexual dysfunction' was based on *yes/no* answers to whether participants had, during the last 12 months, experienced a period of several months or more when they: a) lacked interest in having sex, b) were unable to climax (experience an orgasm), c) came to climax too quickly, d) experienced physical pain during intercourse, e) did not find sex pleasurable (even if it was not painful), f) felt anxious just before having sex about their ability to perform sexually, or g) had trouble lubricating? (Laumann et al., 1999). Some 43% of their sample of 1749 US women answered 'yes' to this question, with 25.7% reporting problems with reaching orgasm, leading the authors to the above conclusion. Although the authors insert the caveat that this is not the same as a clinical diagnosis, nonetheless this figure is widely cited in the academic literature and popular media as evidence that 43% of women have a sexual *dysfunction* (Graham and Bancroft, 2006). Figures for the prevalence of orgasmic disorder in particular vary widely. In a review of 11 studies using a nationally representative sample, the figures ranged from 3.7% to 60% depending on the method of assessment used, the time period considered, and the definition of orgasmic difficulty adopted (Graham, 2010). Controversy over the prevalence of sexual dysfunction abounds, with some alleging that epidemiological studies, particularly those funded by the pharmaceutical industry, inflate the prevalence rates for sexual problems, and consequently create a 'need' for treatment (Mirone et al., 2002; Tiefer, 2001). By creating the impression of a 'crisis' of sexual dysfunction among women, an urgency for quick fix solutions is generated which may benefit pharmaceutical companies or anyone who stands to gain or profit from women's sexual problems. Concern about the *absence* of women's orgasm is a prominent focus for the production of a crisis in female sexuality.

Masters and Johnson's work detailing an apparently universal human sexual response cycle is pivotal in tying orgasm to the physiological and psychological health of the individual. They linked the *presence* of orgasm to healthy, normal and natural sexual functioning and the *absence* of orgasm to sexual failure, dysfunction or abnormality – orgasm became imperative to healthy sexual functioning. Despite being widely criticised for reducing sexuality to biological functions, limiting satisfaction to orgasm during intercourse, privileging male sexuality and ignoring the lived reality of female sexuality (Nicolson and Burr, 2003; Tiefer et al., 2002), their model places orgasm as the pinnacle of sexual response and forms the bedrock of contemporary classificatory systems demarcating normative from dysfunctional sexual functioning – most notably the Diagnostic and Statistical Manual (DSM) of the American Psychiatric Association (APA).

The category of 'Psychosexual Disorders' – including orgasmic disorders – was included in the DSM for the first time in 1980 when the third revision of the manual was published. Although discussion of men and women's sexual difficulties had preceded the development of this document by many years (see Angel, 2012 for an overview), the inclusion of sexual difficulties in the manual had two important consequences. Firstly, it served to establish the absence or mistiming of orgasm as pathological and in need of intervention in ways that are heavily gendered. Men's orgasms are typically constructed (problematically) as inherently present, subject only to problems of (mis)timing – being either (commonly) 'premature' or (more rarely) 'delayed'. These temporal aspects of orgasm, including the intertwining of 'premature' ejaculation with problematic constructions of masculinity, are discussed in Chapter 4. Here, we focus on the imperative to orgasm and on the presence or absence of orgasm as indicative of normal sexual function/ dysfunction. Secondly, this revision marked the start of an intensified biomedicalisation of sexuality in which sexual difficulties were transformed into medical problems characterised by suboptimal genital function and requiring treatment by medical experts. This revision of the manual emerged out of controversies surrounding the psychiatric profession, including a critique of the scientific limitations of the psychoanalytic psychiatry which dominated 1950s America, the rise of randomised controlled trials to test medications, and growing discontentment with psychiatry's misuse of power (Angel, 2012). Collectively, these set the conditions for a revision of the manual which sought to remove assumptions of a psychoanalytic aetiology for sexual problems, and instead focused on the biological aspects of mental illness by identifying discrete disorders operationalised by sets of symptoms (see Table 2.1).

The definition of the orgasmic phase in the manual reflects this physiological focus: '... a peaking of sexual pleasure, with the release of sexual tension and rhythmic contraction of the perineal muscles

Table 2.1 Diagnostic criteria for Female Orgasmic Disorder outlined in the DSM, version 4

A. Persistent or recurrent delay in, or absence of, orgasm following a normal sexual excitement phase. Women exhibit wide variability in the type or intensity of stimulation that triggers orgasm. The diagnosis of Female Orgasmic Disorder should be based on the clinician's judgement that the woman's orgasmic capacity is less than would be reasonable for her age, sexual experience and the adequacy of sexual stimulation she receives.

B. The disturbance causes marked distress or interpersonal difficulty.

C. The orgasmic dysfunction is not better accounted for by another Axis I disorder (except another sexual dysfunction) and is not due exclusively to the direct physiological effects of a substance (e.g., a drug of abuse, a medication) or a general medical condition.

Source: APA (2000: 302.73).

and reproductive organs' (APA, 2000: 494). Not only does this confirm orgasm as the 'peak' or crowning moment of sexual experience, it privileges an understanding of orgasm as primarily a physiological event. Moynihan (2003) has pointed out that

> some clinicians now recommend, along with a physical and psychosocial examination, a comprehensive evaluation that can include the measurement of hormonal profiles, vaginal pH, and genital vibratory perception thresholds, as well as the use of ultrasonography to measure clitoral, labial, urethral, vaginal, and uterine blood flow. (2003: 326)

This has brought with it an increased focus on the physiological changes associated with orgasm, and a growing mistrust or disregard of subjective experience, despite the fact that – as Graham (2010: 265) points out – the subjective aspects of orgasm are the 'reasons why women seek treatment for orgasm problems (i.e., not because they do not experience contractions of the anal sphincter)'.

Ongoing debates about the definition of orgasmic dysfunction have coalesced around two polarised positions. On the one hand are those with a more biomedical orientation who are keen to establish 'objective', physiological markers of sexual dysfunction and to base diagnoses on an evidence base which prioritises randomised controlled trials as the 'gold-standard' for assessing clinical interventions. On the other, are psychologists, feminists and activists who emphasise the social, psychological and contextual factors involved in sexual problems, are keen to retain a focus subjective experience, and are critical of the medicalisation of sexual problems which serves a wide range of financial and professional interests rather than the interests of men and women themselves. A major change introduced into later versions of the DSM (APA, 2000) was the requirement that the absence of orgasm cause 'marked distress or interpersonal difficulty' to warrant a clinical diagnosis. This represents an attempt to avoid pathologising women for normal variation in sexual response and to consider whether the absence of orgasm is subjectively meaningful. Yet few studies adopt this criteria of 'marked distress or interpersonal difficulty' (Simons and Carey, 2001). For example, we do not know whether any of the 43% of women who answered 'yes' to the question posed by Laumann et al. (1999) considered themselves to have a sexual problem that caused them distress. Later surveys that have begun to ask about subjective feelings of distress consistently find that only a proportion of women experiencing orgasm difficulties find this distressing. For example, 31%

of women in a Finnish study reported orgasm problems, but only 16% also reported distress (Witting et al., 2008). Likewise, only 44% of women in a Swedish survey who experienced orgasm problems 'quite often' or 'nearly all the time' perceived these as distressing (Osberg et al., 2004 see also Shifren et al., 2008 for a similar pattern of results in a US study). To complicate matters further, 'objective' definitions of sexual dysfunction bear little resemblance to whether women consider themselves to have a sexual problem (Osborn, Hawton and Gath, 1988) or would like to receive help for their sexual problem (Dunn, Croft and Hackett, 1998). Nearly 20% of women attendees at general practices in England reported that they had a sexual problem despite the fact that their symptoms and behaviour did not meet the criteria for diagnosis according to the International Classification of Diseases (King et al., 2007). Identifying sexual problems on the basis of physical 'symptoms', rather than asking women about their own perceptions of whether this is problematic or distressing may give an inflated estimate of the prevalence of orgasmic dysfunction. This tension between 'objective' and subjective knowledge of orgasmic experience is a recurring one. While the inclusion of distress invites consideration of subjective experience, it does little to explore the social and cultural conditions which might *produce* distress, such as social pressures to orgasm and cultural expectations that orgasm is a natural or inevitable part of sexual interactions. These issues are more readily addressed in the small body of qualitative – mostly feminist – research, which explores the experiences of women around the absence of orgasm.

Experiencing orgasmic absence

Despite the sustained critique of official definitions of orgasmic dysfunction there is a distinct lack of empirical research which addresses women's experience of dealing with sexual difficulties in their day-to-day lives, with the exception of a small body of feminist qualitative empirical work (Cacchioni, 2007; Nicolson and Burr, 2003; Lavie-Ajayi, 2005; Lavie-Ajayi and Joffe, 2009; Lavie and Willig, 2005; Fahs, 2011). This work highlights a number of key findings: (1) that the orgasmic imperative means that women who define themselves as having 'difficulties' with orgasm feel odd, defective or inferior and some experience this as distressing; (2) that women sometimes define themselves as having problems with orgasm if they do not orgasm through intercourse even if they experience orgasm through other sexual activities and types of stimulation; and (3) that women are often more distressed by the reaction of their partners to orgasmic absence than they are by their own lack of physical pleasure. An additional body of work which looks at the phenomenon of 'faking' or pretending to orgasm illuminates how the orgasmic imperative influences the everyday lives of women (see also Chapter 6).

Firstly, then, the absence of orgasm is experienced as distressing by some (but not all) women, not only because of the absence of physical sensation, but because of the pervasive social and personal meanings attached to orgasm which shape their subjectivity (Lavie and Willig, 2005). By positioning orgasm as the 'normal' or 'natural' sexual response, the orgasmic imperative marks 'inorgasmic' women as abnormal. Some women describe feeling 'deprived', 'defective', 'odd', 'not normal', less feminine or a 'failure' if orgasm is not forthcoming during sex (Cacchioni, 2007; Nicolson and Burr, 2003; Lavie-Ajayi, 2005; Lavie-Ajayi and Joffe, 2009; Lavie and Willig, 2005). The Canadian women interviewed by Cacchioni (2007) positioned orgasm as central to their perceptions of positive sexual experiences, with some lamenting that they 'didn't have that feeling of climbing and getting up to that point' (2007: 306). As well as wanting to experience the emotional and physical pleasure they associated with orgasm, these women wanted 'to be normal'. Similarly, women in the UK described the absence of orgasm as being emotionally difficult, distressing, and as evoking feelings of anger or a sense of sadness (Lavie-Ajayi, 2005). As one of the women put it:

> I am still terribly sad that I have never had the experience [of orgasm] (...) I feel that there is a huge experience other people have that inspires people to write things and you know make the most dreadful mistakes in their lives because it is so wonderful and I have never had it and I feel really that I have been denied something. (Lavie-Ajayi, 2005: 61–62)

The representation of orgasm as a peak, perhaps even a transcendental experience, leaves this woman feeling that something is 'missing'. Some women see the absence of orgasm as a sort of defect or deficiency, something which makes them inferior to other women, in part because of the negative social stereotypes of women as frigid, cold, sexually frustrated, tense, or unable to be open about sex (Lavie and Willig, 2005). This is a long way from the feminine 'ideal' of the sexually adventurous woman offered by postfeminist discourse. Although some women attribute their lack of orgasm to poor technique by their partners, many blame themselves, seeing it as a failure in their own ability to orgasm (Fahs, 2011). Feeling unable to orgasm can become a preoccupation where women constantly seek explanations for their apparent difficulties (Lavie and Willig, 2005), and engage in a variety of 'work' to try to experience orgasm so that they can feel 'normal' (Cacchioni, 2007; Lavie-Ajayi, 2005; Nicolson and Burr, 2003).

Secondly, this research highlights the ways in which the orgasmic imperative fuses with the idea that 'real' sex is vaginal–penile penetration (the coital imperative) such that some women feel that they have problems with orgasm if they do not orgasm through intercourse – despite experiencing orgasm in other ways (Cacchioni, 2007). The orgasmic imperative assumes that orgasms are undeniably 'good' and that they represent the peak of sexual experience. But, more frequent orgasms are not necessarily experienced as pleasurable if they are seen as not being produced in the 'correct' way – such as by the introduction of a vibratory stimulus (Marcus, 2011).

Thirdly, a strong finding from this qualitative research is that women experience the absence of orgasm as distressing because of the reactions and concerns of their male partners (Lavie-Ajayi, 2005; Lavie and Willig, 2005). This confirms the importance of the interpersonal relational context for making sense of sexual distress. Some women report being mocked or harassed by male partners who question their inability to orgasm (Lavie-Ajayi, 2005). Moreover, norms of masculinity which position men as responsible for 'giving' women an orgasm, mean that some women experience this as a pressure to orgasm to reassure male partners that their sexual skills are adequate. Women report that their inability to orgasm is problematic because *her* orgasm is important for *his* sexual confidence: 'I think that men find it hard to understand because no matter what you'll say somehow they will see it as an attack upon their masculinity' (Lavie and Willig, 2005: 122). Expecting an orgasm is seen as being too demanding, putting undue pressure on the man to deliver. While 'interpersonal difficulty' is a recognised aspect of the official definitions of orgasmic dysfunction, this qualitative work reveals how this is wrapped up in gendered discourses of sexuality which position men as responsible for 'giving' orgasms to women, and the presence of orgasm as affirming his 'sexpertise' (Potts, 2002). This relational dynamic is reflected in women's accounts of 'faking' orgasm. In the context of a pervasive cultural imperative to orgasm, faking orgasm is seen as a strategy for avoiding self-blame and explicit or implicit pressure from partners to orgasm. Although faking orgasm is not unique to heterosexual couples, research suggests that it is more pervasive in these relationships (Fahs, 2011), with women faking orgasm more often than men (Muehlenhard and Shippee, 2010). Women report faking orgasm to spare their partners feelings, to bring sex to an end, or to respond to a partner's pressure for them to orgasm (Muehlenhard and Shippee, 2010). Women fake orgasm so that 'he won't feel inadequate' (Roberts et al., 1995: 530) or to prevent him from 'feeling insecure sexually' (Muehlenhard and Shippee, 2010: 562). This positions women as responsible for doing the 'emotion work' involved in managing men's feelings and as subjugating their own desires and pleasures to those of men.

Crucially, this qualitative research illustrates that many women are critical of the social imperative to orgasm, locating it in an unrealistic media discourse which represents women as sexually active and experiencing many orgasms, multiply, all of the time. Many women who experience difficulties with orgasm are highly critical of the 'orgasm as the goal' representation of sex:

> I sometimes think, when I listen to things on the radio or women's magazines, that there is a feeling of having to achieve an orgasm. It is a performance and you have got to do well. (65-year-old women in Lavie-Ajayi and Joffe, 2009: 102)

Although some women recognise – and are critical of – this orgasmic imperative, they still measure themselves against this norm (Nicolson and Burr, 2003), although they may not want to see orgasm as the ultimate goal of sex they still see the absence of orgasm as a failure (Lavie-Ajayi, 2005). Despite an awareness that orgasm is represented as problematic for many women, comparing themselves with other women sometimes reinforced their sense of being different, abnormal or less womanly (Nicolson and Burr, 2003; Lavie and Willig, 2005). There is, then, often ambivalence about orgasm for women – especially women who experience difficulties with orgasm – with some seeing orgasm as no 'big deal' (Lavie-Ajayi, 2005). Some women challenge the primacy of orgasm through intercourse as central to sexual satisfaction or intimacy and describe gaining pleasure through a variety of activities (Nicolson and Burr, 2003). Others adopt 'sexual lifestyle changes' in which they challenge normative definitions of sex by privileging activities typically deemed 'foreplay', or by re-evaluating the importance of sex in relationships (Cacchioni, 2007). While there is little evidence of 'outercourse' being taken up as a significant alternative/addition to intercourse in lay accounts, media representations, scientific research or sexology more generally, identifying how, and under what circumstances, these 'alternative' sexual practices become possible is an important area for exploration.

Conclusions

> [Orgasm] represents the ultimate human ecstatic state without recourse to drugs. (Levin and van Berlo, 2004: 83)

Orgasm is often treated as if it is, by definition, a pleasurable and desirable event. In this chapter I have argued that heterosex is subject to an orgasmic imperative in which having or not having an orgasm is not simply a neutral matter of choice – or at least, not an equally valid or valued choice. We saw in Chapter 1 that the three different frames through which knowledge about orgasm is produced all position orgasm as the most appropriate, expected and desirable outcome of sexual activity and even as offering spiritual or transcendental enlightenment. Here, I argue that this constitutes an 'orgasmic imperative' which compels individuals towards orgasmic sex as a goal. The presence or absence of orgasm is worked up as symbolic of the intimacy or compatibility of a couple, the ability of an individual to function or perform their sexuality in a prescribed way, and as indicative of one's status in gender power relations. The coupling of the orgasmic imperative with the neoliberal norm for self-improvement means that pursuing the 'ultimate orgasm' is adopted as the most appropriate attitude (see also Chapter 5). Yet, this is infused with gender ideology in ways which result in different responsibilities and obligations for men and women around orgasmic success. Postfeminist requirements for women to become 'sexual adventurers' who seek to embrace their sexual empowerment, mean that women's ability to orgasm is taken to signify her sexual self-determination, her active and agentic approach to securing her own pleasure, and her status as a modern, liberated woman who has been freed from the constraints of sexual repression. For men, the presence of whose orgasm is rarely in question, sexual success is measured not by the quality of his own orgasm, but by his ability to 'give' a spectacular, unforgettable orgasm to her and in so doing securing access to an endless supply of sex and demonstrating his superiority to other men. His success is affirmed by the presence of her orgasm. Both these discursive moves are only possible against a historical backdrop of constructed uncertainty about the presence of female orgasm in which the *absence* of female orgasm has shifted from being depicted as expected and 'natural' to being unnatural and dysfunctional. The model of sexual dysfunction outlined by Masters and Johnson, and taken up in the DSM rests on a model of sexual response in which orgasm is key. Positioning the absence of orgasm as a dysfunction (rather than, say, questioning the idea that women *should* orgasm through intercourse), or a failure of postfeminist womanhood, serves to stigmatise women who do not orgasm (through intercourse) regularly. While male orgasm is worked up as unproblematically present (for the most part), female orgasm is constructed as problematically absent – an idea which is explored further in the following chapter.

3
Complicated Women, Straightforward Men

Orgasm is a transient peak sensation of intense pleasure that is accompanied by a number of physiological body changes. In men, orgasm is normally accompanied by ejaculation, which makes the event easily identifiable. In women, however, the achievement of orgasm appears to be less facile than for males and recognizing that it has occurred is often difficult for some women.

Meston and Levin, 2005: 194

Yes. I think basically for men, it is a lot more of a physical thing. As a general rule it appears to be that they are more easily excitable and have an orgasm. For women it's a lot slower. Women don't get turned on as easily or have orgasms easily.

Female interviewee in Nicolson and Burr, 2003: 1739

'For me to have an orgasm, I have to be feeling it before foreplay even starts,' says Jamie, 27, a newlywed in Doylestown, Pennsylvania. 'I have to put in a lot of effort, and the stars have to align. But I feel satisfied knowing that my husband is satisfied every time'.

Women's Health, 2007[1]

When it comes to sex, popular discourse argues that *Men are from Mars, Women are from Venus* – and that this extends to the bedroom (Gray, 1992, 1995). In other words, men and women are so different in relation to sex that they can be characterised as coming from different planets. The notion of essential differences between the sexual appetites, desires, beliefs and behaviours of men and women permeates popular culture, scientific texts, biomedical research and psychological reports. It is fundamental to the construction of heterosexuality and the idea that 'opposites attract'. Popular discourse – as well social science research – perpetuates the polarised idea that men are 'more sexual' than women. The much touted belief that 'men think about sex every 7 seconds' is supported by research which finds that men have more sexual thoughts, report more sexual fantasies, experience more frequent feelings of sexual desire, have more permissive attitudes to sex, and rate themselves as having a higher sex drive. Behaviourally, men desire sex more frequently, are more likely to masturbate, have more sexual partners, engage in casual sex more frequently, and choose sexual partners based on their sexual appeal (see Baumeister, Catanese and Vohs, 2001; Peplau, 2003; Petersen and Hyde, 2010; Conley et al., 2011 for comprehensive overviews of this literature).

The idea that men and women are essentially different extends to orgasm – not only are men more likely to experience orgasm in their last sexual encounter, but they are also more motivated to engage in intercourse for physical pleasure (Carroll, Volk and Hyde, 1985), there is a greater connection between orgasm and sexual satisfaction for men (McNulty and Fisher, 2008) and men rank orgasm as more important to sex than women (Mulhall et al., 2008). The above quotes, taken from a scientific paper, a qualitative interview and a woman's magazine, draw attention to the construction of female orgasm as more mysterious, complex, elusive and difficult than the apparently more straightforward and unproblematic male. These extracts illustrate some of the key dimensions of this difference. First, having or achieving orgasm is depicted as somehow easier, more straightforward or more frequent for men than for women. While men are constructed as more 'easily excitable', for women the 'achievement' of orgasm is 'less facile', it involves 'a lot of effort' and they 'don't…have orgasms easily'. Second, male orgasm, since it is normally accompanied by ejaculation, is presented as more 'easily identifiable', unproblematically present, and therefore it has 'never really given any cause for controversy or debate' (Colson, 2010: 8). In contrast, female orgasm is depicted as more elusive and mysterious, such that women themselves (and the scientific establishment) find it difficult to recognise that orgasm has occurred. The mystifying nature of female orgasm is reiterated in debates about the anatomical location of orgasm; male orgasm is unproblematically located in the ejaculating penis, while the location or source of female orgasm is unresolved. Third, the relationship between orgasm and sexual satisfaction is not straightforward for women as it is for men: 'I feel satisfied knowing that my husband is satisfied'. Fourth, for men orgasm is described as a 'lot more of a physical thing', which is typically contrasted with orgasm being described as 'more emotional' for women. Finally, arousal and orgasm are depicted as more rapid for men while for women orgasm is 'a lot slower'. This final issue of timing is addressed in detail in Chapter 4. The presumed complexity of female orgasm, and its positioning as something mysterious and unfathomable, is perhaps most evident in the huge amount of research and writing dedicated to exploring and explaining the female orgasm compared to the paucity of research dedicated to the male orgasm. As Zilbergeld ironically observes, 'there is little or nothing to be learned or said about men and sex. The males after all, are so simple and quite content as long as they're getting enough' (1983: 12). This trend is reflected in popular (as well as scientific) discourse since the content of lifestyle magazines aimed at both men and women frequently focus on the intricacies of the female orgasm giving little space to explicit discussion of male orgasm/ejaculation. In this chapter we concentrate on the construction of female orgasm as physiologically and psychologically more complicated and uncertain than the male orgasm; on the idea of an 'orgasm gap' in the frequency of orgasm between men and women; and on the distinction between the physical and the emotional aspects of orgasm.

The orgasm gap

> Researchers say women have 'more varied' orgasms than men – but males have more of them. Men experience orgasm during sexual activity with a familiar partner 85% of the time on average, compared with 63% of the time for women. (*Daily Mail*, 2014)[2]

Newspaper headlines reporting the latest social scientific research consistently note the existence of an 'orgasm gap' between men and women. The extract above outlines the findings of an internet survey of nearly 3,000 US single men and women which concluded that women 'have less predictable, more varied orgasm experiences than do men' (Garcia et al., 2014: n.p.).[3] As noted in Chapter 1, large-scale national and international surveys of sexual behaviour consistently report such a gap in the frequency of orgasm between men and women (Richters et al., 2006; Laumann et al., 1994; Haavio-Mannila and Kontula, 1997). Without additional explanation or analysis, reports of gender differences are often viewed as depicting the natural capabilities of men and women, and the easy affinity between psychological research findings and cultural discourse contributes to the face-value acceptance of essential gender differences in sexuality. After all, the male sex drive discourse positions men as naturally more sexual than women, so men's greater propensity to orgasm can be seen as reflecting their naturally higher libido. Such figures reinforce the idea that orgasm is more problematic, difficult or troublesome for women than for men.

Some question how 'real' the orgasm gap is, suggesting that it is a methodological artefact – an artificial product of the way that sex researchers (and others) ask questions about orgasmic experience. Critical work has gone further than this, arguing that the 'counting' of orgasm in these surveys is shaped by phallocentric bias which over inflates the orgasm gap by focusing too closely on orgasm during intercourse. Surveys typically focus on counting the frequency or consistency of orgasm solely *during intercourse* (e.g., Haavio-Mannila and Kontula, 1997), often drawing on crude or limited measures of orgasmic occurrence/frequency, and poorly defining or describing the context in which sexual activities occur. Moreover, the concept of 'orgasm during intercourse' is typically taken at face value, overlooking the ways in which these orgasms might be 'assisted' by manual clitoral stimulation or other activities (Lloyd, 2005). For example, Hite's (1976) data showed that 24% of women regularly reached orgasm through intercourse, but that a further 19% regularly reached orgasm during intercourse if direct clitoral stimulation was applied. Similarly, in their online survey of over 14,000 undergraduate students in the US, Armstrong et al. (2012) found that women who stimulated their own genitals during intercourse more than doubled their chances of having an orgasm. Focusing only on orgasm during intercourse *underestimates* the prevalence of female orgasm, obscures the wide range of sexual activities which couples might enjoy, and privileges intercourse as 'real sex'.

For example, in Hite's (1976: 59) study, 82% of women said they masturbated and 95% of these said that they 'could orgasm easily and readily, whenever they wanted'. When men and women in steady relationships were asked to describe their last intercourse and last masturbation, more men and women reported reaching orgasm through masturbation than through intercourse – this difference was small among men but substantial among women (Dekker and Schmidt, 2002). Therefore, researchers have 'inadvertently used male standards (e.g., penile penetration and orgasm) to evaluate women's sexual experiences and consequently ignored activities, such as intimate kissing, cuddling, and touching, that may be uniquely important to women's erotic lives' (Peplau, 2003: 39). Using orgasm during intercourse as a measure of orgasmic frequency *produces*, rather than documents, an 'orgasm gap' between men and women and reinforces the notion that female orgasm is more elusive or difficult to achieve than male orgasm.

A second explanation is that the orgasm gap is 'real' but is a product of the coital imperative which positions intercourse as central to heterosex. The behavioural approach typically treats the orgasm gap as a 'technical' problem. Here 'good sex' is a technical bodily accomplishment – a matter of deploying effective genital stimulation to achieve orgasm. From this perspective, women experience orgasm less frequently or consistently than men because couples are typically not engaging in the kinds of behaviours that might more routinely lead to orgasm for women. Recent surveys taking an 'event level' approach to studying sexual behaviour, ask about the details of the last sexual event/encounter (Richters et al., 2006; Herbenick et al., 2010). Herbenick et al. (2010), for example, asked nearly 4,000 US men and women (aged 18–59) about the details of their most recent partnered sexual event. This revealed a total of 41 different combinations of sexual behaviours across the sample. They found that both men and women were more likely to orgasm if they engaged in a greater variety of sexual activities. This is confirmed by other research. While most men reach orgasm during most of their sexual activities (Haning et al., 2007), for women the inclusion of manual or oral stimulation greatly increases the likelihood of orgasm (Bancroft, 2002; Fugl-Meyer et al., 2006; Herbenick et al., 2010; Richters et al., 2006). The *Australian Study of Health and Relationships* asked about the last sexual encounter of 19,307 Australians aged 16–59 in a telephone survey, including what kinds of activities were involved in this encounter and whether they experienced orgasm. Consistent with other research they found that men (95%) were more likely to experience orgasm than women (69%). However, when they looked at the kinds of sexual activities that were included in the sexual encounter they found that only 50% of women had an orgasm in encounters involving intercourse alone, but this rose to around 70% for encounters involving intercourse plus manual stimulation or plus oral stimulation. However, despite the wide variety of different combinations of sexual activities that are possible, most heterosex follows a predictable pattern that ends with intercourse; surveys which ask *only* about sexual intercourse or which assume that orgasm occurs *because* of sexual intercourse may be misleading (Richters et al., 2006). Studies which specifically ask about the prevalence and frequency of orgasm during alternative sexual practices typically offer a much more optimistic vision of female sexuality than studies which ask about intercourse alone. The idea that women 'need' clitoral stimulation in order to orgasm is commonplace in sexual advice literature and is often presented as commonsense. However, this has done little to unsettle intercourse as the defining act of heterosex (see Chapter 5 for more on this). The fact that female orgasm requires *more* than intercourse alone is itself taken as evidence that female orgasm is more complicated than the male.

As has been hinted at already, feminist researchers argue that gender ideologies track their dirty feet through figures which claim an orgasm gap. They argue that the 'orgasm gap' is not some kind of unfortunate or accidental oversight, but that the lower likelihood of orgasm for women is explained by the centrality of vaginal–penile intercourse in heterosex, which is more likely to result in orgasm for men than it is for women. That this is reported as *news* in a National newspaper alerts us to the symbolic meaning and ideological work done by reporting such figures. The shift to companionate marriage, postfeminist rhetoric about the need for feminism being outdated and the rise of an ethic of reciprocity as a defining feature of heterosex, conspire to position orgasmic *equality* as the right and proper representation of contemporary gender relations. Moreover, the message from the orgasmic imperative is that orgasm is the 'proper' outcome of sexual activity; in an ideal world everyone would report orgasm on each and every one of their sexual encounters. While men come closer to reaching this 'ideal', women fall short. Evidence of an orgasm gap suggests that gender relations are still out of kilter. The orgasm gap is evidence of women's continued sexual subordination. This 'orgasm gap' is troubling both because it indicates that women are failing to meet the demands of the orgasmic ideal, but also because it violates the ethic of reciprocity which structures contemporary heterosex (see Chapter 2). It implies that men are 'getting more' from sex while women are being short-changed.

Complicated bodies

> The female body is complicated and mysterious, and this is especially true when it comes to sex and orgasm. Many women don't understand their anatomy or sexual response, so it's no surprise that men are even more baffled about what makes a woman tick sexually. (Everydayhealth.com)[4]

The historical shift to conceptualising orgasm as an 'event' which happens in the body (Laqueur, 2009) begs the question of where, exactly, in the body this event occurs. For the most part, orgasm is constructed as an event which happens in the genitals. The idea that male orgasm happens in the penis is rarely questioned, but debates about the anatomical source of women's pleasure have raged since Freud (1905) made a dubious distinction between clitoral and vaginal orgasms. The apparent impossibility of pinning female orgasm to a distinct anatomical location is central to the construction of women's orgasm as enigmatic or mystifying. Female bodies are 'complicated and mysterious' by implicit comparison to a male norm, so much so that even women 'don't understand their anatomy' and men are left 'baffled' by the complexity of women's sexual response.

The clitoris was 'discovered' centuries before it was politicised, and initially this anatomical unearthing did little to alter the meaning of orgasm or female sexuality. Since the turn of the 20th century the clitoris has been, and remains, a contested site of meaning about the 'true' nature of female sexuality. For scientists and the medical profession, this is about the role of the clitoris (and vagina) in women's psychological and physical well-being. For feminists, the clitoris represents the possibility of an autonomous female sexuality which is independent of men, while the devaluing or obfuscation of the clitoris and the assertion of vaginal orgasms as 'real sex' is instrumental in the oppression of women and the reproduction of male power and female subordination. In the 19th century, orgasm was seen as essential for women's physical and mental well-being, but experts worried about the role of the clitoris in women's sexuality and specifically that excessive attention to the clitoris would lead to compulsive masturbation, nymphomania or a rejection of intercourse (see Gerhard, 2000 for an overview). Freud's theory made a timely intervention into this arena by asserting that women's psychological health and maturity rested on the transfer of erotic interest from the clitoris to the vagina, infamously describing the clitoris as like 'pine shavings' which help to 'set a log of harder wood on fire' (Freud, 1905: 143). Throughout the 1920s to the 1960s later writers popularised vaginal orgasm, linking its absence to frigidity (lack of orgasm during intercourse), and taking these as indicators of psychological health or ill-health (Angel, 2012; Gordon, 1971; Neuhaus, 2000).

Publication of *The Myth of the Vaginal Orgasm* (Koedt, 1974), a scathing critique of Freudian theory and its application in sexology, established the political significance of the clitoral/vaginal distinction by linking orgasm to a set of concerns about women's sexual freedom and oppression which become a cornerstone of the feminist movement in the 1960s and 1970s. Koedt offered a critique of the role of sexuality and sexual practice in maintaining and reproducing oppressive gender ideologies which limited the social role of women. Vaginal orgasm was attacked as a misogynistic 'myth' which *created* psychological problems for women by perpetuating the idea that sexual passivity was a natural characteristic of femininity and generating anxieties for women about their apparent inability to orgasm. It was one, but perhaps the most well known, of a host of articles published at this time which explored the links between female sexuality and male domination (see Gerhard, 2000 for an overview). This body of work exposed heterosexual intercourse as an institution which eroticises the power differential between men and women and maintains a patriarchal system of the subordination of women (Greer, 1971; Lydon, 1970). As such, intercourse became defined as a sexual act which privileges men's social, economic and sexual interests at the expense of women. The 'orgasm gap' was presented as the manifestation of a sexual system which systematically disadvantaged women, while routinely meeting the sexual interests and desires of men. Freud's emphasis on the importance of vaginal orgasm was dismissed as a patriarchal attempt to institutionalise intercourse, and through this male power, by limiting women's sexual autonomy and privileging the penis and male orgasm. Koedt drew on the work of Kinsey et al. (1953) and Masters and Johnson (1966) as offering scientific 'facts' about women's sexuality to counter the myths of psychoanalysis. In particular, Masters and Johnson's work dismissed the distinction between clitoral and vaginal orgasms, arguing that these were connected through nerves and musculature, which together produced female sexual response. They suggested that the vagina lacked the density of nerve endings to make it responsive to touch, rendering it relatively unimportant to women's sexual response. Making an analogy between the clitoris and the penis, Masters and Johnson argued that clitoral stimulation was more pleasurable for women and more consistently produced orgasm. Feminists condemned vaginal orgasm as an 'invention' designed to shore up heterosexuality, retain the primacy of intercourse as 'real sex' and affirm the centrality of the penis to women's pleasure. In contrast they imbued the clitoris with political significance, seeing it as offering a uniquely female sexuality providing respite from the constraints of masculinist definitions of sexuality and unfettered by ties to exclusively hetero- or homo-sexuality. The clitoral orgasm offered feminists the possibility of an autonomous source of female sexuality, which was separate from men and heterosexuality.

Decades after Masters and Johnson declared that all orgasms were clitoral, the distinction between clitoral and vaginal orgasm remains remarkably tenacious both in scientific research and in the cultural imaginary. The 'discovery' of the clitoris as the source of women's sexual pleasure has largely been adopted by popular writing such as in women's magazines and sexual advice manuals as a key gain of feminism and sexual science, but rather than resulting in a rejection of heterosexuality, the 'orgasm gap' is reworked as a technical problem of technique. Sexual autonomy is repackaged as individual empowerment-through-orgasm, where women (and men) are offered explicit instruction in 'how to' stimulate the clitoris while maintaining the primacy of penis-in-vagina intercourse as the defining act of heterosexuality:

> 'The vagina, urethra and clitoris all need to be stimulated for maximum chances of orgasm,' says neuroscientist Gert Holstege, at the University of Groningen in the Netherlands. 'The key is a combination of external and internal stimulation, best achieved by changing sexual positions'. (*Men's Health* 1)

Ingenious sexual positions which enable clitoral stimulation *at the same time* as 'internal' stimulation of other parts of the female anatomy by the penis are presented as the 'ideal' approach to sex which meets the needs of men and women simultaneously.

In the scientific literature, the search for a vaginal orgasm (an orgasm which can be triggered by penis-in-vagina intercourse) persists, accompanied by an ever-increasing proliferation of different 'types' of female orgasm which purport to be anatomically located. Largely informed by ideas from evolutionary theory, a series of publications by Brody (2006, 2007a, 2007b) and colleagues (2011), for example, claim to demonstrate that penile–vaginal intercourse 'is associated with better psychological and physiological function' (Brody, 2006: 393), although this has received extensive criticism (Levin, 2011, 2012; Prause, 2011, 2012; Laan and Rellini, 2011). Evolutionary theory adds to the clamour about the 'mysteries' of female orgasm by puzzling over the elusive function of female orgasm for reproduction (see Lloyd, 2005 for an overview). The 'discovery' of the 'G-spot', for example, as offering yet another type of female orgasm has gained popular acceptance, although controversy persists over whether it actually exists (Levin, 2003; Jannini et al., 2010) or not (Hines, 2001; Puppo and Gruenwald, 2012; Kilchevsky et al., 2012). In popular advice, the issue is not whether or not the G-spot exists, but the mystery of where to find it:

> The G-spot is more frustrating to find than your lost car keys but worth the hunt, says Dr Yvonne Fulbright, author of *Touch Me There* (Hunter House) [...] While a clitoral orgasm is felt mainly in the clitoris itself a G-spot orgasm can be felt throughout her lower body. (*Men's Health* 16)

A recent academic paper by Puppo and Puppo (2014: n.p.) published in the journal *Clinical Anatomy*, argued for a clarification of anatomical terms used by sexologists and sexual medicine experts and that terms which have come into recent use, such as the internal/inner clitoris, G-spot/vaginal/clitoral, vaginally-activated orgasms and so on, are anatomically 'incorrect terms'. The paper argued that these terms were based more on hypotheses and personal opinions than on scientific evidence. This paper was widely reported in the British media under headlines like 'The vaginal orgasm doesn't exist – it's the clitoris that holds the key to female pleasure, study claims' (*Daily Mail*, 2014)[5], or 'Vaginal orgasms are a "myth", claim researchers' (*The Independent*, 2014)[6]. Nonetheless, the focus on the genitals, and on intercourse, persists despite evidence that orgasms can occur through exercise (Herbenick and Fortenberry, 2011), stimulation of the mouth and anus, skin stimulation, breasts and nipples, through imagery, or during epileptic episodes and by drugs (see Komisaruk and Whipple, 2011 for an overview). At the same time the latest technologies and discoveries are often interpreted in light of this 'mysteries of female orgasm' discourse. For example, reports of some of the first scans of the female brain during orgasm (note that it was just the female brain that was scanned) were reported in one UK National newspaper under the headline 'Scan reveals the secrets of female orgasm' (*The Sunday Times*, 2010).[7] Scientific research about sexual anatomy is often packaged in newspaper headlines as offering to solve the mysteries of, or debunk myths about, female orgasm: 'Scientists reveal mystery behind the female orgasm: When having sex it's all about DISTANCE not size' (*The Mirror*, 2014).[8]

This narrative about a progressively more enlightened understanding of female sexuality, debates about the complexity of women's anatomy, and confusion about the physiological source of women's orgasm, is used to construct, rather than dismiss, the idea that women's bodies and their sexual responses are mysterious, complicated, and unfathomable. Similar sustained attention has not been given to the anatomical location of male orgasm, which is typically presented as arising straightforwardly from the penis. I argue that this simplicity is constructed, rather than reflecting some anatomical truth about male sexuality. For example, the prostate gland is recognised as a source of intense pleasure for men, and although instruction about how to locate and stimulate this gland is (sometimes) given in lifestyle magazines and sex advice manuals, this is not routinely packaged as an 'anal orgasm' to rival a 'penile' orgasm, or as an 'internal' in contrast to an 'external' orgasm. It is not too much of a stretch to see that such classification, evoking the possibility of anal penetration by a penis, would threaten heterosexist sensibilities. The fact that some gay men recognise 'anal orgasm' as a distinct sexual experience which is defined more by its relational properties than its anatomical location (Hoppe, 2011), indicates that such a representation is possible. Moreover, despite evidence that there are different biological mechanisms governing emission (in which seminal fluid is expelled into the prostatic urethra) and ejaculation (in which the semen is ejected), and evidence of a distinction between ejaculation and orgasm, these are typically treated as synonymous and interchangeable under the umbrella of male orgasm. Discussion of the possibility of a 'dry orgasm' (without ejaculation) for men as a choice which enables multiple orgasms (rather than a dysfunction of 'retarded ejaculation') has not been widespread, but again indicates that a more complex conceptualisation of male orgasm is possible if not politically expedient. The complexity of male sexual response is often overlooked or obscured, and there seems to be a collective disinterest in deconstructing men's experience of orgasm. In contrast, and confirming female as a binary opposite of male, female anatomy and orgasm is persistently constructed as anatomically complex, mysterious and a puzzle to be solved by scientists and male lovers alike.

Orgasmic ambivalence

> You know, it's not really the end of the world to me. It wouldn't worry me ... if people said 'oh you'll never have an orgasm again ... '
> (Female interviewee in Nicolson and Burr, 2003: 1742)

Another area of apparent confusion is whether or not orgasms are actually important to women and women's sexual satisfaction. As noted in the previous chapter, the orgasmic imperative suggests that orgasm is essential to sexual satisfaction and that more orgasms equal better, more satisfying, sex. Women's ambivalence about orgasm is both troubling and puzzling in this context. Early research typically conflated orgasm with sexual satisfaction – if an individual had an orgasm then they were, by definition, sexually satisfied. Yet, the research findings are very mixed. The *Global Better Sex Survey*, which surveyed individuals in 27 countries, found that 65% of men compared to 52% of women said that orgasm was a 'very important' aspect of sexual experience (Mulhall et al., 2008). A national probability sample of American heterosexual women aged 20–65, reported that only 29.1% rated 'having an orgasm' as very or extremely important to their sexual happiness (Bancroft, Scott and McCabe, 2011). The *National Survey of Sexual Attitudes and Lifestyles*

(NATSAL) in the UK found that both men and women thought that orgasm was more important to men, but more men (37.4%) than women (28.6%) thought that sex without orgasm cannot really be satisfying for women (Johnson et al., 1994). Other research takes a less direct approach and attempts to explore the role that orgasm plays in men's and women's sexual satisfaction. Some studies report a correlation between orgasm frequency or consistency and sexual satisfaction (Edwards and Booth, 1994; Haavio-Mannila and Kontula, 1997; Philippsohn and Hartmann, 2009; Sprecher, 2002; Waite and Joyner, 2001). Couples in long-term relationships who thought it was likely that they would experience orgasm in their next sexual encounter were more sexually satisfied (Haning et al., 2007), and the frequency of orgasm predicted sexual and relationship satisfaction among married heterosexual couples in the US (Young et al., 1998). Other studies suggest that this relationship is weak or non-existent (Hurlbert et al., 1993). Even when studies do report a correlation, this does not necessarily mean that orgasm is important to sexual satisfaction. Waterman and Chiauzzi (1982), for example, found that orgasm consistency was significantly related to sexual satisfaction in women but not men, but that for most activities (for both men and women) pleasure ratings were significantly higher when the activity occurred *without* orgasm. It is somewhat puzzling, then, that women often report high satisfaction with their sex life in the context of a relatively low frequency of orgasm. In one study, for example, only 29% of women reported always having orgasms compared to 75% of men, yet there were no differences in their physical and emotional satisfaction with their sex lives (Michael et al., 1994). This suggests that women are less interested in orgasm than men, or that orgasm plays a less important role in their sexual satisfaction. The weak relationship between orgasm and sexual satisfaction for women disrupts the orgasmic imperative, and is often presented as more problematic and perplexing than the straightforward relationship between orgasm and sexual satisfaction for men.

Feminist researchers argue that survey data treat satisfaction and the assessment of the importance of orgasm as if it sits outside of gendered cultural norms about sexuality. They have argued that the privileging of male sexuality and orgasm in heterosex, means that women are encouraged to devalue or de-prioritise their own pleasure (Nicolson and Burr, 2003). Assessments about whether sexual experiences are enjoyable (or not) take place in a context in which these activities are infused with meaning – both social and relational. Qualitative work, much of it drawing on feminist approaches, seeks to explore *how* people make judgements about whether or not sex is satisfying and to explore women's ambivalence about orgasm within the context of gendered ideologies about sexuality. In a series of papers Sara McClelland (2010, 2011, 2013) raises interesting questions about the study of sexual satisfaction and women's ambivalence about orgasm. Firstly, she argues that evaluations of how sexually satisfied (or not) women are do not arise straightforwardly from bodily experience, but are influenced by cultural expectations and the sense of entitlement to pleasure and orgasm that are embedded within these expectations. Surveys rarely consider what counts as high or low sexual satisfaction. When asked, female participants described low satisfaction in very negative terms – such as feeling pain, degradation or depressed – while men talk about loneliness or not having adequate sexual stimulation (McClelland, 2009, cited in 2010). If men and women are using very different baseline expectations for 'satisfying' sex, it casts doubt on the validity of group level comparisons. At the other end of the scale, while *all* the male participants described orgasm as an important benchmark of sexual satisfaction, no women described their own orgasm as the *primary* benchmark for their own satisfaction (McClelland, 2011). Instead, women talked about 'being close' as satisfying in the *absence* of orgasm: 'Like, it's satisfying even if you know that realistically you're not going to have an orgasm with that person, you know?' (McClelland, 2011: 311). McClelland argues that individuals are constantly making decisions about whether their experience is going to be good enough rather than ideal (i.e., including orgasm) such that 'just being with' the person becomes the new benchmark against which satisfaction is measured. Similarly, a secondary analysis of the US *National Health and Social Lifestyle Survey*, argued that different gendered thresholds for 'regular enough' orgasms structured assessments of sexual satisfaction (Carpenter et al., 2009). For men, for whom orgasm during sex is anticipated, regularity of orgasm was not predictive of sexual satisfaction. For women, for whom orgasms are less routinely anticipated, climaxing only sometimes (versus always) reduced ratings of pleasure. Understanding the role that expectations play in assessments of sexual satisfaction may help to explain some of the contradictory findings from quantitative research in which the *presence* of orgasm may increase reports of sexual satisfaction, but the *absence* of orgasm does not necessarily result in reports of low satisfaction.

Secondly, McClelland troubles the idea that appraisals of satisfaction are primarily a reflection of *intra*-personal experiences. Self-report measures assume that individuals are reflexively looking inwards to examine their own feelings of satisfaction. 'Feeling satisfied' (or not) is treated as a subjective experience which arises out of the person's own unique experience.

While some describe sexual satisfaction as anchored in the self (ranging from focusing on physiological responses to focusing on feeling close to or comfortable with a partner), for others sexual satisfaction is anchored outside of the self and is dependent on whether they have fulfilled their partner's wishes or desires (McClelland, 2011). More than half the female participants in McClelland's sample described wanting to satisfy their partners and for some this satisfaction was conflated with their own.[9] Survey research also suggests that partner orgasm is important to people's rankings of sexual satisfaction. Feeling that a partner was sexually satisfied was ranked second in a survey of US women (whereas their own orgasm was ranked fourth) (Bancroft, Scott and McCabe, 2011), and frequency of partners' orgasm predicted sexual and relationship satisfaction among married heterosexual couples in the US (Young et al., 1998). In a further study McClelland distinguished two groups of participants who emphasised the importance of the partner's experience and the relative unimportance of their own orgasm. One group consisted of heterosexual men whose own orgasm was consistent, but for whom a focus on their partners' orgasm offered a new form of sexual satisfaction. The second was heterosexual women whose experience did not often (ever) include orgasm and consequently their focus was on their partner's satisfaction (McClelland, 2013). This complicates the relationship between orgasm and sexual satisfaction, highlighting the relational context of orgasmic experience and questioning whether assessments of pleasure and satisfaction are individually experienced. The 'puzzle' of women's apparent ambivalence about orgasm must be understood within these competing demands.

Emotional women, physical men

> Female sexuality is a little more complex. In fact, one of the main differences between male and female sexuality is that guys don't need to feel emotionally connected to the person we're having sex with in order to want to have sex. (Sharecare.com)[10]

A further characterisation of female orgasm as 'more complex' rests on the idea that while for men orgasm is a purely physical experience, for women orgasm (and sexuality in general) is complicated by the need to be 'emotionally connected' to the person. This distinction was neatly captured in Hollway's (1984) description of the (male) sex drive discourse, and the (female) have/hold discourse which positioned men and women as having essentially different motivations and interests in sexual relationships. These discourses are prevalent in social scientific research exploring the reasons that men and women give for engaging in sexual activity. Studies report that men are more motivated to engage in sex for physical reasons, such as physical release or simply because they are 'horny', whereas women are more motivated by emotional reasons, such as feeling closer to a partner (e.g., Carroll, Volk and Hyde, 1985). In a study which explored over 200 different reasons for engaging in sex, men were significantly more likely to report having sex because the person 'had a desirable body' or 'was too "hot" (sexy) to resist,' because they 'wanted to achieve an orgasm,' or because it 'feels good'. In contrast, women exceeded men on only three of the 237 reasons: 'I wanted to feel feminine'; 'I wanted to express my love for the person'; 'I realized that I was in love' (Meston and Buss, 2007: 482–483). Women, it is said, engage in sexual intercourse for the 'spin-offs' such as emotional closeness, commitment, love, affection and closeness (Basson, 2000). The idea that 'the emotional' is distinct and separable from 'the physical' is reified in large-scale surveys of sexual satisfaction, such as the US *National Health and Social Life Survey* (NHSLS), which have begun to routinely incorporate this distinction (Carpenter, Nathanson and Kim, 2009). Nonetheless, these studies typically report sex differences as if they reflect 'real differences' between men and women – often tying them to naturalised explanations of these differences rooted in evolutionary theory (e.g., Buss and Schmitt, 1993) or biological differences.

The idea of 'natural' differences in the sexual motivations of men and women also permeates the ways in which individuals talk about sex, and the advice given in lifestyle magazines. In interviews, women describe the same cultural story about men's sexuality: 'Men have sex, enjoy sex. It is a simple physical act. End of story' (Nicolson and Burr, 2003: 1741). In their qualitative interviews with 45 heterosexual men living in Australia, Mooney-Somers and Ussher (2010) found that men often limited the meaning of sex to the physical, the body, and often only to the genitals. The 'doing' of masculinity means being other than female, a distancing from femininity. These men constructed male sexuality as the pure expression of a physiological drive. A recurrent theme was the tight regulation of the meaning of sexual activity to 'just sex', 'nothing more than sex', or as 'only sex' (2010: 362). For men, sex is positioned as an opportunity to have a physical need met, rather than as having any emotional significance. In contrast, women idealise sex and want intercourse to be about love and romance (Hayfield and Clarke, 2012), and describe orgasms as being 'not so important' when you are in love (Roberts et al., 1995; Nicolson and Burr, 2003). Physical pleasure, and orgasms specifically, were deprioritised by women in favour of emotional connection and ensuring the satisfaction of their partners. As Nicolson and Burr (2003) point out, it is not simply that some women think orgasms are important while others do not, it is that even when an individual woman values orgasm, she puts the needs of her partner above her own (her orgasm is not *as* important as his). While the male sex drive discourse positions men as having an insatiable appetite for sex, where sex is urgent and necessary and men are motivated by physical pleasure, women are traditionally depicted as having little or no sexual desire, and instead are motivated to achieve emotional intimacy through sex. This double standard – in which men are depicted as 'needing sex' and deserving pleasure, while women's pleasure is of little or no importance (Jackson and Cram, 2003) – also sets up heterosexual economy in which orgasms are traded for intimacy. Love and intimacy represent socially approved ways for women to express sexual desire and pleasure, but at the same time they represent a barrier for women to negotiate safe and pleasurable sex (Warr, 2001). Feminists have pointed to the ways in which discourses of love, romance and emotional intimacy serve to put women at a distance to their own bodies and their own physical pleasure, while prioritising the sexual needs of men.

In making this distinction between the physical and the emotional, female orgasm becomes positioned as 'more complex' because of this association with emotionality. While men are positioned as always ready or wanting to have intercourse, women's more complex sexual responses require more preparation or work for them to be ready and willing to engage in intercourse. There is a lot of emphasis in men's magazines on how to get women 'in the mood' for sex, and women's need for emotional intimacy is depicted as making sex more complicated and challenging. Male orgasm is constructed as more *straightforwardly* 'physical', while wrapping orgasm up in notions of love, commitment, intimacy and relationships positions female orgasm as more complicated. In their longitudinal study of sexual satisfaction in newly-married couples, for example, McNulty and Fisher (2008: 231) observed that 'men's sexual experiences appear to be less open to interpretation' and 'may depend less on the contextual aspects of sex and more on the concrete, physical rewards'. Orgasm is presented as rightly, simply or naturally aligned with physical, embodied pleasure.

However, the 'sex is just physical' narrative is only one story that is told about men and sex. This narrative is neatly aligned with causal or 'hook up' sex (an account which is paralleled in women's accounts of hook up sex), while a different is a narrative about 'relationship sex' which involves emotional expression and intimacy which maps onto ideas about maturity. Men's investment in romance and intimacy is seen as part of constructing a mature adult identity (Bertone and Camoletto, 2009; Mooney-Somers and Ussher, 2010; Terry and Braun, 2009), and places different obligations and responsibilities on men – including obligations to deliver orgasm to their partners. Terry and Braun's (2009) analysis of accounts given by 15 New Zealand men of sex in long-term heterosexual relationships, highlights this. From the safety of their relationships they constructed a distinction between the 'enlightened man' they had become and the 'immature' pre-relationship self who was highly focused on penetrative sex for his own pleasure. The sexuality of the pre-relationship self was independent of love and intimacy, and sex was about proving masculinity. In contrast, the 'mature' self sees sex as embedded within relationships in which men are permitted to de-prioritise their own orgasm and become more interested in, and care about, her orgasm. Similarly, Bertone and Camoletto (2009) noted a similar shift in some men's biographical accounts of their changing sexuality, in which men changed from being sexually predatory and operating according to the sex drive discourse, to adopting what they call an 'intimacy' discourse. This discourse is characterised by sex as a way of creating and maintaining a sense of emotional closeness and of mutual disclosure involving the ongoing negotiation of the relationship and the broadening of sexuality beyond the coital imperative. The idea that men's greater commitment to emotional intimacy would be reflected in their commitment to taking on the complexities and burden's of female orgasm is reflected in the accounts that women give of sexual relationships. Some women see a partner's ability to 'give' a woman an orgasm (or his willingness to try) as a sign of his love and commitment and as a measure of their partner's emotional involvement:

> Somehow it also seems to me as an indicator of how much the person loves you, which I find as a positive thing because really if someone loves you he would stay and would do anything for you to enjoy and come. (Ana cited in Lavie and Willig, 2005: 122)

The growing acceptance of the 'permissive' discourse in which sex is depicted as recreational and 'anything goes' as long as it is consensual, presents an interesting context in which to explore how gendered norms of physicality and emotionality operate in 'hook up' sex. Hook-up or casual sex is a sexual encounter which takes place outside of a committed relationship with little or no expectation that a relationship will be forthcoming – it is culturally articulated as 'just sex'. Perhaps not surprisingly, women report having an orgasm less frequently than men in hook-up sex, but more revealing is the ways in which individuals talked about the ethics and norms which governed their understanding of hook-up sex – norms in which women's pleasure is often disregarded (Armstrong et al., 2012). Women report having orgasms more frequently with a 'caring' partner who is 'concerned with her pleasure, willing to take time and perform the practices that worked, and she could communicate what felt good' (2012: 454). In hook-up sex, women often felt that men were 'not even trying to make it a mutual thing' (2012: 455). Men echoed this understanding, arguing that it was not as important for them to 'give' orgasms during hook-up sex as it was during relationship sex:

> But if you're with someone for more than just one night, I think guys, it is important for guys. I think they feel that they should make sure that a girl has an orgasm. And I think that if you're in a long-term relationship, I know I feel personally responsible. I think that it's essential that she has an orgasm during sexual activity. (2012: 456)

Although the ethic of reciprocity coupled with the need to affirm masculine skill places responsibility on men to ensure that their female partner has an orgasm during relationship sex, men have a different understanding of their obligations to women in hook-up sex. The authors conclude that:

> ... the greater gender inequality in hook ups flows, at least in part, from today's version of the sexual double standard – both men and women are seen to deserve pleasure in relationships but women's entitlement in hook ups is not fully accepted. (Armstrong et al., 2012: 457)

For women, the aligning of femininity with a discourse of emotional intimacy and care results in a prioritisation of male orgasm over their own – especially in the context of an ongoing relationship. For men, the aligning of masculinity with the physicality of sex, makes the obligation to 'care' about women's pleasure optional in some circumstances. Women expected more equality in relationship sex, but still felt responsible for their partners' pleasure in hook-up sex. Moreover, the apparent complexity or difficulty of female orgasm serves to position men as 'extra' caring when they do feel some responsibility towards ensuring women's pleasure, while women's caring is invisible, unappreciated or treated as routine. This exchange is predicated on the idea that: (a) men are more motivated by sex and women by emotional intimacy; (b) men are responsible for women's orgasm; and (c) female orgasm is more complicated, difficult and burdensome, requiring more 'work'.

Conclusions

In sum, the female orgasm is typically constructed as more elusive, mysterious, complex and difficult than male orgasm. Female orgasm is depicted as occurring less frequently than male orgasm – women do not orgasm in every sexual encounter (the majority of men do), and some women never experience orgasm. Female sexual anatomy is presented as more complicated than male anatomy. While male orgasm is depicted as arising from the penis, the origin of female orgasm is more mysterious and linked to a proliferating set of anatomical possibilities. In this sense, female orgasm is positioned as more diffuse or difficult to pinpoint. For men, the frequency, consistency or intensity of orgasm is seen as directly linked to men's ratings of sexual satisfaction, but for women this relationship is less straightforward. Finally, men are constructed as having sex simply for physical pleasure, while for women sex is complicated by the messiness of relationships, intimacy and emotionality. Beck (1997: 61) coined the term 'constructed certitude' to describe a means of presenting a clear and unified sense of identity or ideology, especially in times of risk and uncertainty, by obscuring ambiguity or complexity. Despite progressive narratives about the enlightenment afforded by scientific research on female sexuality which promises to solve these 'mysteries', I argue that these discourses produce a 'constructed *uncertainty*' about women's bodies and female orgasm, which is mirrored by the production of 'constructed certitude' in relation to men's sexuality. This constructed uncertainty serves to justify sustained and detailed attention to, and intervention into, women's bodies, while positioning them as fundamentally different from a male norm. At the same time, this male norm is marked as self-evidently unproblematic and therefore uninteresting. Critical scholars too, seem to have had little to say about male orgasm.

Studies reporting sex differences in sexuality, and in orgasm specifically, typically ignore the influence of gendered ideologies and heteronormativity in shaping people's expectations and evaluation of whether sexual activity is emotional, physical, satisfying, important, equitable or fair (McClelland, 2010). Simply documenting when orgasm does or does not occur fails to interrogate the circumstances in which orgasm is made possible (or not), and the meaning that individuals give to this non-event. Following Muehlenhard and Peterson (2005) I argue that

there is a 'missing discourse of ambivalence' in relation to the conceptualisation of orgasm and its relationship to sexual pleasure and satisfaction (although it is very live in women's accounts). Attempts in survey
and questionnaire-based research to establish whether (or how much)
orgasm contributes to sexual satisfaction fail to address ambivalence –
the idea that orgasm might be simultaneously important and unimportant to women, important in some ways but not others, or satisfying in
some ways but not others. Understanding this ambivalence necessitates
an engagement with the ways that gendered discourses present contradictory messages to men and women about their rights and entitlements, duties and responsibilities, in relation to orgasm. This requires a
more nuanced understanding of the negotiation of orgasm (and broader
understandings of pleasure) within local contexts, to understand better
under what circumstances different rights and responsibilities are both
fore-grounded and met. McClelland (2010: 617) offers the 'relative
deprivation framework' as an approach that invites us to ask a different
question about the relationship between orgasm and sexual satisfaction:
When do women who experience orgasm infrequently feel that they
have been unjustly treated and when do they feel that they are simply
inadequate?

4
Coming Together: The Timing of Orgasm

> Since men tend to climax faster than women do (most women need 10 to 20 minutes to peak via intercourse; most men need two), get a head start. Have him tantalize you manually or orally for 10 minutes so you're close to the edge.
>
> *Cosmopolitan 36*

There is a cultural obsession with the timing of orgasm: How long does the 'average' person take to have an orgasm? How long does an orgasm last for? Am I taking too long? How long do you have to wait before you can have a second or third orgasm? Did I climax too quickly? This chapter explores temporality and how discourses about time shape and structure sexuality and our expectations and experiences of orgasm. Drawing a distinction between 'clock time' and the 'natural' timings of the body, researchers have argued that modernity is characterised by attempts to regulate the bodies of individuals by bringing them into line with normative temporal expectations of behaviour. For example, workplace rules and regulations have disciplined the timing of defecation and urination (Inglis and Holmes, 2000), and both mothers and midwives are expected to monitor their own and baby's behaviour in relation to the time and efficiency of the working week (Simonds, 2002). Sexual intimacies, then, have temporal dimensions. The clinical gaze of sexologists, aided by technologies of observation, claim to 'discover' the natural rhythms and timings of the body. Drawing on 'clock time' as an objective measure is central to claiming scientific credibility and establishing the authority of scientific observations about the normal and abnormal timings of the body. Moreover, people hold individual and collective beliefs about how long sex should last to be satisfying, how often they should have sex each week, whether they should orgasm every time they have sex, and how long it should take them to have an orgasm. Lifestyle magazines and self-help books instruct us in how to have long-lasting sex, elongated orgasms, how to climax faster and better. The timing of orgasm is not simply a matter of physiology; cultural assumptions and ideologies shape and frame how this embodied experience is worked up, felt and made sense of. In this chapter, I consider how discourses of time and temporality – including this tension between 'objective' clock time and subjective perceptions of time, and between 'expert' and 'lay knowledge' – shape normative expectations of the timing of orgasm in heterosexual sex. I examine how neoliberal imperatives for fast and efficient orgasms, and the 'gold standard' of simultaneous orgasms, converge with essentialised gender differences in the timing of sexual responses to produce different obligations for men and women. In particular, I examine the construction of 'premature' ejaculation as a problem of timing and a site for the disciplining of men in relation to the demands of hegemonic masculinity and neoliberal intimacies.

Simultaneous orgasm and the 'timing gap'

The melding together of sexual satisfaction, self-actualisation and marital stability with an ethic of reciprocity since the turn of the last century served to position simultaneous orgasm through intercourse (where orgasm occurs *at the same time* for both the man and woman) as emblematic of 'good sex' and relational harmony. For example, in his book *Marriage Counselling* (1948: 123) David Mace argued that 'good sex adjustment for husband and wife means satisfying orgasm for both' with simultaneous orgasm as a 'desirable ideal' (cited in Clark, 1991: 24 – see also Gordon, 1971). Despite (or perhaps because of) numerous sexual surveys demonstrating that penis-in-vagina intercourse often fails to deliver orgasm for women to anywhere near the same degree as it does for men (see Chapter 3), evidence of this 'orgasm gap' fails to dislodge simultaneous orgasm through intercourse as the crowning achievement of heterosex. Indeed, Jagose (2010) points to the difficulty of retaining this information as cultural fact, arguing that 'the fate of such information is to be repeated again and again without ever loosening the cultural imagination's allegiance to heterosexual intercourse' (2010: 527). Similarly, simultaneous orgasm through intercourse retains its hold on the cultural imaginary as the ultimate expression of heterosexual intimacy despite, or perhaps because of, its depiction as something which is difficult to achieve.

Contemporary sex advice literature retains simultaneous orgasm as the yardstick for sexual intimacy between couples. Self-help book

Simultaneous O by Ashleigh Corbiel (2012), for example, is described as providing 'the tools to finally achieve that most spectacular sexual experience', the 'ultimate goal', the 'one thing every couple wants'. Elsewhere simultaneous orgasm is portrayed as 'the natural expression of a beautifully balanced relationship' (2012: 19), and an almost spiritual experience:

> In a very real and beautiful sense, simultaneous orgasm can bring about that special union that prophets referred to when they wrote of how two shall be as one flesh. The act of intercourse accomplishes this in a literal physical fashion, but simultaneous orgasm takes you beyond your physical selves into emotional ecstasy. For some couples it is the gateway into a transcendent, resplendent dimension of human experience. (Riskin, Banker-Riskin and Grandinetti, 1997: 5)

The 'special' status of simultaneous orgasm also circulates in people's attitudes towards and beliefs about sex. Between 12–33% of Canadian undergraduates think that simultaneous orgasm is necessary for a good sexual relationship (Meston, Trapnell and Gorzalka, 1998), and over one-third of men and women in a French survey report that 'Having simultaneous orgasm' was the most important thing in their sexual practice (Colson et al., 2006), with men finding this more important than women (42% and 30% respectively). A survey of Czech men and women found that simultaneous orgasm produced by penile–vaginal intercourse was associated with greater life, sexual, partnership and mental health satisfaction (Brody and Weiss, 2011). Heterosexual couples talk about simultaneous orgasm as a 'golden standard' for sexual fulfilment and intimacy as a couple, describing how 'the better times are when we actually really make love and climax together [...] those are very special times' (Braun et al., 2003: 245). The authors conclude that simultaneous orgasm may constitute an 'ultimate mutuality' or an '*ideal* reciprocity' since both partners are giving and receiving simultaneously.

Regardless of its exalted position as affording special intimacy and satisfaction, it is generally recognised in popular culture, self-help literature and sex therapy that simultaneous orgasms can be difficult to achieve. Simultaneous orgasm is described as 'elusive as winning the lottery' (*Cosmopolitan* 36), 'the stuff of legends' (*Women's Health*),[1] or as the popular website *Netdoctor* puts it:

> The notion that simultaneous orgasm is the norm is simply a myth that's been created over the last couple of hundred years,

by hundreds of romantic novels and erotic stories...But the truth is that, while simultaneous orgasms are nice, they are difficult to achieve...(*Netdoctor*)[2]

Difficult...but not impossible. Positioning simultaneous orgasm as an achievable goal, coupled with neoliberal imperatives for sexual self-improvement, means that rather than being represented as a natural or inevitable outcome of intercourse, couples have to work hard to overcome 'natural' differences to achieve sexual climax at the same time. Some warn against trying too hard to pursue simultaneous orgasm:

> Although sharing the orgasmic moment would be great, doing so is just not always possible. And striving for that achievement can lead to a lessening of sexual enjoyment. If the man repeatedly has to ask 'Are you ready, are you close?' it disturbs the woman's concentration and can put her orgasm further away. (Westheimer, 2011: 169)

The message is that men and women must work hard, develop skills and awareness in order to prepare their own bodies, and the bodies of their lovers, to reach orgasm in synchronicity. Expert advice is on hand to help them in this difficult quest – simultaneous orgasm is a goal which becomes more valuable because of its elusiveness and a point of distinction for the truly compatible couple. The difficulty of simultaneous orgasm reinforces its status as an ideal since only the most dedicated, skilled or well-suited couple will manage it. Simultaneous orgasm needs to be worked at, but this work must appear 'natural', spontaneous, or not too effortful. For the most part couples must 'settle' for the more familiar script in which mutual orgasms are exchanged when she orgasms first (typically through manual or oral stimulation) and his orgasm follows during intercourse (Braun et al., 2003). 'Good sex', including that marked by simultaneous orgasm, is paradoxically constructed as natural and spontaneous *and* as requiring specialist training and technical education founded on expert knowledge from sex therapists, clinicians, sexologists and others (Jackson and Scott, 1997). Two key explanations for the difficulty of attaining simultaneous orgasm are provided: a) it is a mechanical problem of how male and female bodies do (or don't) fit together, or b) it is the result of differences in the timing of male and female sexual responses. In other words, the barrier to simultaneous orgasm shifts from being a problem rooted in heterosex per se, to being a problem of mechanical fit and timing, which are open to resolution. Only couples who are prepared to invest in developing their sexual skills (by following expert advice, training their bodies and consuming commercial products) will be able to achieve this sexual nirvana.

Firstly, then, the widespread acceptance of the clitoris as the crux of women's sexual pleasure, creates a mechanical problem in which the male and female body parts essential for orgasmic sex are not typically brought into pleasurable relief during intercourse. Or as one group of researchers put it, 'the lack of penile–clitoral contact in the conventional "missionary" sexual position' is a particular 'anatomic feature' which affects 'orgasmic capacity and the timing of female sexual response' (Eichel, Eichel and Kule, 1988: 130). To solve this technical problem of anatomical incompatibility, some sex therapists suggest the 'coital alignment technique' as a way for couples to synchronise their sexual responses. This technique involves the careful positioning of the body (the 'man rests the full weight of his body upon the women – not propping his torso up on his elbows' and 'her thighs are bent at an angle not to exceed 45 degrees', Eichel et al., 1988: 131), alongside coordinated sexual movement and careful timing ('it is crucial that partners maintain a steady pace and do not respond to mounting pressure to climax by speeding up and "grasping" at orgasm – or by slowing down and tensing up', 1988: 133). This careful body work is replicated in popular lifestyle magazines which adopt a similarly technical explanation and offer endless advice about different sexual positions which will stimulate the clitoris and the penis to ensure simultaneous orgasm.

> The key to 'synchro-gasming' is control, so try saddling him first – you'll command the pace and position, and can read his expressions too. (*Cosmopolitan*)[3]
>
> Instead of straddling him put your legs together, feet flat between his legs', suggest Brame. The benefits of this are twofold: With your legs together, the fit is even tighter, making the sensations more intense. Plus there's increased G-spot stimulation, which combined with clitoral strokes, make for an explosive orgasm. (*Cosmopolitan* 11)

Such advice rehabilitates intercourse by promising to ensure that (with careful practice) both partners achieve orgasm. Achieving simultaneous orgasm is a mechanical and technical exercise in positioning and moving the body in such a way that the right 'friction' is created to induce an automatic orgasmic response.

The second approach focuses on synchronising the timing of orgasm by overcoming 'natural' differences in the rapidity of male and female sexual responses. Academic, scientific, clinical and popular literature repeatedly promulgates ideas about 'natural' physiological differences in the sexuality of men and women – specifically, that men have rapid sexual responses, while women are slower to become aroused. While the figures reported vary, scientific evidence of a 'timing gap' is routinely reported in magazines aimed at women (see opening quote to this chapter) and men:

> Sexologists at the Kinsey Institute in the US found that the average woman can orgasm after 10–20 minutes of sex. (*Men's Health* 4)

What is often overlooked is that these figures refer specifically to intercourse. There is consistent evidence dating back to Kinsey's research in the 1950s to suggest that women can become aroused to orgasm as quickly as men. For example, Kinsey et al. (1953) note the popular assumption that women are slower to become aroused than men, but go on to point out that during masturbation 45% of their sample took just 1–3 minutes to orgasm and a further 24% took just 4–5 minutes. Hite (1976) also notes that, like men, women can masturbate to orgasm in little over 4 minutes. So, although it is popularly noted that women do not orgasm as readily or as quickly as men during sexual intercourse, the fact that women often have little difficulty reaching orgasm rapidly through masturbation is subject to cultural amnesia. Instead, sex *differences* in the speed of sexual response and time taken to orgasm during intercourse are often elided with arousal in general, and the clear message is that women are 'slower' to orgasm:

> A man's sexual response time averages 2.8 min while a woman's takes an average of 13 min [...] which is why only 20% of women can climax during intercourse. It is no ones fault, simply a fact. (Renshaw, 2007: 96)

A second solution, then, is for couples to have to address this natural 'timing gap' by putting in the hard work and effort needed to develop the skills and control necessary to synchronise their arousal.

> In some ways simultaneous orgasm is the ideal solution to the 'problem' of human sexuality: the fact that men and women are running on unsynchronized watches. The fact that men tend to be easily and quickly aroused; women tend to be slowly and intricately aroused; and the whole sweet task of loving is to slow him down and speed her up so you meet somewhere in the middle. When you

both explode in the same shared moment, it is truly a kind of bliss. (Bechtel and Stains, 1996: 273)

Numerous self-help books and therapeutic interventions attempt to guide the heterosexual couple through the intricacies of timing their mismatched sexual responses to peak in orgasm at the same moment. Specifically, women must train themselves to orgasm through intercourse more rapidly and readily, and men must train themselves to control and delay their ejaculation. In other words, women need to speed up their sexual response, while men need to slow theirs down.

Speeding up women, slowing down men

To minimise the apparent discrepancy in male and female sexual response, women are encouraged to 'speed up' their orgasms, by getting 'a head start' (*Cosmopolitan* 36):

> there are occasions when you want to speed up the satisfaction [...] masturbating to the brink – but not allowing yourself to peak – ensures that you'll be bursting at the orgasmic seams by the time your man walks through the door [...] When you peak faster, your guy can cross the line sooner too. So do what works to speed up your orgasm – ultimately, it benefits you both. (*Cosmopolitan* 6)

Masturbation is often presented in women's magazines not as a source of sexual pleasure in its own right, but as a mechanism for enhancing 'readiness' for intercourse (Moran and Lee, 2011). Magazines reinforce the neoliberal message that faster and more efficient orgasms are 'better', but also recognise that this speed is better suited to male sexual response. Moreover, in the example above, the idea that men need to wait for her orgasm *before* he can orgasm or 'cross the line too', creates the urgency for women to speed up, with this being presented as something which 'benefits you both'. Women are urged to work on themselves, using masturbation as a tool, to prepare themselves for a rapid sexual response. Men's magazines also target their advice primarily towards giving men tricks and tips to help speed up women's sexual responses – often these techniques are embedded in scientific, typically biological, knowledge:

> Invest at least three minutes of your total 15 in kissing. Studies by Lafayette College in the US found that *kissing* reduces levels of the stress hormone cortisol, quickening the time it takes to turn you both on. (*Men's Health* 4)

Men are tutored in the art of seduction and how to build a woman's arousal before intercourse by suggestions such as 'Flirt with her via text or email throughout the day' (*Men's Health* 50) or 'Turn her on instantly' with sensual tricks to get her in the mood (*Men's Health* 49). Men are also advised about where (and how) to touch women so that their responses will be faster. When talking about the 'anterior fornix' or 'A-spot' which is a patch of nerve endings, *Men's Health* describes it in the following way:

> It sends sexual signals to the brain, so touching her here speeds up the arousal process. 'She'll be lubricated enough to have sex in 5–10 seconds and close to orgasm in 1–2 minutes,' says Dr Chua Chee Ann, the sex therapist who reported the discovery in the *British Journal of Sexual & Marital Therapy*. (*Men's Health* 16)

The timing of women's response is often reported in articles aimed at men, with various 'experts' espousing that their own specialist techniques of intercourse, oral sex or manual stimulation will help 'most women' orgasm in just a couple of minutes.

Paradoxically, women's magazines also advise women not to rush sex. For example, in one article addressing the 'Reasons you don't have an orgasm', women are advised that 'racing through foreplay' is a problem:

> Here's the scenario: Your guy is eager to get to the main event. Problem is, you're not exactly ready and you're afraid that if you ask for a little pregame action, he might think that you're too high-maintenance in bed or just get frustrated. Plus like a lot of women, you may feel self-conscious about just lying there and receiving pleasure. But don't rush through the warm up. (*Cosmopolitan* 29)

In a neoliberal context in which speed and efficiency are validated, the 'slower' female sexual response is perhaps especially problematic. In this example women are encouraged not to rush, at the same time as anxieties about pace are rehearsed. Men are presented as ever ready, eager and willing for sex (intercourse is positioned as 'the main event'), while women are 'afraid' to ask for more time to become aroused. Using the imagined voice of the reader ('you') as separate from the authoritative editorial voice allows the articulation of women's anxieties whilst maintaining a distance from these views. In this way, women's apparent belief that their sexual needs are too demanding or unreasonable ('you're too high-maintenance') and that receiving pleasure is problematic ('like a lot of women you may feel self-conscious') are articulated as normative but mistaken. This is brought into sharper focus when the article goes on to explain that women need at least 20 minutes of 'arousal time' before adding: 'We know that 20 minutes might sound like a long time, but trust us, the good guys don't mind'. This both reinforces the idea that women's orgasms are hard work or burdensome (see Chapter 5), but also that 'good guys' are the ones who are prepared to put in this hard work. The ethic of reciprocity creates temporal obligations and responsibilities – women should ensure that they are ever ready for sex to meet men's more rapid response, but 'good men' will be prepared to invest the time to ensure that women orgasm.

Most advice in lifestyle magazines is aimed at ensuring that women reach orgasm as fast as possible, but there is also advice which is aimed at helping men to slow down their responses:

> Try holding your penis and 'dipping' it in and out of the entrance to her vagina. This is a great way to delay ejaculation if you want to, and playing in the shallows means a satisfied customer who'll come again and again. (*Men's Health* 42)

This advice, aimed particularly at men who are worried about the size of their penis, presents 'delaying ejaculation' as optional, but the economic metaphor of a 'satisfied customer' reinforces the idea that it is men's responsibility to provide a sexual service to women using their sexual skill to bring them to orgasm 'again and again'. Sexual positions can be used to slow down the male sexual response by ensuring that the penis receives less stimulation:

> 'Rate your sexual excitement on a scale of one to 10,' says Dr Ian Kerner, author of, *She Comes First* (Collins) 'Try keeping yourself at seven by slowing down and decreasing the amount of stimulation to your penis. You can do this by asking her to go on top; not only will your penis be less stimulated, she is more likely to orgasm faster in this position so it will bring you in sync'. (*Men's Health* 23)

Men are encouraged to engage in careful surveillance and monitoring of the body to be able to identify when his climax is close. Moreover, the man can deploy a range of bodily strategies to discipline his performance into one which is slow enough for her to orgasm first or so that they can be 'in sync'. Lifestyle magazines aimed at both men and women often draw on techniques commonly used in sex therapy to instruct readers in how to delay ejaculation, as this advice aimed at women illustrates:

> To do this, try the stop–start method: During foreplay, stroke his shaft to get him excited, but have him signal to you when he's about to orgasm so you can stop the stimulation for a short period of time. When his arousal level subsides, you can resume, repeating the cycle a few times before bringing him to orgasm. (*Cosmopolitan*)[4]

The purpose of this technique, according to the article, is not only for him to last longer but for him to be able 'to actually train himself to hold back from coming'. Individuals are encouraged to regulate the speed of their own, and each other's, sexual functioning by adopting techniques and principles of bodily self-assessment, surveillance and modification. With so much emphasis on the 'correct' timing of orgasm, it is perhaps not surprising that failure to coordinate timing appropriately becomes defined as dysfunctional.

Cuming 'too soon': premature ejaculation

> Size may not matter but length of sexual performance is important to both men and women so delay the inevitable orgasm with double strength Stud D-Lay Cream for longer-lasting, fulfilling sex that ticks everyone's box again and again. (Advertising for Stud D-Lay Cream™ for premature ejaculation)[5]

Nowhere is the cultural chatter about the timing of orgasm more apparent than in discussions of premature ejaculation (PE). As the above advertisement illustrates, there is a preoccupation with longer-lasting sex as definitive of good or satisfying sex, while climaxing 'too soon' marks an inadequate sexual performance. Products such as these, which bind sexual performance and masculinity tightly together, are marketed to heterosexual men with the promise that their 'inevitable' orgasms can be controlled, that this can compensate for other 'inadequacies' (e.g., a small penis), and allow them to meet the obligations of hegemonic masculinity by bring their partners to orgasm 'again and again'. The 'timing gap' and demands for men to 'delay' their orgasm and to be 'longer-lasting' in order to ensure that their female partner is fully satisfied, has meant that (despite a focus on rapidity and efficiency) longer-lasting sex has become culturally coded as better sex, and men who can last longer, as better lovers. A man's endurance during intercourse, his ability to keep going, becomes both a physical feat and an exercise in willpower, and a marker of his virility and masculinity. It is perhaps not surprising then that, against this cultural backdrop, 'premature ejaculation' (PE) is positioned as a sexual 'dysfunction'. It is one which is under increasing scrutiny in the academic and scientific community, although it is fair to say that this has not received nearly as much attention as erectile dysfunction, especially in the wake of the commercial success of sexo-pharmaceuticals and its re-branding as a bodily malfunction.

While all men can be encouraged to 'last longer' the positioning of some men as 'suffering' from PE marks an especially troublesome performance. Hegemonic masculinity perpetuates what McCarthy and Metz (2008) call, the 'perfect intercourse performance', as one of the foundation stones of male identity. Emphasis is placed on the physical performance of 'real sex', which is narrowly defined as the insertion of an erect penis into a bodily orifice culminating in ejaculation and orgasm. Medical and sexological discourses reproduce and legitimate this heteronormative masculinity by presenting a penis which is erect for the purposes of vaginal penetration as the model for healthy and functional sexuality (Tiefer, 1994). This has been demonstrated through a range of critical work which has explored the construction of erectile difficulties and the marketing and consumption of drugs designed to enhance performance by producing hard, more reliable and longer-lasting erections (Marshall, 2002; Grace et al., 2006; Potts et al., 2004). In contrast, very little academic consideration has been given to ejaculation as a marker of masculinity despite its interpellation in the naming of commercial products like Stud Delay™ cream. A rare exception is Johnson's (2010: 239) analysis of ejaculation in which he examines how this 'innocuous physiological function' and its timing and performance become equated with the masculine ideal'. He argues that males learn that ejaculation is the most important sexual event with which all sexual encounters must end, and that time 'is a frame through which sexual success becomes measured' (Johnson, 2010: 241).

Here, we examine how ejaculating at the 'right time' is regulated through the interweaving of neoliberal shifts towards the rational management of sex, and the demands of hegemonic masculinity, for a 'perfect intercourse performance' (McCarthy and Metz, 2008). In particular, we expose the ways in which these imperatives are embedded within, and legitimated through, the construction of PE as a sexual dysfunction in key national and international organisations: The World Health Organisation's International Classification of Diseases (ICD) and the American Psychiatric Association's Diagnostic and Statistical Manual of Mental Disorders (DSM). Exploration of the ways in which premature ejaculation (also known as rapid ejaculation) is defined in the key scientific and medical literature illuminates the ways that masculinity and sexuality intersect. In the World Health Organisation (WHO), premature ejaculation is defined as the 'inability to control ejaculation sufficiently for both partners to enjoy sexual interaction', and diagnostic criteria include 'occurrence of ejaculation before or very shortly after the beginning of intercourse (if a time limit is required: before or within 15 seconds of the beginning of intercourse)' (WHO, 1992: F52). Similarly, the American Psychiatric Association (APA) defines premature ejaculation as the 'persistent or recurrent ejaculation with minimal sexual stimulation before, on, or shortly after penetration and before the person wishes it' and includes evidence of 'marked personal distress or interpersonal difficulty' as a criterion for diagnosis (APA, 2000). These definitions are highly contentious as powerful groups with vested interests (including urologists, pharmaceutical companies and psychologists) jostle to position PE as a mental disorder requiring psychological intervention or as a sexual dysfunction requiring medical intervention (see Waldinger and Schweitzer, 2006 on the historical development of these definitions). Here, I draw attention to four key features of these definitions:

- *Timing* – the timing of ejaculation is central to this 'disorder' but exactly what is meant by 'premature' or 'rapid' is unclear with some disagreement about whether this is an objective cut-off (15 seconds or less) or a subjective judgement (before the person wishes).
- *Distress* – the definitions require that ejaculating 'too soon' or 'before one wishes' results in subjective distress before a diagnosis of PE can be given.
- *Control* – according to the ICD, premature ejaculation is the inability to *control* the timing of ejaculation and although this has been included and subsequently dropped from the APA definitions, it has remained central to men's experience of PE and is often included in outcome measures testing the efficacy of interventions.
- *Relational difficulties* – the definitions position PE as a relational problem. The ICD refers specifically to the sexual *enjoyment* of the partner. Despite some use of gender neutral language (e.g., partners or penetration), the definitions (and corresponding literature) are underpinned by heteronormative assumptions about the timing of male and female sexual responses.

This chapter considers each of these aspects in turn – drawing both on the scientific and academic discussions about PE and also on cultural products and popular discourse.

How soon is 'too soon'?

A dysfunction called *premature* ejaculation begs consideration of exactly what is meant by premature; in other words how soon is too soon? A range of commercial and professional interests converge with this question. Identifying and treating men who 'have' PE and differentiating them from men who do not, is essential for establishing the legitimacy of an intervention into the lives of a group of men who are 'different' from the norm and are therefore in need of expert knowledge and practice. Time represents an important dimension by which such men and their sexual performances can be distinguished from the majority. Moreover, establishing clear and measurable benchmarks against which the success of treatment (including newly-emerging pharmaceutical treatments) can be assessed is essential for the approval, credibility and marketability of drug treatments and increasingly of psychological treatments which require a scientific evidence base. Yet, the question of how soon is too soon has received little attention until recently, and has proven difficult to answer with any degree of certainty. Debates in the clinical literature oscillate between attempting to establish objective measures of ejaculatory timing using 'clock time' on the one hand, and men's subjective perceptions of being 'too quick' on the other. Recent attempts to formalise clinical definitions and to establish clear norms or standards of sexual function, have given renewed attention to 'clock time' as a way of distinguishing the premature from the 'on time'. Intravaginal ejaculatory latency time (IELT), defined as the time from vaginal penetration to the start of ejaculation inside the vagina (thus neatly side-lining gay men who experience PE), has been suggested as an appropriately objective measure of PE. In one study, female partners of men who thought they had PE used a stopwatch to measure the amount of time it took for their partner to ejaculate after the start of vaginal penetration, at home, on each occasion of intercourse, for four consecutive weeks (Waldinger et al., 1998). Using this approach, and based on the distribution of IELTs in a sample of 1,587 men, Waldinger (2003) have suggested a clinical threshold of one minute.

One problem is that this 'objective' measure often does not map neatly onto men's own perception of whether they experience PE or not. 'Clock time' and 'subjective time' do not coincide. There is considerable overlap in the time it takes men to ejaculate (as measured by a stopwatch) between those who are labelled as having, or not having, PE based on DSM criteria, with some men defining themselves as having PE despite having IELT scores of 25 minutes (Patrick et al., 2005). In one study, 87% of men who had been diagnosed with PE reported ejaculating within two minutes of intercourse, but 22% of the non-clinical sample reported the same (Hartmann et al., 2005). Therefore, clock time may not be sufficient in itself for identifying whether orgasm can be considered 'premature' – feelings of subjective distress and control continue to be important (Rosen and Althof, 2008). Not all men who consider themselves to orgasm prematurely find this distressing or troubling. Analysis of data from a large observational study in the United States using validated patient reported outcome (PRO) measures found that distress was one of the most important variables in determining the diagnosis of men with PE (Rosen et al., 2007).

On the other hand, relying on men self-defining as having PE is often treated with suspicion. Within the therapeutic literature there is the suggestion that men (and women) are unduly swayed by cultural preoccupations which elide staying power with masculinity. For example, in their workbook for clients, Wincze and Barlow advise that:

> Many people have unreal ideas about how long a man should be able to last. They have these ideas because of 'locker-room bragging', folklore and porno movies. Research has been done on how long it takes a man to ejaculate after penetration. The results show that the average time is between 2 and 8 minutes for most men. (Wincze and Barlow, 1996: 50)

Part of the solution, then, is to educate men and their partners so that they develop more realistic expectations. Clearly, the interaction between what is happening in the body (i.e., when ejaculation occurs) and men's perceptions of this (and their female partners) interact in complex ways. Men's perceptions of being 'too soon' may bear little resemblance to the amount of time it actually takes them to ejaculate. Whilst clinicians and pharmaceutical companies may be keen to fix the timing of ejaculation so as to delineate the normal from the abnormal, the timing of men's ejaculation needs to be considered in relation to the socio-cultural meanings given to long-lasting sex, and to men's ability to control their sexual arousal.

Controlling the body

The inability to control ejaculatory timing is one of the defining features of premature ejaculation, and is a central part of the ICD categorisation of premature ejaculation, although it has disappeared from the DSM description of the dysfunction which retains the idea that ejaculation occurs involuntarily (before the person wishes it). Lack of control remains key to men's subjective experience of PE. Men describe lacking a sense of control as a central feature of their experience of PE ('Well, for me, I don't feel like I really ever have control') and regaining control as an important goal of successful interventions ('I mean, the ultimate success would be ultimate control') (Revicki et al., 2008: 36). Indeed, men who regularly ejaculate without any subjective feeling of control, even if their 'clock time' is longer than 2 or 3 minutes, are likely to self-define as having PE (Rowland et al., 2005). Moreover, feeling that one has poor or extremely poor ejaculatory control distinguishes well between men with PE and those without PE (the majority of whom consider themselves to have 'very good', 'good' or 'fair' control) (Hartmann et al., 2005). When asked what they mean by 'ejaculatory control' men describe this as being able to 'stop' or 'hold back' ejaculation if desired, the time to ejaculation and as 'the ability of the man to prevent ejaculation' (Revicki et al., 2008: 40). PE is constructed in both medical and lay discourse as a problem of control – a problem of mind over matter, of disciplining the body and bringing it under the control of the individual.

With the rise of Viagra™ social scientists have explored the ways in which dominant scripts of masculinity are predicated on the idea that normal sexual functioning requires the ability to generate and sustain an erection, and to be able to engage in penetrative sex to orgasm (Marshall, 2002; Potts, 2000b). Premature ejaculation has received rather less scrutiny than erectile dysfunction, but both interweave discourses of performance with discourses of control. Traditionally, gender roles have positioned women as being more aligned with the emotionality and the body, and men as being more aligned with rationality and the mind (Roberts et al., 1995). Male sexuality is presented as a natural drive that needs to be civilised or controlled by rational man. One of the ways in which this is represented is the construction of the penis depicted as a miniature male person with desires and a mind of its own which often conflict with the conscious control of the man's cerebral-brain/mind (Potts, 2000b). In interviews, heterosexual men in Australia treated the need to exercise control over their sexual drive, and specifically to exert mastery over their bodies and especially their penis, as a natural, inevitable and unquestioned aspect of male sexuality (Mooney-Somers and Ussher, 2010). Male sexuality is paradoxically constructed as uncontrollable and urgent, and as needing to be controlled. Consequently, descriptions of losing an erection or otherwise losing control over the male body during intercourse became stories of 'the failure of control' (2010: 359). The emphasis on 'mindful mastery' of the body fuses neoliberal concerns with a managerial approach to sex, with the rationality of hegemonic masculinity. Viagra™, by purporting to offer an erection 'on demand', promises to protect masculinity from sexual 'failure', thereby affirming the mastery of mind over body and intensifying normative expectations of heterosexual sex (Loe, 2001, 2004; Potts et al., 2004). Viagra becomes a pill to not only repair sexual problems, but to enhance and improve sexual performance by promising harder erections, available on command, and which are longer lasting. The shift from understanding erectile dysfunction as a psychological problem to a mechanical failure transforms a failure of the mind into a failure of the body and paves the way for the widespread acceptance of a techno-fix which reaffirms the authority of the rational sexual actor. Men experiencing depression, for example, have sometimes felt 'more of a man' and compared themselves jokingly to 'porn stars', because a side effect of their anti-depressant medication is their ability to 'keep going for hours' (Emslie et al., 2006). Redefining PE as a physiological problem which rests outside of the conscious control of men, may allow a similar shift to take place. The construction of PE as a failure of control, and specifically as a failure of the conscious mind to control the body, is embedded in the DSM which describes PE as ejaculation that occurs 'before the person wishes it'. The message for men, then, is that sex requires the mastery of mind over body and the natural propensity to become aroused quickly and easily needs to be monitored and managed.

Relational trouble

'Unsuccessful' sexual interactions with a partner are often an implicit criterion for sexual dysfunctions, but PE is *explicitly* constructed as a problem which arises in the context of partnered sexual interactions. The ICD describes PE as the 'inability to control ejaculation sufficiently for *both partners* to enjoy sexual interaction' (emphasis added). When asked how long they felt a man ought to be able to delay or control his ejaculation for, the majority of men (regardless of whether they did or did not experience PE) indicated that this should be 'until the partner has experienced her orgasm' (Hartmann et al., 2005: 98). Indeed, Masters and Johnson suggested that the 'stopwatch' approach to defining PE should be avoided and replaced by a consideration of the relationship context and that the satisfaction of the partner should be the defining issue. They go on to point out that the same woman might on one occasion be satisfied by 30–60 seconds of 'intravaginal containment' but desire substantially more on another. Therefore, they suggest that a better definition of PE is if a man 'cannot control his ejaculatory process for a sufficient length of time during intravaginal containment to satisfy his partner in at least 50% of their coital connections' (Masters and Johnson, 1970: 92). Certainly, feeling distressed about not satisfying existing partners (or being reluctant to establish new relationships) was the second most commonly reported concern for men with PE in one interview-based study (Symonds et al., 2003). Men with PE also reported that they did not feel 'manly', and that 'When you can't satisfy your woman, you somehow feel like there's a large part of you that is missing or failed' (Revicki et al., 2008: 38). Not only do these representations of PE affirm intercourse and an erect (but non-ejaculating) penis as essential to female pleasure, but the idea that men are responsible for women's orgasm and sexual satisfaction is institutionalised in 'official' definitions of PE as a sexual dysfunction. The construction of a 'timing gap' between men and women places an obligation on men to delay their own orgasm until they have 'given' an orgasm to their female partner, and so doing affirms both their masculinity and their commitment and care to their partner. Men who ejaculate before their partner, who are defined or define themselves as ejaculating prematurely, are conversely positioned as failing to fulfil their obligations as men.

The positioning of orgasmic timing as 'problematic' is something which must be worked up (or not) between the couple within the context of their relationship. Norms and expectations of orgasmic timing have to be negotiated, made meaningful and personalised within the context of a particular relationship. This being the case, there is surprisingly little research which looks at the processes by which couples come to regard PE as a problem, attempt to solve this problem for themselves, or come to seek professional help in solving this problem. Most research on partner dynamics is quantitative and highlights the negative impact of PE on partner sexual satisfaction and on the relationship (Patrick et al., 2005; Rosen et al., 2007). Partners have an important role in prompting men who define themselves as having a problem, to seek help for this problem. An internet-based survey found that although most men had not sought treatment, of those that did 74.6% did so because they wanted to better satisfy their partner sexually (compared to 61.2% who wanted to increase their own pleasure (Porst et al., 2007). Furthermore, 21.2% sought help because their partner became concerned, upset or angry when they climaxed quickly, and 14.9% said that their partner asked them to seek help (Porst et al., 2007). In a large-scale qualitative piece of research in the US and Europe, Revicki et al. (2008) explored the impact of PE on the everyday lives of men and their female partners. Both men and women felt that they 'lacked something that could bring more fulfilment', that 'something was missing' from their sex lives, and that this 'affected their sense of intimacy' (2008: 35). Indeed, even when they find other ways to satisfy their partners, men still feel that their performance is inadequate: 'But even when she's completely happy, I feel like I am not lasting as long as I should' (2008: 37). In a rare study, Byers and Grenier (2003) asked men and their female partners to complete questionnaires about his ejaculatory behaviour. Their findings concluded that women have little understanding of men's subjective experiences of PE. Women thought that men had more control over their ejaculation, and thought that they were less concerned about ejaculating sooner than they wanted (Byers and Grenier, 2003). Of course, some women may not be distressed about PE, and may even feel relieved because they do not feel that they have time for lengthy sex (Revicki et al., 2008).

Conclusions

Orgasm is subject to temporal discipline – orgasm must be delivered, experienced or performed in a timely way. Temporal norms are structured by sexual science, which creates standards and benchmarks against which temporal performance can be monitored with the use of a stopwatch. But, they are also structured by neoliberal drives for speed and efficiency, and by expectations about 'natural' differences in the sexual responses of men and women. Women worry about taking 'too long' to orgasm, while men worry about not lasting 'long enough'. There is a considerable amount of 'body work' which goes into delivering orgasms 'on time' – work performed on the body to bring the body into line with social expectations. As we have seen, women are compelled to speed up their bodily responses while men are encouraged to slow theirs down. Men who seek professional treatment for premature ejaculation have often tried a number of different strategies to delay their orgasm before seeking treatment. These include: 'wearing multiple condoms, applying desensitization ointment to the penis, repeatedly masturbating prior to intercourse, not allowing their partner to stimulate them, or distracting themselves by performing complex mathematical computations while making love' (Althof, 2006: 846). In a web-based study of men who identified as having premature ejaculation, over half reported using special positions during sex, interrupting stimulation, masturbating, focusing on something else, and having intercourse more often than usual to try to delay orgasm (Porst et al., 2007). In addition, around one-quarter (24.9%) reported using creams and ointments, and others had used alcohol (42.1%) and recreational drugs (15.6%) to attempt to manage the timing of their orgasm. Men work hard to ensure that the feelings in their bodies match the 'rules' they have for appropriate emotional (and physical) responses to sexual stimulation. Considerable work goes into controlling and disciplining the male body, so that an orgasm is produced 'on-time'. Beyond these statistics we know very little about the work that individuals do to manage the timing of their sexual responses to meet cultural expectations, and we know even less about how couples share, negotiate or manage this work as they navigate the everyday details of their sex lives. Questions about how and when some couples decide there is a 'problem' with timing, or the contexts under which they do not interpret a rapid ejaculation as troubling, are rarely addressed.

Debates about the relative importance given to patients subjective perceptions of time and distress about ejaculating 'prematurely', and the utility of objective measures time which promise to distinguish between the dysfunction and the anxious, represent different concep-tualisations of the body and bodily experience. They also represent a 'turf war' between psychologists and medical professionals about claims to expertise. As the success of sexo-pharmaceuticals has highlighted, there is money to be made from sexual distress. A focus on 'clock time' treats the body as a mechanical system which is either functioning in a timely way, or is malfunctioning. Striving to produce objective measures of premature ejaculation is driven as much by the need for measurable outcomes by which to demonstrate the efficacy of pharmaceutical inter-ventions, as it is by a desire to better understand this phenomenon. Moreover, in pursuing 'objective truths' and clinically useful norms, such research serves to create and perpetuate new standards against which sexual 'performance' can be judged, and sometimes deemed defi-cient. As Steggall and Pryce (2006) point out, since heterosexual men rarely have the opportunity to observe other men during sexual encoun-ters, how do individuals know what an 'appropriate' or 'normal' amount of time is? Scientific/medical discourse is a powerful force in demarking the normal or usual from the abnormal and unusual. Of course, this is not the only potential source of information. We do not know, for example, whether and under what circumstances men use pornography as a measure for their own performance, or rely on information from partners (who may have other partners to compare to), or draw on infor-mation from magazines or the internet to make evaluations about their own orgasmic performance.

Moreover, the definitions of premature ejaculation included in classificatory systems are far from value-neutral. As we have seen, gendered ideologies permeate these definitions at the same time as they are obscured as objective science. Knowing that ejaculating after a short time is *experienced* by (some) men as a lack of control and as emasculating, is only understandable by acknowledging the influence of gendered ideologies about heterosexual performance. It is not enough to know what the body does (or doesn't) do and when, this bodily event is interpreted in relation to a set of norms about the appropriate, right and proper timing of orgasm. These norms are infused with heteronormative assumptions about 'natural' differences in the timing of male and female sexual responses, and a strong ethic of reciprocity and mutuality permeates a concern with premature ejaculation. These norms circulate through popular culture, but are also embedded within the formal systems by which sexual performance is deemed normal or dysfunctional. These norms evoke different entitlements and obligations for men and for women. The cultural requirement that men delay their orgasm until they have 'delivered' an orgasm to their female partner, is written into formal definitions of sexual dysfunction making this a requirement of masculine performance, rather than optional. In contrast, women are obliged to speed up their orgasm to meet the more urgent needs of men.

5
Orgasmic Labour: Training the Body for Orgasmic Success

Okay, you've heard of a clitoral orgasm and you've heard of the G-spot kind – both damn good in their own right. Now imagine if you blended the two types for one phenomenal fireworks-like finale. Yep, you can actually do that. It takes some specific techniques – which we teach you here – and a bit of practice, but experts say it's a skill you can master.

(*Cosmopolitan* 7)

Train hard to stay harder

Use the gym to strengthen bedroom stamina

Olympic performance in the bedroom is as simple as sticking to your training schedule. You'll have better erections, longer orgasms and increased all-round sexual satisfaction if you are burning 1,400kcal or more a week in your workouts. (*Men's Health* 9)

Orgasms don't just come naturally – they require hard work. Contemporary sex advice positions orgasm as something that needs to be worked at, improved, practiced and mastered. Sex is an arena for self-improvement as we exert ourselves in an effort to become better or more skilled lovers, able to deliver an 'Olympic performance in the bedroom'. It is not enough to have an orgasm, we are impelled to have bigger, better, stronger, longer, frequent, multiple orgasms which offer a 'phenomenal fireworks-like finale'. This chapter examines the neoliberal drive towards sexual self-improvement in the pursuit of rapid, reliable and intense orgasmic experiences, and demonstrates that orgasms are increasingly constructed as effortful, requiring skill and hard work – both to induce orgasms in the self, and to evoke orgasms in the other. The intersection of neoliberal imperatives for work and self-improvement with discourses of masculinity (including stamina, hard work, skill and perseverance) and postfeminism (sexual adventurousness and empowerment) determine what kinds of 'work' are undertaken in the pursuit of orgasmic success. We focus on the ways in which lifestyle magazines – specifically *Cosmopolitan* and *Men's Health* – offer a 'pedagogy of the body', teaching men and women how to hone, develop, improve, move and shape their bodies to achieve the ultimate orgasmic experience. Tricks, tips and techniques to achieve these super-orgasms, we are told, can and should be learned, and lifestyle magazines offer expert advice to 'teach' us how to train ourselves and our bodies. The sexual body is depicted as needing to be whipped into shape through intensive 'workouts' in the gym, and through continued 'practice' and by 'sticking to your training schedule' in order to 'master' the sexual skills and techniques which will deliver the ultimate orgasmic experience.

Working at orgasms

The entry of a neoliberal 'performance imperative' (Tyler, 2004) into the organisation of contemporary sexuality has meant that sex is increasingly reframed as 'work' requiring effort, knowledge and skill. Chapter 2 explored the role of the orgasmic imperative in this discourse of rational management. If the performance imperative involves a drive for 'great sex' (Ménard and Kleinplatz, 2008), for outstanding rather than ordinary or mediocre sex, then 'great sex' is increasingly characterised by quicker, longer, intense and more frequent orgasms. As neoliberal rationality comes to infuse intimate spaces, and sexuality becomes a project of continual self-improvement, expert knowledge (from sexual science, celebrities, lifestyle coaches, sex therapists, etc.) comes to have extra significance as a route to sexual self-transformation. In the context of sexual self-actualisation and the imperative to develop technologies of sexiness, expert knowledge forms part of what Bernstein (2001) refers to as the 'Totally Pedagogised Society' where instruction and learning pervade every aspect of life over an individual's lifestyle and extends well beyond formal schooling. In this context, expert knowledge – especially as it is communicated through mass media, comes to serve not just an information function, but a pedagogical function and consequently adopts a more instructional tone explicitly 'teaching' individuals how to transform their sexual selves in the pursuit of sexual fulfilment.

Lifestyle magazines depict 'great sex' simultaneously as resting on natural, chemical or magical elements beyond individual control, and on the mastery of sexual techniques which can be explicitly taught

(Duran and Prusank, 1997). Continually acquiring and perfecting new sexual skills is presented as essential for maintaining intimate relationships in which sex is positioned as the glue which holds the relationship together. Women are frequently depicted as seeking emotional intimacy and commitment through sex (Durham, 1996; Duran and Prusank, 1997), and attaining and retaining monogamous heterosexual relationships are presented as essential for women's happiness (Ménard and Kleinplatz, 2008; Moran and Lee, 2011). Women are required to develop sexual skills in order to keep themselves and their partner satisfied (Farvid and Braun, 2006). The emergence of men's lifestyle magazines in the 1980s which were self-consciously about what it means to be a man (rather than focused on leisure pursuits such as sports), opened up for public discussion previously neglected areas of male experience – including personal relationships (Jackson et al., 2001; Rogers, 2005). 'Lads mags' promote a hedonistic lifestyle oriented around pleasurable consumption and celebrate a ferocious autonomy (Jackson et al., 2001; Attwood, 2005b). They adopt a predatory attitude towards women and eschew intimacy and emotional engagement with women in favour of male-bonding (Benwell, 2004; Edwards, 2003). In contrast, in other magazines (such as *Men's Health*) intimate relationships become reworked as the most effective route to 'good' (i.e., adventurous and varied) sex, allowing men to take intimacy seriously while maintaining the 'natural' sexual drive of traditional masculinity (Rogers, 2005). Sex advice is typically seen as more common in magazines aimed at women (Ménard and Kleinplatz, 2008; Duran and Prusank, 1997), but Taylor (2005) found that improving one's sex life was the third most popular theme in the editorial content of *Maxim*, *FHM* and *Stuff*. *Men's Health*, the focus of this chapter, has been described as an anomaly since it regularly features more sex advice than is typical of men's lifestyle magazines (Ménard and Kleinplatz, 2008). If sex is the glue that holds relationships together, the emphasis in neoliberal discourse is on how to capitalise on the hard work involved in developing sexual expertise as efficiently as possible. If orgasm is the desired 'end product' of sex, we can identify a number of characteristics of the way in which sex is constructed in magazines which are aligned with the rational management of work, including: the breaking down of sex into manageable stages; the presentation of discrete tips and techniques to improve sex as a technical or mechanical achievement; the drive towards fast and efficient orgasms produced with minimal effort; and the invocation of an 'intimate entrepreneur' who invests in his or her sexual skills.

Firstly, in describing sex as 'Taylorised', Jackson and Scott (1997) evoke the notion of a finished product (orgasm) manufactured through the linear progression of a series of simplified actions (foreplay). Sex is broken down into constituent parts which magazines assure are more easily learned and mastered (Rogers, 2005). One article promising to teach men how to *Give her an orgasm in 15 minutes* (*Men's Health* 4), breaks the 'job' down into handy time segments advising men to 'spend 3 minutes of your time kissing' and articulating each activity in a count-down to 15 minutes. Similar articles offer '10 ways to upgrade your sex life' (*Men's Health* 10), promise to 'break down how to achieve that ulti-mate pleasure' with five tips (*Cosmopolitan* 7), or show men how to 'Build her stage-by-stage towards the best orgasm of her life' (*Men's Health* 24). In each case, the task of 'achieving' or 'giving' an orgasm is broken down into an easily manageable production line of tasks with specific instruc-tions about what to do at each stage.

Secondly, advice and tips about improving the technical, mechan-ical or physical factors involved in producing 'great sex' constitute a considerable proportion of magazine content. The magazines claim to offer economy of effort – although sex is work, various tricks, tips and techniques are offered to make this difficult job (of securing female orgasm in particular) as easy as possible: 'a few extra tricks so the road to bliss is even more of a sure thing' (*Cosmopolitan* 11), 'It really is possible to climax for that long if you follow the instruc-tions in a new book' (*Cosmopolitan* 28), 'the trick to having a mind-blowing orgasm'(*Cosmopolitan* 40), 'Follow this technique to give her great orgasms' (*Men's Health* 14). Techniques are offered which promise fail-safe ways to make female orgasm a certain outcome, to make the effort put into sex guaranteed to produce the required orgasmic result: 'Guarantee her more orgasms' (*Men's Health* 14), 'Make her orgasm every time' (*Men's Health* 17), or to guarantee that women will 'reach orgasm every single time' (*Cosmopolitan* 11). Such tricks and techniques are portrayed as universally effective (Ménard and Kleinplatz, 2008), ensuring maximum efficiency of effort such that orgasms are produced effectively and with assured outcomes.

Thirdly, the magazines focus on producing orgasms quickly. Readers are invited to learn how to 'hit bliss in record time' (*Cosmopolitan* 6), 'Make her orgasm in 3 minutes' (*Men's Health* 22), or given 'Great tech-niques to get her to the big O sooner rather than later' (*Men's Health* 42). As noted earlier (Chapter 4) it is women's orgasms which are typically seen as in need of 'speeding up'. As well as certain outcomes, the maga-zines promise long-lasting effects for minimum effort: 'How to have a 15 minute female orgasm' (*Cosmopolitan* 24), 'Give her a 30 minute orgasm' (*Men's Health* 11), 'can an orgasm last all day?' (*Men's Health* 18), or '3 ways to guarantee all-night sex' (*Men's Health* 20). Orgasms should be quickly and easily achieved but with long-lasting effects. Women and their bodies are not people with individual tastes, desires, responses and sensitivities, but are interchangeable bodies which each function in the same way (Ménard and Kleinplatz, 2008). Inducing orgasm becomes a matter of applying the right trick, technique or bit of knowledge – regardless of the partner. The performance imperative involves a rationalisation of techniques for producing pleasure, techniques which are fast, efficient and effective and 'guaranteed' to produce orgasms.

Finally, the self-conscious and reflexive improvement of sexual 'performance' is intimately bound up with new forms of sexual subjectivity in which the individual becomes the manager of the sexual self. The 'performance imperative' encourages a form of 'sexual entrepreneurship' (Harvey and Gill, 2011), in which men and women are encouraged to 'invest' in sexual selves and to develop their 'sexual capital', guided by the advice of 'experts' (Tyler, 2004). Developing and maintaining one's repertoire of sexual skills and techniques involves a constant appraisal of one's current performance and skill level with a view to 'upgrading'. For example, a quiz in *Men's Health* (1) encourages men to ask themselves 'Are you good in bed?' – low scorers are advised to 'Improve your performance by going running three times a week' while top scorers are warned that there's 'no reason to be complacent'. Elsewhere men are advised to 'Make the most of your manhood' (*Men's Health* 2), to 'Improve your foreplay technique' (*Men's Health* 6), are advised about 'How to be a better lover', and are told to 'Improve your performance in the sack with these simple tricks' (*Men's Health* 34). Men and women are impelled to 'invest' in themselves as skilled sexual actors, and to become effective problem-solvers who utilise 'quick fix' solutions guided by the advice of mediatised 'experts' (Tyler, 2004). This offers 'constructed certitude' (Rogers, 2005), the advice given in magazines shores readers up against the uncertainties of relationships, claiming to make them better equipped to be successful, providing them with a toolbox for increasing the sexual satisfaction of themselves and their partners.

In the rest of this chapter we focus specifically on what kind of work men and women are pressed to undertake in the pursuit of the ultimate orgasm. In particular, we explore the idea that contemporary sexuality is characterised by the accumulation of 'technologies of sexiness' (Radner, 2008; Gill, 2009), and the acquisition of a 'sexy body', as valuable assets with which to stake a claim in the sexual marketplace. In her articulation of the postfeminist sensibility, Ros Gill (2009) describes a shift towards developing 'technologies of sexiness' – the accumulation of sexual knowledge and skills – as replacing (or overshadowing) sexual innocence and virtue as defining features of femininity. Although originally discussed in relation to postfeminist female sexuality, I argue that these ideas apply equally (albeit differently) to men who are also required to transform themselves into sexual champions. However, the construction of the female orgasm as more elusive, hard to achieve or problematic, coupled with the making of men as responsible for 'giving' women orgasm, means that lifestyle magazines aimed at both men and women focus overwhelming on the work involved in producing the female orgasm. Specifically, I am interested in exploring the work involved in transforming the sexual or 'sexy' body, and identifying the ways in which individuals are tutored in how to manage, manipulate, move and modify their own bodies (and the bodies of their partners) to achieve orgasmic success.

'Sexual adventurers' and the female body

To understand how this focus on sexual labour becomes centred on training the sexual body – on developing particular embodied performances – we need to pay attention to key cultural shifts in the representation of sexual subjectivities and bodies of women in popular culture. In particular, I argue that the shift from objectification to subjectification and the intensified focus on the 'sexy body' as emblematic of femininity noted by Gill (2009), gives rise to a different relationship between the female sexual adventurer and her body. Gill (2007, 2008) noted a cultural shift away from representing women as passive objects of the male gaze, towards a representation of women as active, independent and sexually powerful. Using the example of 'midriff' advertising (the rise of advertising displaying this part of the body) Gill argues that such imagery demonstrates four central themes: an emphasis upon the body, a shift from objectification to sexual subjectification, a pronounced discourse of choice and autonomy, and an emphasis upon empowerment. This mobilises a particularly pernicious self-disciplinary form of power in which the making over of the sexual self is performed not to meet the demands of an external 'male' gaze, but to please the self (Gill, 2009). While disciplinary pressure on women to meet normative standards of heteronormative beauty by presenting an able-bodied, white, young, feminine body has been a strong stand of feminist work on visual representations and beauty work (e.g., Bartky, 1990; Bordo, 2008), Gill notes a shift towards presenting the body as the primary source of women's capital such that femininity itself becomes redefined as a bodily property replacing the idea that femininity might be defined by caring or mother-hood or other structural or psychological elements. The possession of a 'sexy body' is positioned as central to women's identity, and women are depicted not as objectified sex objects, but as knowingly playing with their sexual power. This expression of sexual power is not about seeking men's admiration, which is present but incidental, but about women pleasing themselves. The possession of a 'sexy body' requires constant monitoring and improvement in order to effectively capitalise on this power (Gill, 2009). In the analysis presented below, I argue that the possession of a 'sexy body' goes well beyond managing the appearance of a buffed, depilated, lithe, and (to-be-read-as) attractive body which has been the focus of much feminist work. Investing in a 'sexy body' requires a more thorough working on the materiality of the body than this implies, and impels women to take control of, and master, their bodies in pursuit of (freely chosen and desired) orgasmic bliss. I outline four forms of embodied labour which lifestyle magazines propel women towards: (1) developing expertise on bodily sensations and responses; (2) exercising the sexual body to improve bodily responses; (3) learning and mastering sexual positions which enhance orgasmic experience; and (4) teaching men bodily knowledge.

Sensate sexpertise

Readers are assured that they can acquire the bodily knowledge necessary to experience quick, intense and long-lasting orgasms by developing a clear understanding of their own body. This involves not just knowing *about* the body, but knowing *through* the body – through bodily prac-tices and sensate experience of the body. The magazine emphasises the importance of personal knowledge and experience ('you know better than your boyfriend exactly what it takes to make your head spin', *Cosmopolitan*1), but at the same time offers generalised information about women's sexual anatomy and responses. Personalised descriptions of the embodied sensations and feelings ('It's like an overwhelming feeling of tingles throughout your body', *Cosmopolitan* 41), sit along-side information about the physical signs associated with sexual arousal similar to that which might be found in text books ('rapid breathing, vaginal lubrication, pelvic thrusts, clenching of the fingers or toes', *Cosmopolitan* 13), which allow women to compare their own bodies and responses. This kind of sensate information is rarely available in formal sex education – a fact much criticised by feminist researchers as contrib-uting to a 'missing discourse of desire' among young women (see also

Fine, 1988) – and goes beyond the mechanics of sex. Masturbation is depicted as key means for knowing and understanding the body, and to achieving orgasmic 'success': 'If you suspect, then, that you aren't climaxing, you can learn to by becoming familiar with your body and how it reacts to sexual stimulation' (*Cosmopolitan* 14). This bodily awareness is pressed into service for achieving more speedy or intense orgasms: 'The more you learn about your own body's responses, the more adept you'll be at quickly reaching orgasm' (*Cosmopolitan* 6). Often depicted as a means to an end, rather than as pleasurable or meaningful in its own right (Moran and Lee, 2011), masturbation is frequently portrayed as a training ground for achieving orgasm with a partner ('Masturbation is perhaps the most crucial step to peaking with a guy. It allows you to feel out your climax triggers and then show them to your man', *Cosmopolitan* 7), or for mastering a new technique ('You might be more successful if you start experimenting, during your solo sessions, since you'll be able to focus totally on yourself', *Cosmopolitan* 21).

Exercising the sexy body

Women are instructed that the body needs to be trained to meet the requirements of a (multi) orgasmic sexual subject. This includes both training the body to be responsive, and ensuring a mindful mastery over the body. The body is depicted as having both 'natural' orgasmic capabilities ('The average woman is built to come again and again', *Cosmopolitan* 7), and as a machine which can be made to work more effectively and efficiently. Aligning sexual labour with other forms of exercise, readers are advised to capitalise on these natural capacities, by training their muscles and bodily responses by adopting a 'workout' regime. Women are warned that sex is 'acrobatic' (*Cosmopolitan* 11), and that they should 'Step up the sexercises' (*Cosmopolitan* 7), mould the body into 'peak condition' (*Cosmopolitan* 22), and flex, clench, pump or squeeze their muscles to ensure efficiency of function:

> Consider this your ultimate down-there workout motivator: Strong PC (pubococcygeus) muscles have been demonstrated to be a crucial component to having multiples, says Beverly Whipple, PhD, coauthor of The G Spot: And Other Discoveries About Human Sexuality. (*Cosmopolitan* 7)

Precise anatomical detail about which muscles to move, and which methods for exercising the body are effective is provided by 'experts' (typically sexologists and/or book authors) and translated into more colloquial terms by the editorial narrative: 'Remember, when they're not making you moan, these Kegel muscles – which surround the vaginal canal – are the ones that enable you to withhold urine' (*Cosmopolitan* 7). Readers are depicted as already knowledgeable sexual subjects (who 'remember' the function of these muscles), but who need further guidance to hone their skills. For example, readers are presented as familiar with Kegel's exercises, but these are also briefly explained: 'By now, you know the Kegels drill: Flex the muscles until you feel them tighten. Release. Tighten again'. The article then goes on to offer further advice to *extend* readers' knowledge further by offering the 'Pelvic Connecting Crunch' – an exercise which 'uses your transverse abdominals and inner thighs to engage the PC muscles and work it harder'. Exercises like these are recommended on the premise that 'Fit pelvic muscles can result in more powerful orgasms' (*Cosmopolitan* 22), or will enable readers to enjoy 'easier, stronger orgasms' (*Cosmopolitan* 6).

Readers are induced to exercise in order to adopt a particular kind of mindful mastery over the body where the body performs whenever and however the woman/owner desires. This rational control over the body is more typically associated with men, but is integral to neoliberalism and its postfeminist variant. The body has natural and automatic reactions which can be exploited by those who know how to 'trick' the body into performing. Women can fool the body into delivering multiple orgasms, for example, by 'moaning out loud, breathing faster and harder, and tightening and loosening your pelvic muscles' (*Cosmopolitan* 12). Readers are told that this will 'send your body signals that it's time for another orgasm' and the 'expert' concludes that 'you may even condition your body to become excited again automatically'. This mastery requires hard work to learn the necessary skills and techniques, and readers need to 'practice, practice, practice' (*Cosmopolitan* 32). But, mastering the body is not enough. Women must prevent the 'natural' orgasmic response of the body being disrupted by intrusive thoughts, lack of confidence or self-consciousness. Women are told that being 'single-minded' holds them back from experiencing multiple orgasms, and are advised to develop a new attitude which includes 'knowing that your body is fully capable, even built, to experience deeper, longer, and more frequent orgasms' (*Cosmopolitan* 7). The promise, then, is that women can 'master' their bodily responses to be able to call on orgasm at will, although only the most adventurous and most disciplined women will: 'Though all females have the potential to be plural peakers, not all women are able to master it' (*Cosmopolitan* 21). The 'expert' gives credibility and 'scientific' legitimacy to the advice offered, but a delicate balance needs to be struck between 'instructing women' about how to train their bodies and treating women as already knowledgeable sexual subjects. Through precise anatomical detail which facilitates a mechanised understanding of the body, women are instructed in how to discipline their muscles and their bodily responses to 'guarantee' their own sexual pleasure.

Positioning the body

To ensure orgasmic 'success' the magazine offers explicit training about how to coordinate male and female bodies during intercourse. Again maintaining the balance between knowledgeable readers and readers-in-need-of-instruction, sometimes readers are assumed to already know certain positions – such as 'missionary' or 'doggie style' – whilst more 'sophisticated' or elaborate variations are explained. The following description of the 'Lusty Lap Dance' position is illustrative:

> This one's always a fan favorite – he sits and you straddle him so you're face-to-face. 'You have a lot of control over the speed, angle, and motion because you can use your arms and legs to help you maneuver,' says Berman. 'Rather than just moving up and down, which can be especially tiring for you, sway forward and back, rubbing your clitoral area against him.' In addition to the freedom of move-ment, there are a few other benefits to this booty move. 'If you lean back just a little bit, you'll get greater G-spot stimulation and he'll be able to *play* with your clitoris,' Brame explains. Plus, your breasts will be perfectly aligned with his mouth, adding a whole other layer to the sexual experience. (*Cosmopolitan* 11)

Drawing on the expert advise of authors Berman and Baume, women are given very precise instructions about how to *position* their own bodies for sex, about where to place their arms and legs and so on, and about how to *move* the body ('sway forward and back'). The merits of these positions centre on their ability to offer stimulation to different parts of the body typically the clitoris and g-spot ('If you lean back just a little bit, you'll get greater G-spot stimulation and he'll be able to play with your clitoris'), presenting sex as a mechanical exercise akin to scratching an itch. In addi-tion, women's empowerment is affirmed as the positions afford greater opportunity for women to exercise control ('You have a lot of control over the speed, angle, and motion'). Elsewhere women are given instruction about how to move the body during intercourse to ensure effective stimu-lation; they are advised to 'grind against his penis' or 'gyrate your hips in an oval rather than up and down' (*Cosmopolitan* 6). Sex is presented as a technical exercise in ensuring the right body parts are stimulated by the right kind of movement. Moreover, women are invited to understand their bodies, and the sexual architecture of their bodies, in relation to the bodies of men: 'During doggie-style, have your guy suddenly go really deep, so he strokes your G-spot with each thrust. It's an extra push that'll help you reach blast off' (*Cosmopolitan* 24). Women are often addressed as if they are in control of, and managing, the sexual action – not only are they in control of the pace, timing, depth of penile thrusting – but they are also controlling what their male partners do to ensure an orgasmic ending. I take up this point in more detail in the final theme.

Teaching the boys

Women are addressed by the magazines as already sexually knowledgeable and as extending their sexpertise with the advice offered. As experts, women are expected to take responsibility for teaching men how to please them in bed:

> Try giving him a tutorial by masturbating in front of him, which can make for an incredibly erotic encounter. Or, give him a demo with your hand over his, then have him mimic your moves. (*Cosmopolitan* 1)

Women are entreated to 'show' or 'teach' their partners how to arouse them by giving embodied performances and by guiding and moving their hands: 'You can also clue him in by illustrating what you want, by putting your hand over his and directing his fingers to where you'd like to be touched' (*Cosmopolitan* 2). This is not simply about giving information, but about 'showing' through bodily practices. Far from being 'sex-perts' (see also Potts, 2002) in the bedroom, or more knowledgeable about and experienced in sex than women, men are constructed as willing students who need instruction and are open to 'feedback':

> But, from now on, you need to take more responsibility for your pleasure and really let him know what works and what doesn't work. (The truth is, guys crave guidance, but we're too inhibited to ask for your feedback.) (*Cosmopolitan* 2)

Although women are still advised to carefully manage the feelings and emotional sensitivities of their male partners (see Roberts et al., 1995), they do so whilst solving sexual problems, taking 'responsibility' for their own orgasm, and instructing men in how they should be touched. Women are depicted as orchestrating sexual interactions and directing men's actions: 'have him enter your vagina from behind' (*Cosmopolitan* 12), 'have him bring you to climax with his tongue' (*Cosmopolitan* 21), or 'have your guy suddenly go really deep' (*Cosmopolitan* 24). Describing a 'new' sexual position, women are told to:

> Have your partner enter you at a higher angle than usual (the pillows will help), planting his hands on the floor beside your head. He should move inside you with slow, languid figure-eight motions, so that you feel his whole package – his penis plus pubic region. Remember: The figure-eight motion is key to this manoeuvre. (*Cosmopolitan* 43)

This includes instruction about how he should position his body ('planting his hands on the floor beside your head'), how he should move his body ('with slow languid figure-eight movements') and how he should place his body relative to the women ('enter at a higher angle than usual'). With a flagrant disregard for gendered power relations in which women experience great difficulty negotiating safe and pleasurable sex with male partners (see Holland et al., 1998), mediatised representations depict women as in control, sexually experimental and adventurous, and able easily to direct men to do their bidding. So, responsibilities for sexual success are newly-formed in contemporary women's magazines as women are given responsibility for ensuring their own orgasmic pleasure by instructing and training men in how to please them. This 'teacher' role is the route to the empowered, autonomous sexuality of postfeminism.

Championing the male body

The emergence of men's lifestyle magazines is typically interpreted as a response to the growth of consumer culture and associated 'crisis' of masculinity. As relationships become detached from reproduction and status, and instead offer a valuable route to self-fulfilment, magazines offer a commentary on contemporary gender relations in which mutual attraction, sexual compatibility and emotional egalitarianism are aspirational. The emergence of 'new man' characterised by sensitivity, nurturance and caring in the 1980s gave way to the 'lad mag' in the mid- to late-1990s marked by a return to 'traditional' male values of sexism, male bonding and homophobia (see Benwell, 2002; Edwards, 1997; Jackson et al., 2001; Nixon, 1996). The more 'downmarket' 'lad's mags' (such as *Loaded*, *Maxim*, and *FHM*), can be seen as much as a reaction against the middle-class 'new man' offered by 'upmarket' magazines (such as *GQ*, *Esquire*), as a backlash against feminism and changing gender relations (Benwell, 2004; Edwards, 1997). 'Lad's mags' often reduced women to sexual objects, depicting 'some kind of prepubescent world of masturbation and drunken one-night stands' (Edwards, 2003: 139). What Attwood (2005b: 91) describes as this 'Playboy' ideology resists domesticity unless it is 'saturated with sex', as suggested by the 'reader's wife and the babe girlfriend' who exist solely for sexual gratification and display. These magazines orient towards sexual variety and in particular celebrate 'bizarre' or unusual sex, with the message that women want to engage in these behaviours as much as men 'exemplified by articles in which women are quoted as they enthuse over bondage, sex in public, group sex, and the use and imitation of pornography during sex' (Taylor, 2005: 162). 'Lad's mags' are characterised by an 'unrelenting gloss of knowingness and irony: a reflexivity about its own condition' (Benwell, 2007: 539), which enables a distancing of themselves and their readers from accusations of sexism, whilst presenting the contradictions of masculinity at a safe distance (Benwell, 2004; Jackson et al., 2001).

Yet, despite depicting committed romantic relationships as limiting and restrictive, they are also portrayed as normative (Taylor, 2005), and the emphasis on autonomy sits alongside an emphasis on intimacy. Magazines offer advice about how to manage sexual relationships in the increasingly complex modern world (Jackson et al., 2001), constructing both certainty and uncertainty about intimate relationships for their readers (Rogers, 2005). On the one hand, sex is depicted as easily available, unproblematic, natural and inevitable, and men are presented as sexually confident with eager sexual partners who enjoy their activities. On the other, sex is also constructed as necessarily difficult, women as both demanding and unpredictable, and sexual relationships as a source of anxiety and a threat to masculine self-esteem.

Men are obligated to develop a 'technology of sexiness' to meet both their own mediated desire for frequent and varied sex, and the pressure from women's increasing demands for better sex amid their unpredictable sexual responses. Magazines generate uncertainty about intimate relationships, *and* offer a 'constructed certitude' in how to manage these anxieties (Rogers, 2005). Sex is depicted both as a site of fun and pleasure, and as a site for serious contemplation and work. 'Good sex' becomes a sign of distinction (Bourdieu, 1984); a way of marking oneself out and maintaining a place in the socio-sexual hierarchy. Notwithstanding their differences, collectively these magazines are characterised by: a relationship with or response to feminism; the sexualisation and sexual objectification of women; an ironic tone; a consideration of intimacy and relationships; an engagement with consumer culture; and the construction of masculinity as a bodily property.

Here we explore how working on the body and developing 'technologies of sexiness' are integral to becoming a 'sexual champion'. In the face of increasing uncertainty around employment and work, and the intensified focus on consumption as a route to identity, men's bodies have become a vehicle for the 'doing' of masculinity in new ways. Men's lifestyle magazines promote the consumption of lifestyle products – including or especially those aimed at bodily transformation and grooming – as integral rather than antithetical to masculinity (Nixon, 1996; Mort, 1996; Edwards, 1997). Changing visual codes have meant that men's bodies are increasingly depicted as a spectacle for male consumption, and the use of increasingly sexualised poses means that men are encouraged to look at themselves (and other men) as objects of desire. Masculinity becomes wrapped up in the ability to create a particular appearance – a hard, stylish body (Alexander, 2003). Bodily insecurities are both fuelled and doused as magazines provide solutions in the form of branded products, advice about diet, health, exercise and grooming, and guidance in how to minimise fat and tone muscles. Here we focus specifically on the ways in which men are impelled to work on the 'sexy body' by: maintaining sexual health; working out; and using sexual science and mastering her body.

Maintaining sexual health

Articles about health, fitness and diet feature prominently in men's magazines and play a pivotal role in the medicalisation of men's bodies (Boni, 2002). Gupta and Cacchioni (2013) argue that contemporary sex manuals offer a new rationale for the importance of working on the sexual self – a focus on sex as a route to maintaining health and wellness. This 'sex as health' discourse is also prominent in men's magazines in which men's bodies are positioned as at risk and in need of protection from illness, disease and even death (Boni, 2002). For example, one article entitled 'How sex can save your life' (*Men's Health* 8) claimed that 'Sex can beat cancer, heart disease and even banish wrinkles'. It went on to explain that 'A study in the journal *Biological Psychology* found men who had had sex the previous night responded better to stressful situations', and that men could 'side-step stress' by harnessing the 'soothing power of another person's touch' and adopting certain sexual positions:

> 'Positions that maximise bodily contact, such as spooning or your partner sitting facing you on a chair, have the greatest beneficial

effect on cortisol levels,' says Brody. If only stress relief was available on the NHS[1] (*Men's Health* 8).

The male body is depicted (both explicitly and implicitly) as continually at risk and under threat often from stereotypical 'male diseases' such as stress, cardiovascular disorders, and high blood pressure (Boni, 2002). Being healthy also means maintaining sexual function – typically erectile function. Extolling the benefits of exercise, for example, one article reporting a study published in *The Journal of Sexual Medicine* noted that:

> The study was building on previous research showing that older men are able to maintain better sexual performance through exercise. This is the first time it's been proved that younger men also benefit. (*Men's Health* 9)

In another article readers are warned that 'the only thing stopping your erection from wilting is the release of nitric oxide from nerve endings in your penis' (*Men's Health* 39). Fortunately, readers are offered simple solutions for maintaining a 'sustained erection and heightened sensitivity'; just '13 minutes running at 10kph boosts nitric oxide levels for 24-hours' and a 'fistful of pumpkin seeds packs 2g of L-arginine which is proven to increase nitric oxide in exhaled breath by 15%'. In the context of the biomedical imperative of 'sex for life', in which men are challenged to maintain a youthful sexual function (erections hard enough for the purpose of penetration) into later life, erectile 'health' has a special status (Potts et al., 2006). The majority of the sex advice manuals sampled by Gupta and Cacchioni (2013) promulgated the message that it is important to continue having sex into old age, as regular sex is required to prevent sexual dysfunction. Individuals are tasked with engaging in self-care regimes to avoid or minimise the risks of ill-health (Boni, 2002).

As well as avoiding ill-health and sexual dysfunction, healthy practices were also linked to maintaining an active sex life and securing access to frequent sex. For example, with the tag line 'Keep a little something up between the sheets' one article reported that a poll (conducted by a vitamin supplement firm) had found that 'energy levels among Brits are the key cause for lacklustre performances in the bedroom' (*Men's Health* 50). Advice on how to manage this problem included having sex at particular times of the day when energy levels are naturally higher, drinking a juice made from Acai berries, or avoiding sexual positions which expend more energy: 'missionary and "doggy" positions are particularly draining – burning up around 25kJs a minute apparently'. Similarly, avoiding stress is not just valued for its health benefits, but is seen as a way to 'Supercharge your sex drive' or 'Boost your libido' (thereby maintaining frequent sex and/or an ever-ready desire for sex) and improve performance to give her 'a night to remember':

> Often, adds Brewer, a decreased libido is simply the result of stress – and all you need to get back on tip-top form is to learn how to relax. Something as simple as taking a bath can significantly lower the cortisol (the stress-inducing hormone) levels in your body. (*Men's Health* 43)

With the neoliberal focus on speed and efficiency, men's magazines offer numerous opportunities for men to deal with stress quickly and without wasting precious time or effort (Boni, 2002). Sex is presented as a pleasurable shortcut to doing the body work of maintaining good health – this reiterates the idea that men are ever ready for sex and keeping fit and healthy at the same time is an added bonus which offers efficiency of effort. The magazines also draw on familiar discourses of health to talk about how to enhance sexual experience as well as sexual performance. After explaining that a greater volume of semen is associated with a more intense orgasm, one article gives advice about what healthy foods to eat to 'supercharge your orgasm':

> Spanish research published in *Fertility and Sterility* found upping your intake of folates (found in spinach, asparagus and lentils), vitamin C (in broccoli, oranges and strawberries) and lycopene (tomatoes, watermelon, and grapefruit) increased semen volume for every man in the study, with one guy increasing his by 45%. (*Men's Health* 15)

The language of diet, calories, exercise, energy, stress, cortisol, etc. – are harnessed and put to work in the disciplining of the sexual body in a neat elision of bodily regimes.

Working out

Working on the body by working out and building muscular strength is a familiar cornerstone of hegemonic masculinity. In sex advice, exercising the body is presented as serving the dual purpose of enhancing men's sexual pleasure and improving their sexual performance. Exercise regimes to develop 'your love muscle' are a regular feature of the magazine:

Great abs may help you get lucky, but if you want to get the most from the experience you need to work on your pubococcygeal (PC) muscle. At the floor of your pelvis, it controls peeing and spasms during climax [...]. Kegel exercises will develop PC power. Squeeze the muscle you use to hold back your pee. Once you've identified this muscle, tighten it, hold for two seconds, then release. Repeat 20 times, three times a day, gradually holding it tight for longer. And keep at it. (*Men's Health* 3)

Readers are advised that doctors and sex therapists recommend these exercises in order to 'improve orgasm and reduce the chances of premature ejaculation'. Men are sold the benefits of exercising to improve their sexual stamina – in other words that they will be able to keep going for longer if they are fitter and stronger. One article entitled 'Improve your sex life with yoga' claims to teach men 'how to boost your flexibility and stamina in bed' and warns that:

When you lean over your partner in the missionary position your quadriceps need to lengthen as your hamstrings contract. 'If the hamstrings are weak and the quads tight, then these muscles will soon fatigue and the rhythm and fluidity during the height of passion will be lost,' says Lee. (*Men's Health* 12)

The implication is that men's performance will suffer and fail (passion will be lost). Exercises to improve stamina and strength are offered, detailed anatomical information about which muscles are being used is given, and men are told that they should see 'significant improvements in your bedroom performance in less than a month'. Men are encouraged to monitor, assess and quantify their own 'exercise regime' and sexual performance. In a quiz purporting to assess 'Are you good in bed?' men are asked to rate their level of exercise (e.g., 2–3 high-intensity, 45-minute sessions a week) and are awarded points on the basis of their answers. The article then informs them of the sexual benefits of regular exercise:

According to research at Colorado State University, moderate 30-minute runs three times a week for a month will get you panting in more ways than one. Of the study's 3,000 participants, 75% reported a higher sex drive, 72% were 'more sexually responsive' and over 60% reported they could go for another lap around the bedroom within 10 minutes. (*Men's Health* 1)

Low scorers on a quiz are told that they should 'Improve your performance by going running three times a week'. Like women, men are
encouraged to exercise their muscles to improve their own sexual
pleasure, but more often the emphasis for men is on enhancing their
sexual *performance*.

The science of the body

In her analysis of men's magazines, Rogers (2005) argues that the 'scien-
tization of sex' is a key mechanism for moving the reader from chaos
to control, from uncertainty to certainty in his negotiation of sex and
intimacy. Science is depicted as providing credible evidence that the tips
and techniques presented are guaranteed to produce the results that
men desire. The body is presented as a mechanised, biological system
which can be tricked and bent to the will of the individual, if they are
knowledgeable and skilful enough to manipulate the natural capabilities
of the body. As demonstrated in the examples above – 'expert' evidence
drawn from the reporting of academic journal articles, interviews with
academics and scientists, or quotes from sex therapists or book authors
are presented as adding credibility to the advice that is presented in
the magazines. More than this, technical knowledge about the body is
an important way for men to master their own body (and that of their
partner – see below):

> Watch Saturday's big match. Or work out. Or rent *The Godfather Part II*.
> Or go for a run. All of these activities have been shown to raise testo-
> sterone level [...] researchers at Athens' Military Hospital in Greece
> found that the more testosterone a man has in his bloodstream, the
> better his chances of achieving orgasm. (*Men's Health* 3)

> ... set the ball rolling with a sirloin supper. 'The protein in the meat
> will naturally boost levels of dopamine and norepinephrine, two
> chemicals in the brain that heighten sensitivity for both of you
> during sex,' says Dr Sarah Brewer, author of *Increase Your Sex Drive*
> (Thorsons). (*Men's Health* 1)

Improving sexual performance is simply a matter of knowing how the
body works and making small adjustments to one's usual routine –
working out, watching a film, eating steak – the 'science' of hormones
and neurotransmitters will naturally and inevitably do the rest. Rogers
(2005) argues that 'science' is used to present men's sexual urges as
natural, antithetical to intimacy, and advice as incontrovertible, factual
and objective. Essential differences in the physiological functioning of

men and women, as established by science, are often used to explain or justify men and women as having naturally different sexual needs, motivations and desires:

> 'Orgasm is all about brain activation,' says Gert Holstege of the University of Groningen in the Netherlands, who has studied men's and women's brainwaves during orgasm. 'The brain activates the genitals and controls everything.' Unlike women, though, who experience intense activity in the area of the brain connected with emotion, men experience most activity in the secondary somatosensory cortex, which deals with physical sensations. The upshot? For better orgasms, your partner needs to focus more on your penis and you need to focus on the sensations coming from it. (*Men's Health* 3)

This familiar trope that women are emotional while men are physical is presented as scientific 'fact' leading to simplistic conclusions about how this information might be used in embodied sexual interactions.

Mastering her body

> When your partner feels she is about to come, watch and feel for the regular two-second contractions in her genital area, which indicate orgasm is imminent. Once they start, stop stimulating the clitoris and immediately move to stroking the inner vaginal walls. Using your fingers either push them in or out or sweep them in circles, slowly and steadily, in and out of the vaginal entrance. (*Men's Health* 11)

Perhaps one of the most prominent features of the construction of sexuality in men's magazines is the very detailed anatomical information about *women's* bodies, including how women's bodies *should* look and feel leading up to and during orgasm. Men are invited to 'watch and feel' women's bodies for indicators of arousal, and are given step-by-step instruction about how and where to touch women's bodies – to stroke, sweep, push, or circle. This is not just anatomical, 'factual' information, but information about sensations and feelings – about what her body should feel like and look like, and how her body should move. Particular attention is paid to the genitals as the focal point for sexual stimulation – although men are often instructed that women need to be finessed into the 'right mood' first. Men are given detailed instructions in how to touch, stroke and stimulate women's bodies, and how to move their own bodies in order to provide the most effective stimulation to 'give' her an orgasm. This includes intercourse and how to use/move the penis, but more commonly refers to oral or manual stimulation. Here is a description of the 'Kivin Method' of cunnilingus, promoted as 'the fastest way of getting there':

'With one hand, pull up her clitoral hood,' he says. 'Then lick from side to side across its base, just above her clitoris.' Place one finger of the other hand on her perineum (the area directly below the opening of her vagina). When you can feel her pre-orgasmic contractions, you'll know you're in the right place. (*Men's Health* 4)

The magazine offers 'A guide to her vagina' (*Men's Health* 29), a 'master-class' in oral sex (*Men's Health* 30), advice on 'How to hit her G spot' (*Men's Health* 13) and a guide to becoming 'cliterate' (*Men's Health* 26). In contrast to women's magazines, men are presented as being poorly informed about sexual anatomy and lacking in sexual skills. This is not least because female anatomy is depicted as bewildering:

According to a recent survey conducted by Ann Summers, 55% of men have never found their partner's G spot – and 36% don't even know what it is. Though it's true that the G spot can be frustratingly elusive, it's well worth searching for. (*Men's Health* 13)

Expert knowledge about the female body is presented as essential for seducing women, and arousing them so that women will want to engage in intercourse. Readers are encouraged to get their partner 'in the mood' through various forms of 'foreplay,' ranging from doing the dishes to sending a partner an erotic text message. In addition, knowledge about the body is seen as giving a shortcut to arousal:

Take her to live comedy or meet up on a day she has a spinning or yoga class. This preps her core-gasm because ab exercises stimu-late the vagus nerve running through her pelvis. As the countdown draws closer, have some quiet drinks back at your flat. University of Florence research found that women who drink a glass or two of red wine are more aroused. (*Men's Health* 4)

These techniques and skills are presented as valuable commodities, or assets to be traded for an enhanced status as a lover or for enviable sex:

Speed isn't everything in the bedroom, but bringing her to climax in the time it takes to whip up a late night snack is a valuable skill. This step-by-step guide shows you the buttons you should press to earn an enviable sexual reputation. (*Men's Health* 10)

In men's magazines, these skills serve to place men within the socio-sexual hierarchy – in the eyes of female lovers and amongst their male peers – producing an 'instant spike in your approval ratings' (*Men's Health* 4). The reward for men of putting in the effort – the 'pay off' for investing in developing their sexual self – is the promise of more frequent sex with a more responsive partner (Krassas et al., 2003; Taylor, 2005).

Conclusions

In pursuit of the ultimate orgasmic experience, men and women are compelled to work on and improve their sexual skills to achieve the best orgasmic experience with the minimum of effort and maximum efficiency. The 'sexy body' becomes a site which is subject to intense rational control, self-examination, measurement and improvement. Responsibility for 'sex work' (Cacchioni, 2007) is placed on the shoulders of the individual, echoing a neoliberal commitment to personal choice and agency. In her study of women who self-defined as experiencing difficulties with orgasm, Cacchioni (2007) found that in order to achieve 'normal' heterosexuality, women undertook different kinds of 'sex work' on their own minds and bodies (and those of their partners). One of these types of sex work which she terms 'discipline work', which refers to 'changing one's mental and physical sexual response to standard heterosexual practices' (2007: 307), is the one which is more likely to be advocated by sex 'experts'. This work is characterised by a quest to implement a certain skill and/or degree of concentration to manipulate the body or the mind. While this kind of discipline work may be particularly acute or pernicious in relation to 'sexual dysfunction', it is possible that in the guise of 'pedagogy' these magazines could be seen as part of this disciplinary regime in which men and women are being encouraged to mould and train their bodies in ways which better meet the requirements of heterosexual sex and the orgasmic imperative.

Working on the 'sexy body' involves much more than the transformation of the surface of the body into something which is read as (hetero) sexually attractive. Capitalising on the corporeal capital afforded by the body requires a working on and working over of the musculature, hormonal, and neurochemical aspects of the body through exercise, diet and an accumulation of atomistic tricks and tips for enhancing sexual experience and expertise. Lifestyle magazines offer a detailed and explicit 'pedagogy of the body' with specific instruction on bodily techniques, anatomy, fit and functioning. Individuals are tutored in how their own body (and that of their partner) should be touched, stroked, smacked, pushed, pulled, penetrated, and so on. This expert tuition prompts a genitally focused, mechanistic approach to sex and to the body, and invites a different subjectivity in relation to embodied experience. Readers positioned as willing students waiting to be taught – who choose to engage in these lessons for their own self-enhancement and pleasure – are ready to reap the rewards of their sexual investment. They are also invited to develop a technical mastery of their own body, using the body as a tool which can be called upon to do their bidding, whenever, wherever and however they choose. For women, this embodied knowledge is presented as offering them control over their own body, and presents them as being empowered in interactions with men, orchestrating sexual encounters and directing men and their bodies. This representation bears little resemblance to empirical research which highlights women's difficulty in negotiating safe and pleasurable sex with male partners. For men, distance from this traditionally feminine area of concern is maintained by a focus on the strength and functioning of the body. The male body is presented as having an 'uncertain future', being more precarious in its functioning and 'at risk' from illness and disease (Boni, 2002). The ironic tone of men's magazines and a focus on health enables a resistance to the feminisation implied by male grooming. Moreover, men's bodies are given relatively little attention. Although some articles do outline techniques to enhance the orgasmic experience, the vast majority focus on mastering the mysterious female body. Men are expected to hone their sexual skills to deliver 'mind-blowing' orgasms to their female partners – thus firmly leaving men in the driving seat of heterosexual sex.

6

Performing Orgasm: Blurring the 'Real' and the 'Fake'

Faking it happens. A lot. In fact, studies show that 60 percent of women have delivered an Oscar-worthy performance between the sheets [...] While there's little harm in the occasional bluff, here's why you should curb the counterfeit climaxing and find your true peak potential.

(*Women's Health*)[1]

It's also a good idea to spend some time thinking about why you were pretending. Maybe you were afraid of bruising his ego, or perhaps you worried that he'd reject you if you told him the truth. You could have even felt like you had to live up to some false ideal of porn. Then, if he asks you point-blank if you were faking... or, if you feel compelled to 'fess up about your 'performance'... you will be able to focus the discussion on your actions rather than his 'action'. Making it about you and shouldering the responsibility will help prevent him from feeling like a lousy lover.

(*Cosmopolitan* 2)

Faking orgasm is a widespread phenomenon. Simulating orgasm is simultaneously presented as both relatively harmless and as a highly sensitive matter, the discovery of which must be handled carefully. Women are encouraged to take responsibility for the problem of faking by identifying their own 'insecurities' about orgasm, protect their partners from feeling like 'lousy lovers', and to 'curb' the self-defeating practice of faking and pursue authentic orgasms. Faking it, then, requires work. There is work involved in putting on an 'Oscar-worthy performance', and work involved in confessing to this performance and managing the emotional reactions of partners to this news. This chapter builds on ideas about the labour required to orgasm by considering the idea that 'faking' or 'pretending' orgasm is one kind of 'orgasm work' undertaken largely by women. Moving away from neoliberal ideas about a rational and managerial approach to sex, this chapter draws primarily on the theory of 'emotion work' (Hochschild, 1983) to explore the gendered dynamics of faking orgasm. In this chapter I argue that we need to shift from seeing pretending orgasm as an unfathomable practice rooted in the insecurities of individual women, to seeing it as an 'inventive bodily technique' which embodies the tensions of unequal access to sexual pleasure in the context of cultural discourses of work, care, and reciprocity (Jagose, 2010: 529). Moreover, I take issue with the idea that the distinction between 'real' and 'fake' orgasms can be seen as resting in some authentic bodily experience and argue that the bodily experience is always already social. As a way into these debates, it is useful to explore the prevalence of faking, and the cultural stories that surround its pervasiveness.

Faking it happens. A lot

Over a 40-year period using varied methodologies, studies consistently report that between 50–65% of women have at one time or another faked an orgasm. Schaefer (1973: 248) found that 57% of the 30 white middle-class women she interviewed had 'felt it was necessary to "pretend" or "fake" orgasm'. In Hite's (1976: 154) study, 53% of the more than 3,000 women who returned questionnaires distributed via magazines and mail responded positively to the question 'Do you *ever* fake orgasms?' Some 58% of the 805 professional nurses sampled by Darling and Davidson (1986) reported *ever* pretending orgasm. Of the 232 female university students recruited by Wiederman, 55% said that they had 'at one time or another, pretended to have an orgasm *during intercourse*' (1997: 134, emphasis added). Over a decade later, 50% of the 101 female university students recruited by Muehlenhard and Shippee (2010: 554) reported that they had 'pretended to have an orgasm'. An online survey of over 3,000 women, found that 74% had faked an orgasm in their *current or most recent relationship* (Mialon, 2011). Finally, 53.9% of 453 young American women (mostly university students) agreed that they had 'pretended that you were having an orgasm when you really weren't' during *sexual intercourse with their current partner* (Kaighobadi, et al., 2012). Despite variations in questions about whether women had *ever* faked or had faked *in their current relationship*, and about faking during intercourse or other sexual activities, the figures suggest the practice is widespread. Of course, faking is not a practice limited to women in heterosexual relationships. Of the nearly 2,000 men who responded to an online survey, 27% reported faking in their current or most recent relationship (Mialon, 2011), while 45% of the 180 male university students reported having pretended to have an orgasm at some time (Muehlenhard and Shippee, 2010). There is some evidence that lesbian women fake orgasm (Califia, 1979; Fahs, 2011; Schreurs, 1993) and there is no reason to think that some of the men who fake are not simulating orgasm during sex with other men (although this is difficult to discern from the limited literature). But, this does not detract from fake orgasm as a traditionally feminine practice nor does it preclude an analysis of faking as paradigmatically heterosexual (Jagose, 2010).

Despite the prevalence of faking orgasm, the dominant cultural story about this practice is that it is outdated, disappearing and soon to be extinct (Jagose, 2010). According to this story, the understanding of female sexual response has historically been so poor that heterosexual women routinely faked orgasm during intercourse since there was little hope or expectation of genuine pleasure. In more enlightened and liberated times, with improved information about female sexual anatomy, the 'discovery' of the clitoris, an egalitarian ethic of reciprocity, and the recognition of women's sexual agency, the need for this orgasmic sleight of hand is diminished. For example, Masters and Johnson (1966) were confident that their ground-breaking studies identifying the characteristics of human sexual response would make feigning orgasm unnecessary for two reasons. Firstly, that improved knowledge of physiological responses would enable women to gain adequate sexual stimulation, making the 'age-old foible of orgasmic pretense' redundant (1966: 138). 'With orgasmic physiology established', they argued 'the human female now has an undeniable opportunity to develop realistically her own sexual response levels' (1966: 138). Secondly, that growing recognition of the visible signs of orgasm would make faking untenable:

> With the specific anatomy of orgasmic-phase physiology reasonably established, the age-old practice of the human female of dissimulating has been made pointless. The obvious, rapid tumescence and corrugation of the areolae of the breasts and the definable contractions of the orgasmic platform in the outer third of the vagina remove any doubt as to whether the woman is pretending or experiencing orgasm. (Masters and Johnson, 1966: 134)

With their scientific knowledge, Masters and Johnson believed that they would be able to definitively distinguish the 'real' from the 'fake' in the hitherto elusive and mysterious female orgasm. Cultural anxieties about the invisibility of female sexual response, which places its authenticity in perpetual doubt, would be soothed and eliminated, and women's access to genuine pleasure would be secured. Fake orgasms, then, speak to both the authenticity of the experience of orgasm and to the accurate recognition (or not) of this experience by others – both lovers and sex researchers.

Yet, Masters and Johnson's confidence that sexual science would make faking unsustainable appears misplaced. The success of women's attempts to deceive their partners, and men's inability to distinguish the real from the fake, remains a well-rehearsed dilemma in popular discourse. This cultural anxiety provides the comedic zeal behind the infamous *When Harry Met Sally* scene in which Sally (Meg Ryan) simulates an orgasm in a New York deli to prove to Harry (Billy Crystal) that he cannot tell the difference between this and an authentic orgasm. The impetus for this demonstration was Sally's claim that while most women fake, most men believe that their own partner's orgasms are genuine – as Sally says 'you do the Maths'. Social scientific research confirms that women are more confident about being able to fake an orgasm without being detected (only 25% of women believe that their partners can tell if they fake compared to 66% of men), and are more confident in their ability to detect whether their partner is faking an orgasm (75% of women believe that they can a spot a fake compared to only 55% of men, Mialon, 2011). Men's angst about being able to distinguish the real from the fake is fuelled by the prevalence of websites that offer advice about 'Signs She's Faking It'[2] which promise to minimise the uncertainty they simultaneously create. For example, readers are assured that they can 'use the following signs that she really is having an orgasm to distinguish the faux from the bona fide, and catch her in the act'. Similarly, an article in *Men's Health* magazine entitled 'Is She Faking It?' offers a multiple choice test where men can test their knowledge of the visible signs of authentic climax:[3]

> Next time she's in the throes of passion, watch out for the following sign to find out whether that passion is bona fide or a 'buncha' lies.
>
> Take a look at her chest. It's:
>
> a. Mottled with a sort of red, blotchy rash.
> b. Normal, apart from a sweaty sheen.
> c. Plump, cool, the perfect place to rest a drink.

Lifestyle magazines repeatedly reiterate scientific knowledge about sexual response to reassure readers that they will be able to spot a fake orgasm – in the article above, readers are told that 'a process called vaso-congestion, where the blood rushes to the chest and genitals' results in 'a rash-like flush across the chest, something a faking woman can't reproduce'. The promise that improved knowledge and careful attention to the visible signs of sexual climax will enable individuals to distinguish the real from the fake permeates the cultural imagination (see Frith, 2014).

Forty years after the publication of Masters and Johnson's research, faking orgasm is continually depicted afresh as an unnecessary, defunct, and soon-to-be-obsolete sexual practice which is inappropriate for contemporary sexual relationships. Like Masters and Johnson, women's magazines present faking as unnecessary since 'real' orgasms are readily achievable if women are prepared to learn more about their own bodies and to 'teach' men about how to pleasure them (see previous chapter). Women are encouraged to give up faking in the pursuit of authentic orgasms. Problem pages urge women who fake orgasms to 'take more responsibility for your pleasure' and that 'communicating about what does... and doesn't... turn you on can only make sex better for both of you' (*Cosmopolitan* 2). The practice of faking is attributed to women's psychological deficiencies ('Nervousness and self-consciousness with a new partner and the pressure to climax are common concerns for many women', *Cosmopolitan* 4), and they are encouraged to overcome these anxieties to reach for sincere pleasure. If orgasm is emblematic of the modern, liberated, postfeminist woman, faked orgasm is seen as an outdated hangover from less enlightened times and indicative of (some) women's lack of sexual confidence, or worse as signifying submission to male needs and desires. When *Cosmopolitan* magazine launched an 'International Don't Fake It Day', women were encouraged to 'sign our pledge to make faux Os a thing of the past' (*Cosmopolitan* 41). Figures from the latest sex research demonstrating the prevalence of faking are reported with a weary sigh, but provide the impetus for renewed efforts at its eradication. Women are advised that faking 'has to stop', that it is time for an 'orgasm revolution' since we will 'never truly be equal if we don't' (*Cosmopolitan*).[4] Faking orgasm is not just old-fashioned, then, it is downright unfeminist.

So, the recognition that large numbers of women fake orgasms and that this practice is relatively routine is both widely acknowledged, and simultaneously treated as both trivial and as a source of cultural anxiety. This ambivalence alone makes it worthy of greater academic attention. One assumption of both the scientific literature and popular discourse, is that the distinction between the real and the fake lies in the unmediated bodily signs of authentic orgasm; that if these signs can be identified then faking orgasm becomes an impossibility or at the very least implausible. Yet, in the 40 years which have passed since Masters and Johnson's laboratory work identified the physiological signs of orgasm, and despite the widespread circulation of these biological indicators in popular discourse, the practice of faking remains prevalent. This alerts us to the idea that this scientific knowledge does not signal the death of faking as a practice, but forms part of the network of ideological discourses which sustain and perpetuate this practice. Yet this sits alongside the representation of faking as an outmoded, somewhat dishonest, practice which is unsuitable for postfeminist women in modern relationships. The practice of faking remains impervious to sexological dissection, which invites a detailed consideration of *why* women fake that goes beyond the simplistic assertion that it is 'because they can'.

Why do women fake?

While the literature which explores why women fake orgasm is relatively small, two distinct approaches have emerged which are briefly outlined below. The first is an individual differences approach that attempts to identify the intrinsic characteristics which distinguish women who fake from women who do not. Both Wiederman (1997) and Darling and Davidson (1986) adopt this approach, hypothesising that perhaps women who are less sexually experienced or have lower sexual self-esteem would be more likely to fake orgasm. In fact, they found the opposite. Wiederman suggested that this 'unexpected' finding could be explained by the idea that such women hold themselves to a higher standard of sexual performance and thus fake orgasm to 'compensate for perceived deficits in sexual responsiveness' (1997: 138). Evolutionary psychologists explain individual differences in faking as part of a broader strategy of 'mate retention' in which access to 'good genes is assured by decreasing the 'likelihood of a male partner's infidelity or defection from the relationship', and by signalling her own pleasure and thus 'manipulating his commitment to the relationship' (Kaighobadi et al., 2012: 1122). In their questionnaire-based study of 453 young women (mostly students) in the US, Kaighobadi and colleagues found that women who perceived a greater risk that their partners would be unfaithful were more likely to fake orgasm. While women may adopt the strategy of faking orgasm in order to preserve a relationship (discussed below) this does not mean that evolutionary psychology offers the most convincing explanation of this behaviour – particularly if we accept Jagose's contention that faked orgasm is a 20th century invention

(2010). This individual differences approach typically serves to pathologise women, to reduce women to their reproductive function, and to overlook the interpersonal dynamics of faking and how these might be situated in contemporary gendered discourses of heterosex.

The second approach addresses the question of why women fake by asking women directly, in order to draw out the *meaning* of pretending orgasm and locate these meanings within broader cultural discourses about sexual and intimate relationships (Hite, 1976; Roberts et al., 1995; Muehlenhard and Shippee, 2010; Fahs, 2011). This research identifies a number of key reasons women give for faking orgasm. Perhaps the most widely cited reason is *to avoid hurting their partner's feelings* (Hite, 1976; Schaefer, 1973, Roberts et al., 1995; Trice-Black, 2010; Muehlenhard and Shippee, 2010). Reflecting the representations in women's magazines, the absence of orgasm is seen as a sensitive issue which is likely to damage men's self-esteem and bruise their fragile egos. Faking orgasm is presented as an act designed to protect men from these difficult feelings. As one of the US women in Fahs' (2011) study explained, 'I fake often because, you know, he's going to feel bad about himself or he's going to feel that I haven't enjoyed myself, so I just feel like I need to have one to make him happy ...' (2011: 60). Similarly in her small-scale study on women's sexuality during transition to motherhood Trice-Black (2010: 157) found that women put the sexual needs of their partners above their own and faked orgasms in order to 'protect his ego' and to 'ensure that he 'feels good' about his ability to please.

A second reason that women fake orgasm is in order *to avoid problems in the relationship* (Darling and Davidson, 1986; Fahs, 2011; Hite, 1976; Muehlenhard and Shippee, 2010). Women report that male partners sometimes become upset, frustrated or angry by the absence of women's orgasm (Fahs, 2011; Roberts et al., 1995; Muehlenhard and Shippee, 2010). Some women fake in response to this direct pressure from partners to orgasm (Fahs, 2011), or to avoid awkward conversations or questions (Muehlenhard and Shippee, 2010), or the 'difficult encounters' they experience when they do not perform a (fake) orgasm (Roberts et al., 1995: 529). Faking orgasm, then, is seen as a way of avoiding disruption or damage and a way of avoiding confrontation or difficulties (Hite, 1976).

Thirdly, women report faking because orgasm was unlikely or taking too long and they **wanted to end the sexual encounter** (Muehlenhard and Shippee, 2010; Fahs, 2011). In one study, 61% of women reported that they pretended to orgasm to bring sex to an end, typically because they were bored, not in the mood, or tired and wanting to sleep

(Muehlenhard and Shippee, 2010). Women describe faking orgasm because they are physically and emotionally drained from the demands of doing both paid work and/or the majority of work within the home: 'I faked it because I just wanted to be done with it, I guess, like it's 2.00 a.m., and I'm tired and want to put an end to it' (Fahs, 2011: 62).

Finally, a further reason that women gave for faking orgasm was **to avoid feeling abnormal** (Darling and Davidson, 1986; Fahs, 2011; Hite, 1976; Roberts et al., 1995; Schaefer, 1973; Wiederman, 1997). Fahs (2011) found that some women who find it difficult to orgasm, and who blame themselves and their 'faulty' bodies for this orgasmic inconsistency might fake orgasm to avoid feeling or appearing abnormal.

In making sense of what women say about *why* they fake, feminist researchers have identified the sociocultural discourses which make faking orgasm a reasonable or necessary practice for some women to adopt, and demonstrated how these serve to privilege male sexuality and perpetuate sexual oppression. Researchers have drawn tentatively on the theory of 'emotion work' to explain why women privilege male sexuality and fake orgasm to protect the feelings of their partners (Roberts et al., 1995; Jackson and Scott, 2007). This work draws connections between faking orgasm and gendered discourses of care and sexual performance, such that faking orgasm becomes a practice of emotion management through which masculinities and femininities are done. In this chapter, I want to push the application of emotion work theory further to explore the affective dynamics of faking, to examine the relationships between emotion and embodied practice, and to unsettle the distinction between the real and the fake. I briefly outline the origins of theory of 'Emotion Work' in commercial interactions, before exploring its application to the private sphere and intimate relationships.

Emotion work

Emotion work refers to the effort that people engage in to try to induce or suppress feelings to make them 'appropriate' to the situation. The concept was popularised and developed by Hochschild (1979, 1983) who outlined a social theory of emotion management. She argued that such emotion management was inherently ideological since 'feeling rules' govern not only what it is appropriate, expected or legitimate to feel in a given situation, but also the relationships that people have and their responsibilities and obligations towards each other. Hochschild was interested in the commoditisation of feelings in service work, such as that performed by flight attendants, asking in whose interests such feeling rules operate. For

example, exhortations for attendants to 'be cheerful' and to induce positive feelings in travellers may boost profits but be at considerable cost to
workers in terms of effort expended, burnout, stress and alienation from
'true' emotions (Zapf, 2002). Hochschild (1983) made a key distinction
between 'surface acting' where people mask or disguise what they really
feel (e.g., supressing disgust or feigning desire), and 'deep acting' in which
women work to actually *feel* differently. Emotion work may involve work
on the emotions of *others*, and/or work on the feelings experienced by the
self. She identified three (intertwined) techniques through which people
'do' emotion work – cognitive, bodily and expressive – although subse-
quent work has most focused on the cognitive dimension. Cognitive work
is the effort to change images, ideas or thoughts; bodily work attempts to
change the physical or experiential aspects of emotion (such as trying
to breathe slower or trying not to shake); and expressive work involves
changing expressive gestures (e.g., trying to smile or trying not to cry).
The concept of emotional labour has since been used to explore the social
regulation of emotion in a wide range of settings including nursing (James,
1992), teaching (Hebson et al., 2007), clerical work (Wichroski, 1994) and
in commercial sex work where workers engage in emotional labour to
induce the appropriate feelings of arousal and pleasure in clients, while
protecting themselves from the emotional and psychological demands of
this work (Brewis and Linstead, 2000; Sanders, 2005; Bernstein, 2007).

Parallel work has explored emotion work in the private sphere of
family life including sexual and intimate relationships. This includes the
work that mothers do to manage the emotional relationships between
children and their fathers following divorce or separation (Seery and
Crowley, 2000), the work that wives do to bring their partner out of a
bad mood (Minnotte et al., 2007), or the work that women undertake
to maintain emotional intimacy in long-term relationships (Duncombe
and Marsden, 1993). This emotion work represents a 'third shift'
(Hochschild, 1989; Erickson, 2005) alongside housework and childcare
since it involves the expenditure of time and effort essential for maintaining family and intimate relationships, and for which women bear
the greater responsibility. This unequal division of emotional labour
can be understood in relation to ideologies of love and intimacy which
position women as primarily responsible for, and ideally suited to,
doing emotion work, and men as unwilling or incapable of so doing
(Duncombe and Marsden, 1993, 1995, 1996). The association between
caring and nurturing and femininity means that emotion work affirms
and reproduces gendered conceptions of self, and that women are held
more accountable for performing this work (Erickson, 2005).

Surface acting, 'sex work' and faking orgasm

Sexual intimacy has also been identified as a site for emotion work. Duncombe and Marsden (1996: 220) argue that heterosexual couples in long-term relationships can be seen as performing a kind of 'sex work' (which parallels emotion work) to bring their sexual feelings into line with the feeling rules of how they think sex 'ought to be' experienced. The couples in their study talked about trying to manage the disappointment that their intimate lives did not match the emotional and sexual fulfilment promised by cultural discourses about the couple relationship. By feigning desire, by trying, working on, or forcing themselves to have sex, women attempted to maintain a sexual relationship. Often this effort was undermined by a building resentment that this work was not recognised or reciprocated with greater intimacy by male partners. Faking orgasm is a particular kind of 'sex work' which, despite its apparent prevalence and recognition, has received little sustained academic attention (although see Roberts et al., 1995; Jagose, 2010). As noted earlier, the literature on faking orgasm has typically brushed up against the theory of 'emotion work' rather than engaging with it in depth. In describing this work, then, I have taken certain liberties in imposing the emotion work framework on top of the research in order to draw conclusions about how fake orgasm is conceptualised, and to move towards a troubling of the distinction of fake orgasms from real or authentic orgasms. We revisit the reasons that women give for faking orgasm in light of feminist theorising about how this practice becomes meaningful in the context of gendered ideologies in which the doing of sex (and the faking of it) is swept up in the re-articulation of gender and sexual identities. Emotion work theory gives us a conceptual apparatus through which we might be able to understand faking orgasm – specifically the importance of sociocultural 'feeling rules' for shaping individual experience, the distinction between emotion work done on the self and work done on others, and the differentiation of 'surface acting' (e.g., pretending to feel pleasure) and 'deep acting' (changing to actually feel pleasure).

Faking orgasm is typically conceptualised as a form of surface acting to meet the cultural demands of feeling rules – women work to appear *as if* they are experiencing orgasm on the surface, but their 'real' feelings remain unchanged. We have already explored some of what we might call 'feeling rules' (or sociocultural discourse about orgasm) which might give rise to faked orgasms in previous chapters. The orgasmic imperative (Chapter 2) suggests that men and women are *supposed* to experience orgasmic bliss during sexual interaction particularly intercourse (preferably at the same time); the ethic of reciprocity (Chapter 2) suggests that partners *should* work to evoke mutual orgasm – that they *should* be able to 'give' orgasms to one another; and the performance imperative (Chapter 5) that individuals *should* work on themselves to improve their sexual skill and technique to ensure orgasmic performance. As previous chapters have illustrated, these feeling rules are heavily gendered and the obligations and entitlements that they incorporate are wrapped up in sexual ideologies of masculinity and femininity. In addition to these 'feeling rules', emotion work theory draws attention to the rule that women are held accountable for doing and managing emotions (both their own and those of others) in relationships. Feeling rules suggest that sexual activities should be pleasurable and that they should 'naturally' result in orgasm. If sex is not pleasurable, if an orgasm is absent, it is accountable and has to be explained (Frith, 2013a). Feminist research argues that the practice of faking orgasm is a rational response to these sociocultural feeling rules which position orgasm as an obligation for women in a cultural context in which they have unequal access to sexual pleasure.

Men and women frequently account for an absent orgasm in one of two different ways: either there is something wrong with the women and her sexual functioning; or there is something wrong with her partner – that his skills as a lover are inadequate (Roberts et al., 1995). In both cases, the need to account for orgasmic absence raises the potential for relationship problems and difficult or awkward conversations. We noted earlier (Chapter 2) that the orgasmic imperative positions women who do not experience orgasm as dysfunctional, abnormal or as sexual failures. Lifestyle magazines emphasise that every woman *can* experience orgasm, at the same time as presenting women's 'inability' to orgasm as relatively common (Lavie-Ajayi and Joffe, 2009). Responsibility for solving this problem is seen as lying with women who need to become more confident and knowledgeable about their bodies, and to be less repressed and more adventurous in their sexuality. Women describe feeling pressure to orgasm – they feel pressure to demonstrate their pleasure to partners, but they also feel pressure to *feel* pleasure (Fahs, 2011). Within this context, one of the reasons that women fake orgasm is to avoid feeling abnormal, or to avoid feeling inadequate as lovers. In her research with women who identified as having sexual difficulties, Cacchioni (2007) found that women engaged in different kinds of 'sex work' to achieve what they saw as 'normal' heterosexuality – including both avoidance work (being busy or falling asleep to avoid sex) and performance work (faking or pretending pleasure and desire). Women may feel particular

– Please Steve but also look desirable to Steve.

♦ Would be a Secondary reference.

pressure to fake during intercourse where there is a greater pressure to orgasm (since feeling rules position intercourse as the most satisfying sexual experience), and perhaps the least likelihood of experiencing a 'genuine' orgasm. Muehlenhard and Shippee (2010) found that women were most likely to fake during penile–vaginal intercourse – with oral sex a distant second. Others have found that the absence of orgasm is more problematic in relationships in which penetrative sex predominates (Lavie-Ajayi, 2005). Some women report that their partners' react to their lack of orgasm by harassing or mocking them – making them feel that they are sexually inadequate (Lavie-Ajayi, 2005). Faking orgasm involves surface acting on the self, in which women disguise their own feelings of boredom, fatigue, or lack of arousal by giving the appearance of sexual ecstasy. Of course, although the orgasmic imperative might be felt particularly keenly by women who experience difficulties with orgasm, its disciplinary effects are felt by all women. The assumption that only sexually inexperienced or unconfident women, or women who do not experience orgasm, would fake orgasm has been contradicted by research evidence showing that women who are more sexually experienced and who can experience orgasm are more likely to fake (Darling and Davidson, 1986; Wiederman, 1997; Muehlenhard and Shippee, 2010). As orgasm becomes a benchmark of how women are as lovers, their femininity, how liberated they are and how in touch with their bodies they are, faking orgasm allows women to escape the guilt and shame of not experiencing orgasm as often as they feel they should or in the context of sexual practices that they feel should result in orgasm (i.e., intercourse) (Fahs, 2011).

In contrast to work performed on the self, faking orgasm is more often positioned as a form of emotion work done on partners – a means of protecting men from feelings of inadequacy, ensuring that men feel confident in their sexual performance, and avoiding problems in the relationship. In their ground-breaking paper on faking orgasm, Roberts et al. (1995: 523) identified two narratives (or feeling rules) which were woven through people's accounts of their sexual experiences: a narrative of love and relationships, and a narrative of work and skill. These highly gendered discourses about sex and gender create the possibility for emotion work and reveal how the doing of emotion work is implicated in the making of gendered and sexual subjectivities. The first feeling rule positions sex and love as intimately intertwined. Sex is, as one of their respondents put it, 'the ultimate way of showing someone that you care about them' (1995: 525). Articulated primarily by women, here sex is seen as a route to securing intimacy and as essential to the relationship; moreover, the stability of the relationship was placed above women's own sexual pleasure. The absence of orgasm is seen as a problem for their relationship, rather than for their own sexual pleasure or sexual self.

The second feeling rule, one that was particularly adopted by men, was the idea that evoking orgasm in a partner requires the application of sexual skill and technique. Since men's capacity for orgasm is typically seen as 'natural' and unproblematic there is (so the story goes) little need for sustained work. The female orgasm, in comparison, being more elusive and difficult to attain is dependent on men's work and the application of skill. 'Giving' women an orgasm was seen as a 'demonstration of the man's sexual capabilities and skill' (1995: 526), and women's pleasure as dependent on men's work. As noted elsewhere, this feeling rule places obligations on men to 'give' orgasms to women:

> I feel like my partner is more central to the experience than me so I have to, I'm in a way there for her, to please her, so I have no problem with having an orgasm, so, I feel like it's my duty to make sure she has one as well.(Male participant cited in Roberts et al., 1995: 526)

Heterosexuality becomes an 'economy' in which 'the woman's orgasm is exchanged for the man's work' (1995: 528). The presence of women's orgasm therefore confirms the work and sexual skill of the man and affirms his status as a 'good lover' – especially when women's orgasms are seen as more problematic or difficult to achieve. Within this economy, the absence of orgasm is problematic since it casts doubt on men's sexual capabilities and skill. Women's accounts of faking orgasm reveal that they are well aware of both the orgasm-for-work exchange, and the possibility that orgasmic absence may be read as a lack of male sexpertise. For example, women see faking as an attempt to reward the 'hard work' that men have put into attempting to 'give' their partners an orgasm – 'I didn't want him to think his effort was worthless' (Muehlenhard and Shippee, 2010: 562) – and recognise that one of the consequences of not faking is that men may feel inadequate, less manly or unskilled in the bedroom. Women report that their partners want them to experience orgasm, and that often their biggest problem with not experiencing orgasm was their partner's reaction to this (Lavie-Ajayi, 2005).

A focus on emotion work draws attention to the ways in which these accounts are shot through with an ethic of care in which the 'feeling rule' is that women have responsibility for managing their own, and their partners, emotions. Here, faking orgasms can be seen as an act of care:

> I fake it when I care about the person, cause I'm not going to fake it if I don't really care. That's almost as much energy as having one! (Cited in Fahs, 2011: 61)

[handwritten: Ø Get original citation for this.]

Therefore, Fahs concludes that 'faking orgasm may symbolize deeply internalized oppression (e.g., one's own pleasure as frankly less significant than one's partner's pleasure), but faking orgasm can also represent, for women, a gesture of care, affection, love and nurturance' (2011: 62). The coupling of caring and nurturance with femininity means that women are charged with the responsibility for maintaining relationships and intimacy through the expression of care. However, whether or not men 'care' about women's pleasure is also a source of ambivalence. Men's investment in women's orgasms is sometimes seen as a 'pressure' to orgasm, in which men care more about their own performance than pleasing their partner. For example, one 23-year-old in Fah's research observed:

[handwritten left margin: • Men's 'care' for females mainly pleasure is anti-feminist]

> I would say that mostly guys don't really seem to care, but I think they enjoy it, and they like you to orgasm because that makes them feel better about themselves. (Fahs, 2011: 56)

In this case, men's investment in women's orgasm is seen primarily as a selfish one if men are concerned predominantly with the affirmation of their own sexual prowess. Women express resentment at the requirement to produce an orgasm (real or faked) to meet this expectation. At other times, men's concern with women's orgasm, and the work, effort and skill that they put into attempting to satisfy women is interpreted as an act of care. Both men (Gilfoyle, Wilson, and Brown, 1992) and women (Roberts et al., 1995) position men as being generous, kind, skilled or caring lovers if they wait for their partner to orgasm before 'taking' their own, or conversely of being selfish and inconsiderate if they do not. The work that men put into 'giving' their partners an orgasm is seen as a sign of their love and commitment, an act of care which may be accompanied by feelings of accomplishment or pride (Fahs, 2011). This is reflected in the way that both men and women talk about relationship sex as being characterised by men's care and concern for female orgasm in contrast to 'hook-up' or casual sex in which it is acceptable and expected for men to be 'selfish' (Armstrong, England and Fogerty,

[handwritten bottom margin: Ø boosts their ego. Believe they gave a greater performance / better at sex.   → Contrast to Steve in paragraph.   Ø Contrast (Monogamy) to elaborate point.]

2012). In response to the care shown by men in being considerate lovers who invest time and effort into women's pleasure, faking orgasms can be seen as a reciprocal act of care – an exchange for the care he has shown in 'working hard' to please her.

Faking orgasm, then, can be seen as a creative response to tensions invoked by competing feeling rules and how these are played out in individual relationships. Faking orgasm is not attributable to women's insecurities, lack of sexual experience or inability to orgasm. To describe them as such ignores the sociocultural conditions in which women's access to pleasure is being negotiated. There is more at stake in sexual interactions than sexual pleasure; faking orgasm reveals the ways in which masculine and feminine sexual subjectivities are negotiated in the context of orgasmic and coital imperatives which serve to disadvantage women. Calls for women to stop faking, to engage in clearer communication, and to take responsibility for their own pleasure ignore the gendered power dynamics which make faking a sensible and perhaps necessary strategy to get through the day/night. Women's faking may be a reasonable, strategic attempt to manage the dynamics of particular relationships within the context of an orgasmic imperative which structures the experience of sexual relationships. Faking orgasm can: bring to an end an unwanted sexual encounter which women may have felt pressured into or acquiesced to; it may prevent arguments, disagreements or awkward discussion about why an orgasm is absent and who is to 'blame'; it may help women to avoid feeling sexually inadequate or abnormal; it may maintain a relationship and allow the illusion that 'we are happy really'. The emotion work theory places an ethic of care as central to these negotiations – faking orgasm is a way of caring for a male partner. While gendered discourses place an unequal burden on women for performing emotion work, this work is not exclusively female. Faking orgasm can be positioned on part of a reciprocal exchange of caring in which the care that men put into 'providing' an orgasm is rewarded with an orgasm – sometimes one which is fake. Faking orgasm, then, reveals something of the complex interplay of feeling rules which serve to maintain heteropatriarchy.

Deep acting, the real and the fake

So far, emotion work has provided a useful theory for understanding why women fake orgasms. As demonstrated, research has concentrated on identifying feeling rules and understanding how these shape the practice of emotion work (including the gendered division of such work), and on outlining faking orgasm as a kind of surface acting in which women suppress their own feelings in order to evoke positive feelings in their male partners. In this work the idea that there is a clear distinction between what one feels and what one shows to the other person has been treated as unproblematic. In this section, I cast doubt on this distinction.

Surface acting rests on the distinction between what one really feels and how one acts. While researchers have explored the reasons why women fake – few have asked about how women fake or the nature of this performance. Muehlenhard and Shippee's (2010) qualitative survey research with 180 male and 101 female college students is a rare exception. They asked how people fake orgasm and found that most (78% of men and 90% of women) acted out an orgasm in four different ways: (a) bodily acting (using movements such as moving or thrusting, freezing or clenching muscles); (b) vocal acting (making sounds such as moaning or breathing faster and louder); (c) verbal acting (saying 'I'm coming'), and (d) vague descriptions ('I just acted the same way [as when experiencing orgasm on a previous occasion]'). Faking orgasm is, then, an embodied *performance* – a performance which is enacted through the body. The notion of performance rests on a distinction between 'acting' and 'experiencing' which is reflected in their definition of 'pretending' orgasm: 'Acting like you were having an orgasm when you weren't really having one, or saying that you had an orgasm when really you didn't' (2010: 554). The notion of faking or pretending orgasm rests on the distinction between this and a real or authentic *experience* of orgasm. But here I want to explore the idea that this distinction – while held strongly in the cultural imagination – is not so easy to maintain.

Firstly, Muehlenhard and Shippee's own research casts doubt on this distinction – since both men (16%) and women (23%) reported experiences which were neither straightforwardly faking, nor real or authentic – they had not pretended orgasm but had done *something similar*. Moreover, based on the content of their narratives, the researchers reclassified 18 of the responses from this 'something similar' category as having pretended orgasm, and reclassified three people who indicated that they had pretended into the 'did not pretend' category. At the very least this suggests that the distinction between pretending to orgasm and other activities is not clear-cut. Similarly, in the same study a large percentage of participants indicated that they had pretended to be more aroused or enthusiastic about sex than they really were (69% of women and 57% of men) suggesting that pretending orgasm may be only one of a number of performances taking place in sexual interactions. Where would one draw the line between pretending to be more aroused or enthusiastic and pretending to orgasm?

Secondly, the notion of deep acting also promises to blur the boundary between the real and the fake. Rather than acting as if something is felt or experienced, deep acting requires a shift in the lived experience of the body such that pleasure or desire is felt rather than feigned. While generally under-explored, there is some indicative evidence to suggest that this may be part of what happens when some women fake orgasm – at least some of the time. Elliot and Umberson (2008) conducted in-depth interviews with 31 married couples about their experiences of sexual intimacy in long-term relationships. Participants saw sex (and orgasm in particular) as a barometer of marital success and the health of the relationship, yet as simultaneously fraught with difficulties because of the 'naturally' different sexual desires of men and women. Consequently, a high proportion of the sample (74%) reported conflict over sex – especially around sexual frequency. Elliot and Umberson argue that men and women engage in emotion work to reduce this conflict, enhance intimacy and facilitate their spouses' well-being. Primarily this emotion work involved 'performing desire' (2008: 398) by actively working on the self to alter their own sexual feelings, attitudes and behaviours. Women make a conscious effort to be more sexual, to want sex more or to be more willing to have sex, while men make a conscious effort to reduce their sexual feelings and to focus on the quality rather than quantity of sex. In other words, they attempt to induce desire, reduce desire or perform desire. Some women report faking orgasm to enhance sexual excitement for their partner or *for themselves* (Hite, 1976). For example, in a study that interviewed 481 women who fake orgasms, Cooper, Fenigstein and Fauber (2014) found that a subset of women faked orgasm to increase their own arousal. Rather than involving the suppression of their own desires, for these women faking orgasm was one way of achieving more positive sexual experiences. Similarly, some women report faking their level of arousal to ensure that their partner continues to pleasure them (Opperman et al., 2013). One explanation for this could be the idea of 'empathetic sexual arousal' – becoming more aroused in empathy with the heightened arousal of a partner. Haning et al. (2008) argue that the ability to perceive the feelings of another person is one of the most fundamental aspects of empathy. Over 90% of the 1177 young male and female participants in their study agreed that 'I find that it is a turn-on for me when my sex partner is really sexually excited'. They note that faking orgasm may be advantageous for women since it benefits their sexual relationship by increasing the sexual response of their partner, and that this practice may allow women to avoid negative reactions from their partner (i.e., loss of erection, ending the sexual interaction or anger). However, they give no consideration to the idea that increasing a partner's arousal might, in turn, also increase the woman's own arousal – although their theoretical approach would support this interpretation. Moreover, popular self-help literature – often written by sexological experts – also offers faking as a route to increased sexual pleasure and genuine orgasm. For example, Heiman and LoPiccolo's (1976) classic *Becoming Orgasmic: A Sexual and Personal Growth Program for Women* suggests 'role-playing' orgasm as a way of discovering the ways in which women are afraid to 'let go' in having an authentic orgasm. Similarly, lifestyle magazines encourage women to '*Fake it till you make it*' and to induce multiple orgasms by intentionally mimicking the bodily signs of orgasm such as 'Moaning out loud, breathing faster and harder, and tightening and loosening your pelvic muscles' [*Cosmopolitan* 12].We could argue that the type of 'discipline work' advocated by 'sex experts' which is characterised by 'a quest to implement a certain skill and/or degree of concentration to manipulate the mind or the body' is, if successful, also a form of deep acting (Cacchioni, 2007: 308).

A final complication to the distinction between 'real' and 'fake' orgasms is offered by several commentators who have noted that since women's orgasms are considered to be largely invisible, and because women's orgasms function to affirm the 'success' of men's labour, there is 'a demand for noisy and exaggerated display' (Roberts et al., 1995: 528). If a noisy, writhing orgasm arises out of a need to reassure male partners of the adequacy of their sexual performance – this performance will be required whether the orgasm is genuinely experienced or feigned. How an orgasm is recognised *as* an orgasm both by partners and by the self involves a large degree of interpretation – how to communicate an embodied experience to a partner, how to interpret one's own physical sensations, and how to recognise a partner's responses as an orgasm involves a set of cultural competencies which must be learned (Jackson and Scott, 2007). Women may be required to 'show' their embodied experience in ways that are recognisable as authentic to partners. Cultural representations have an important role to play in shaping our understanding of what an orgasm looks and sounds like (as does the sexological research). These representations may bear little resemblance to the way women actually look during orgasm. As Shere Hite notes in her ground-breaking research on female sexuality:

> Picture book and pornography examples of female orgasmic passion
> often show women writhing and arching like wild horses during

orgasm. This is more accurate as a depiction of passionate arousal than as a picture of a woman during orgasm. During orgasm women (and men) become rigid and tense and for most women this means lying still. (Hite, 1976: 124)

Some of the women in her research complained that their partners did not believe that they were experiencing orgasm because they did not display ecstasy in the way that their partners thought that they should: 'A lot of my partners think I am very strange because I get very quiet and very much into my head when I have an orgasm. They think because I don't pant, scream and claw I haven't had one' (1976: 126). As well as being able to display orgasm in a way that is recognisable, women need to also be able to recognise the sensations of orgasm and be able to label these as orgasm in order to distinguish effectively between what is real and what is fake. As we discuss in the following chapter this is not as straightforward as it might initially appear. Consequently, the cultural conventions by which orgasm is typically represented, may blur the distinction between real and fake orgasms since even genuinely felt orgasms (if indeed there can be such a thing) must be presented in particular ways in order to be recognised.

Conclusions

Fake orgasm is typically understood as an unpolitical, unfeminist practice – as a poignant instance of women's submission to men's sexual needs and desires, or a manifestation of patriarchy in practice. The typical reading of faking orgasm as a form of emotion work to appease male anxieties and boost men's egos would fit with this reading. Jagose (2010) offers a delightfully alternative reading of faked orgasm, in which faking orgasm is seen as 'an inventive bodily technique' (2010: 529). Jagose wants to understand orgasm not as a problem – as a poor imitation of the real thing – but as a 'positive cultural practice, an erotic invention that emerges from a specific set of circumstances as a widespread observance, a new disposition or way of managing oneself in sexual relations' (2010: 535). Fake orgasm is interesting not simply (or not only) because of what it reveals about the normalising of sexuality, about a practice of mimicry, but also for what it reveals about 'authentic' or 'genuine' experience.

One aspect of this is the idea that the distinction between real orgasm and fake orgasm lies in embodied experience – that a real orgasm is felt, while a fake orgasm is performed. The notion of deep acting draws this distinction into question. While I would not deny that orgasm has a physiological element, nor that specific physical changes occur in the body, the idea that we can distinguish between a real and fake orgasm simply by looking at bodily processes is a fallacy. A woman who is told that she is experiencing orgasm simply because a certain part of her brain lights up on a PET scan, or because a set of muscles is contracting, is unlikely to be convinced unless the experience looks, sounds or feels as she culturally expects it to. Indeed, it may only be experienced as pleasurable in a context in which matches her (culturally shaped) desires. Whether or not a woman 'really' has an orgasm is not knowable by recourse to the body alone – orgasm (fake or otherwise) requires interpretative processes. Orgasms – both real and fake – are enacted and performed through the body. These performances are necessarily shaped by cultural expectations and understandings, such that even performances which are interpreted as genuinely felt may be read as inauthentic by lovers. Moreover, in contrast to the cultural story that orgasms happen naturally and are evidence of a body out-of-control, the notion of deep acting exposes the considerable work that goes into experiencing an (authentic) orgasm. Emotion work is helpful and unhelpful here since it rests on the idea of a distinction between surface- and deep-acting – both involve acting (or enacting). Attending to the slipping and sliding between these two forms of work, and the impossibility of drawing hard and fast lines between them, is important. This draws attention to the labour involved in producing orgasms that might be interpreted (by self and others) as genuine, and those that might also be interpreted as fake. The important question is not, then, how can we distinguish a 'real' orgasm from a 'fake' orgasm – although this is a question that preoccupies scientists, permeates popular culture and generates anxieties between lovers. Rather, the question becomes why is the distinction between 'real' and 'fake' orgasms culturally necessary? What purpose does this serve? In whose interests does this distinction operate and who does it disadvantage? Under what circumstances – culturally and interpersonally – does this distinction become meaningful? We need more nuanced research which goes beyond asking how many women fake and for what reasons, to asking how women fake, under what circumstances and with what consequences. We need research which explores the functions which a public discourse on faking serves.

A second way in which faking draws our attention to its opposite – the 'authentic' – is through attempts to imagine an alternative sexuality. Feminists have a tendency to reach for a supra-social sexuality (see also Jackson and Scott, 2007) – a sexuality which is transcendental, magical or potentially transgressive – as an antidote to a sexuality which is shaped and constrained by disciplinary cultural discourses. In the context of palpable inequalities in sexuality, the transformative possibilities of desire and pleasure (for example) as markers of 'healthy sexuality' and routes to sexual empowerment, represent an attractive alternative. Yet, Jackson and Scott (2007) argue that there can be 'no "revolutionary", "productive", disruptive or subversive desire beyond the social' (2007: 103). In her analysis of faked orgasm Jagose is equally sceptical about the 'transgressive' possibilities of sexual acts – she attempts to queer our understanding of faking by articulating its political possibilities while challenging our understanding of agency. Dominant accounts of sexuality place orgasm as a privileged site of authentic personhood – a place in which the social is stripped away, leaving bare the essence of the person. Fake orgasm, by contrast, is impersonal – it resists being an authentic expression of one's personhood. Jagose argues that this impersonality is key, and she outlines three ways in which fake orgasm is impersonal. Firstly, it draws on conventional codes of representation which circulate through popular culture, making each orgasm indistinguishable from the individual's previous orgasms or from those of others. This also makes a fake orgasm indistinguishable from an authentic orgasm. Secondly, faking orgasm is impersonal since the intimacies of the couple are lost and replaced with a feigned intimacy. Finally, fake orgasm produces a hyperconsciousness of what one is doing and therefore represents a break in the usual self-continuity. In a context in which sexuality is seen as key to personhood, this impersonality is problematic. But Jagose encourages us to 'queer' this understanding. If we put this into the context of emotion work then, fake orgasm resists the typical exchange of heterosexual relationships – an exchange in which men give women orgasm and women give themselves; and an exchange in which women give orgasms in exchange for men's work. In faking orgasm, women withdraw the labour involved in producing authentic orgasms. They hold themselves back. Faking orgasm subverts the idea that sex is an authentic exchange. Jagose insists on the 'counter-intuitive possibility that pleasure does not necessarily feel good', that pleasure might be 'difficult, might be demanding, intricate, perhaps even difficult or disagreeable' (2010: 531). Faking might be a desirable – even pleasurable – alternative since it requires less of the self. This does not mean that we should see women as strategically and agentically engaging in subversive political acts when they fake orgasm – indeed this may be experienced by women as frustrating and undesirable. Jagose offers an alternative view of agency which is much more humble than the 'apparently heroic, self-authoring subjects' who resist normative sexuality, where agency is action which is 'ineffectually repetitive' (2010: 534). Jagose's reading of fake orgasm demonstrates how something which is typically seen as unfeminist can be recognised as political, agentic and even pleasurable and always as situated within the constraints of the present. This allows for 'a respectful rethinking of a common feminine practice, where it can be seen as political without (most likely) having political intent and as agentic without *therefore* being empowering' (Gavey, 2012: 720).

7
Embodying Orgasmic Sensation

How do I know if I'm having an orgasm?

> Q: I've recently become sexually active, and I'm not sure if I am reaching orgasm. Can you tell me what it feels like?
>
> (*Cosmopolitan 14*)
>
> [...] I want to know if I had an orgasm because I'm not really sure. Do you feel like you have to pee when you are about to have an orgasm? I need answers please. ASAP!!!
>
> DearCupid[1]

Posed as questions to 'agony aunt' or advice columns, these two requests for information speak to the indeterminacy and ambiguity of orgasmic sensation – 'How do I know if I'm having an orgasm?' These questions both evoke an uncertainty about the presence or absence of orgasm (a recurring theme throughout this book), and raise questions about the status of the bodily experience as a way of addressing this uncertainty. It would be easy to dismiss these appeals as arising from the inexperience of the protagonists and to assume that in time they would naturally learn to correctly identify their physical sensations as orgasm (or not). Instead, I want to consider this as a practical problem to be addressed by all sexual beings – how do we know what an orgasm feels like, and how do we learn to identify our own bodily sensations as an orgasm? I want to problematise what it means to 'know' the experience of orgasm, not as concrete and objective factual information, but as something which is felt through the body. This chapter is concerned with the embodied, sensate experience of orgasm. Male embodiment has been woefully neglected – a point which is picked up in the final chapter – so we know very little about men and boys' embodied experience of ejaculation and orgasm. In contrast, cultural chatter about women and their bodily experience is loud and pervasive – not least because the sexual bodies of girls and young women are positioned as particularly troublesome. We saw in Chapter 3 the ways in which female orgasm is constructed as more elusive or trouble-some than the male, and this extends into the articulation of embodied experience, which is our focus here. Feminist debates about the 'missing discourse of desire' in girls' formal sex education have drawn attention to girls' embodiment and the alienation of girls from their sensate experience (Fine, 1988). Building on the idea of embodied pedagogy introduced in Chapter 5, this chapter explores the informal instruction in the embodied experience of orgasm – the felt sensations of orgasm and how to recognise and make sense of these sensations – offered by magazines and internet forums providing sexual advice. Building on the work of Jackson and Scott (2007), this chapter explores the idea that 'having' an orgasm is a practical accomplishment that must be learnt through embodied processes that are socially mediated. To start, I come back to the initial question with which this chapter started – 'How do I know if I'm having an orgasm?' – to explore the tension between objective and subjective accounts of bodily experience offered in the scientific literature.

Orgasmic ambiguities

Despite the best efforts of scientists to answer this question defini-tively, identifying objective bodily mechanisms and markers of orgasm remains persistently and stubbornly elusive. Attempts to demystify orgasm through visualising technologies reaffirm the idea that orgasm is an embodied event that can be located and known with the increasing precision and careful measurement that these technologies afford. Yet, at the same time, orgasm is ineffable, obscure and resists specification. A particular puzzle and one which has cropped up in various guises throughout this book, is the mismatch between objective measures of sexual arousal and orgasm which focus on blood flow, muscle contrac-tions, vaginal vasocongestion or penile tumescence (swelling caused by increased blood flow to the genitals), brain chemistry and the like, and subjective accounts of sexual pleasure and climax as reported by indi-vidual men and women. Not only have scientists failed to identify defin-itive physiological markers of orgasmic experience – although several have been suggested including heart rate (Levin and Wagner, 1985) and rectal pressure (van Netten et al., 2008) – but these bodily signs often fail to coincide with the subjective experience of research participants.

Ideally, it seems, objective measures of physiological changes would align perfectly with subjective experience, allowing assertions about orgasmic presence to be made with supreme confidence and enabling accurate counting (and accounting) of orgasm for the purposes of clinical trials and therapeutic practice. While greater credibility is often accorded to the scientific/objective measures of orgasm (at least in scientific circles) the 'failure' of men and (more typically) women to give accounts of their orgasmic experience which map onto these measures is a persistent thorn in the side of scientific certainty. Not only is female sexual response (including orgasm) seen as more difficult to accurately measure (requiring more complex equipment), but also psychophysiological research consistently shows that the relationship between women's sexual feelings and their genital responses are generally weaker than they are for men (see Laan and Everaerd, 1995 and Chivers et al., 2010 for overviews). This both affirms the construction of female orgasm as less visible and knowable than the male (since ejaculation is often taken as indicative that an orgasm has occurred), and also positions female orgasm as more puzzling, complex and elusive (see Chapter 3). While many men seem to infer their sexual feelings from changes that take place in their genitals (Sakheim et al., 1984), women seem to rely less on this information.

Researchers have typically taken the presence of pelvic contractions as definitive proof of orgasm, but a number of women claim to experience orgasms without such contractions (see Levin, 2004). Moreover, in self-report studies some women report uncertainty in being able to identify whether or not they have had an orgasm. In a small-scale study exploring women's self-regulation of sexual response, only 22 (67%) of the 33 women who reported having orgasms stated that they were 'very sure' they actually were having orgasms (Prause, 2011). This is consistent with an earlier study in which 10 of 67 women were unsure if they had experienced orgasm (Clifford, 1978). Using physiological measures, Hartman and Fithian (1994) discovered a number of women in their sample who were 'having orgasms' but who did not 'realise' that they were. Once the orgasm was identified to these women, they were able to identify further orgasms. They did 'experience' orgasms but they did not recognise this experience *as* an orgasm (cited in Lloyd, 2005). A review of the literature on female sexual arousal reveals that there is little agreement between reported genital sensations and changes in genital vasocongestion, while correlations between genital and subjective sexual arousal in men are usually significantly positive, despite differences in methodology and procedures (Laan and Everaerd, 1995).

Evidence of greater concordance between subjective and objective measures of arousal for women who orgasm more frequently (Adams et al., 1985; Brody, Laan and van Lunsen, 2003; Brody, 2007a), are taken as suggestive that greater concordance is linked to better sexual functioning. Therefore lack of agreement between objective measures and subjective experience is generally interpreted as a female 'lack' – women are depicted as 'less able' to recognise and interpret physiological signs of arousal or lack the ability to integrate bodily cues.

Several explanations have been put forward to account for the poorer relationship between genital and subjective arousal in women. The first is that anatomical differences mean that men have more cues to sexual arousal than women; when men's genitals press against trousers, for example, this provides recognisable feedback about arousal (Laan and Janssen, 2007). In addition, some argue that men pay greater attention to, and are more aware of, their bodily cues than women who are more readily influenced by the meaning of sexual behaviours and stimuli. Evidence from assessments of heart rate have found that men are more accurately able to assess changes in their heart rate than are women (Jones, 1995), and that men rely more on internal physical cues to define their emotional state than do women (Pennebaker and Roberts, 1992). This leads some to suggest that:

> men may have high sexual concordance because their subjective sexual arousal is highly influenced by their perception of the internal sensory cues that indicate the extent of their penile erection (e.g., fullness in the penis and groin, tightening of suspensory ligaments). Women, on the other hand, are more likely to be influenced by their attitudes, beliefs, and values regarding sexuality. (Chivers et al., 2010: 48)

The second explanation is the idea that sexual arousal response is automatic and non-conscious. Laan and Janssen (2007) suggested that in order to feel sexual arousal individuals need an amalgam of sexual stimulation (of varying content and intensity), unconditioned and conditioned autonomic nervous system (ANS) responses, *and* conscious assessment of the response as 'sexual'. Researchers have drawn on evidence which suggests that men's and women's bodies sometimes respond automatically during unwanted sex or when viewing depictions of sexual assault to suggest that this response is automatically activated by exposure to sexual stimuli, whether or not this is accompanied by a subjective appraisal of these stimuli as sexually arousing or desired (Laan and Janssen, 2007; Bullock and Beckson, 2011). Reports of genital response and orgasm during sexual assault for women (Levin and van Berlo, 2004) and men (Bullock and Beckson, 2011), suggest that genital responses do occur under conditions of sexual threat. Such responses are often confusing for victims, and may be used by perpetrators to argue that the victim 'really wanted' the assault, but marking these responses as automatic and outside of conscious control mitigates against such interpretations (Bullock and Beckson, 2011). Indeed, this line of reasoning suggests that physiological responses occur separate from a conscious assessment of the responses as 'sexual', suggesting that some conscious interpretation of bodily signs is necessary in order to feel or experience sexual arousal or pleasure.

Third is the suggestion that women have learned less well than men to become aware of their sexual responses. For example, that perhaps women have missed out on learning experiences, such as masturbation, which would allow them to more accurately perceive of bodily signs of sexual arousal. In western cultures, more men than women masturbate and the women that masturbate do so less frequently than men (Oliver and Hyde, 1993). Women who masturbate often demonstrate a closer relationship between their physiological arousal and their subjective experience of arousal than women who do not or only rarely masturbate (Laan et al., 1993). Typically this is treated as a 'technical' issue although some (feminist) researchers link this lack of learning to the masculine bias in sexual science which perpetuates women's alienation from their bodies, and to the operation of gender ideologies which reinforce a sexual double standard. I return to this shortly.

Our purpose here is not to assess the accuracy of these three explanations, but rather to acknowledge that despite intense scientific scrutiny, orgasmic experiences remain somewhat ambiguous and ineffable. All three explanations suggest that physiological changes in themselves are not enough to mark out orgasmic experience, and that some kind of interpretation is needed in order for these changes to be experienced *as sexual*, and moreover *as sexually pleasurable*, by the individual. While all three adopt a cognitive approach to thinking about the nature of this interpretation – ranging from conscious attention to experiential learning – a more socially-embedded understanding of these processes is possible. Knowing that one has had an orgasm involves a recognition and interpretation of bodily response; but this interpretation does not take place anew for each individual, rather these processes takes places not anew or afresh from each individual but rather these processes are mediated by gendered ideologies about the nature of orgasm as an embodied experience.

Embodiment and orgasm

Taking up this question of what it means to know that one has experienced an orgasm, and exploring the connections between bodily experience and 'knowing', it is helpful to reflect on the ways social scientists have theorised the body. One of the central tensions in debates about the body concerns the extent to which the body is constituted through language, knowledge and practices, and the extent to which the body has material or essential attributes. Crawford (2012) outlines three theoretical approaches which have been at the heart of this debate, each of which have their own limitations: social constructionism, phenomenology and structuration. Social constructionist approaches have shifted researchers away from the idea of a 'natural' or biological sexual body and towards examining the ways in which sexuality is organised and shaped through economic, social, cultural and political conditions. This has been the predominant approach adopted in this book. Within these approaches, the body is devoid of essential attributes, instead meaning is inscribed onto the body through discourse in the context of particular relations of power. Social constructionists have demonstrated the role of discursive and normative regimes in disciplining, governing, representing or politicising the body. A weakness is its over-emphasis on social structure at the expense of exploring the lived experience of embodiment. While this approach established sexuality as inherently symbolic and social, it often fails to address sexuality as 'a lusty, bodily, fleshy affair' (Plummer, 2003: 525). Work focuses on identifying the scripts, discourses, identities, cultures and politics through which sexuality is constituted, but rarely focuses on bodies as living, breathing, sweaty, felt, touchable, writhing, humping, juicy, noisy, penetrating, enveloping, orgasmic bodies. In contrast, phenomenological approaches to the body and embodiment prioritise thick description of lived experience, and see meaning as inseparable from our embodied experiences of the world. These approaches prioritise the experience and materiality of the body, since it is through the body, through embodied experience, that we practically engage with the world. The body is a sensing body which touches, hears, smells and sees the world. However, these approaches are criticised for neglecting the role of power relations and external constraints on shaping the body and the lived experience of the body. Finally, structuration theory was presented as a way of overcoming the divide between agency and structure by pointing to the fundamentally dialogical and recursive nature of the relationship between bodies and societies. This approach invokes the notion of a reflexive self who is involved in body projects through which identity is managed. In this book we have explored the idea of the neoliberal pursuit of orgasmic success as a body project through which individuals might 'do' particular versions of masculinity and femininity.

Shilling (2005) encourages researchers to move beyond these theoretical divisions, since an effective theorisation of the body needs to embrace all of these ideas:

> It is one thing to acknowledge the body's importance as a location on which the structures of society inscribe themselves [social constructionist], as a vehicle through which society is constructed [phenomenology] or as a circuit which connects individuals and society [structuration theory] but any comprehensive theory of the body needs to take account of *all three* of these processes. (2005: 18, original emphasis)

Recently, Jackson and Scott (2007) have suggested that interactionist sociology can provide a helpful way of understanding the socially embedded nature of embodied experience. They do not offer this as a complete sociology of the body (or even the sexual body) but instead argue that this approach can make us attentive to aspects of embodiment which are overlooked by other approaches. Usefully for the purposes of this book, they discuss orgasm as a case study for exploring how 'even this most individual, "private", "physical" experience is always also social' (2007; 96). Symbolic interactionism is a constellation of related theoretical frameworks which are loosely drawn together by the pragmatist tradition (Waskul and Vannini, 2012), but is characterised by: an understanding that the body is more than a physical, corporeal object, it is a social object which is imbued with symbolic meaning; an understanding that the body-as-object and the body-as subject cannot be separated and embodiment is a fluid, emergent, productive and negotiated process of being; and a focus on mundane, everyday bodily encounters and interactions through which embodied experiences are negotiated and made meaningful. Jackson and Scott offer three ways of conceptualising embodiment in sexual encounters, which are analytically distinct but are interwoven through embodied selves which are reflexively constructed and reconstructed in everyday sexual encounters. The *'objectified body'* is the material body which is an object of desire or another's touch. This physical body is not 'natural', but made meaningful through symbolic systems of classification (as raced, classed, gendered, etc.) and associated processes of recognition – for example, recognising a body as a person, a particular kind of person, or as sexually attractive/desirable. The '*sensory body*' refers to our reflexive capacity to experience the world not only through our physical senses but by making sense of and interpreting these bodily sensations by drawing on available cultural scripts. Finally, the '*sensate body*' is the means through which we experience pleasure, which requires a reflexive engagement with our own embodied state. As Jackson and Scott point out, this view of embodiment does not deny the physical materiality of bodies, but draws attention to the way that bodies are not meaningful in themselves. They conclude that:

> All of us are embodied within social contexts which profoundly affect how we experience our own and others' bodies. Interpreting bodies as sexual requires a set of culturally acquired competencies as does experiencing our own lived bodies as sexual. (Jackson and Scott, 2007: 101)

This begs the question of *how* these competencies are acquired. Jackson and Scott's model invites a thorough reconsideration of the ways in which the interpretation of the sexual body is embedded in sociocultural meanings which is beyond the scope of this chapter. Here, we explore some of the cultural scripts which may mediate how individuals develop the cultural competencies necessary to interpret their sensory and sensate embodiment. We consider the role of popular culture (specifically women's magazines and internet forums) in 'teaching' women how to acquire the cultural competencies necessary to interpret bodies as orgasmic, and the messages about embodiment contained in these texts. This is, of course, not the same as exploring the ways in which women *actually* acquire these competencies, and popular culture may play only a limited part in this process for some women. Nevertheless, an exploration of cultural texts does illuminate some of the cultural scripts through which embodied experience is socially mediated. Moreover, as we shall see, popular culture offers different messages about embodied experience, and a different kind of embodied pedagogy, from that which is available through more formal sites of instruction such as school-based sex education.

Embodied pedagogy

Embodied pedagogy – instruction about the lived experience of the (sexual) body – is notably absent from school-based sex education. Feminist analyses have pointed to the ways in which sex education constructs notions of 'normal' adolescent sexuality in ways which shape, regulate and discipline the sexual identities, experiences and behaviours of young people as much through what is excluded from the curriculum as through what is included (Bay-Cheng, 2003; Haywood, 1996). Academics, educators and young people alike criticise sex education for omitting information about sexual pleasure, enjoyment or orgasm (Allen, 2008; Hirst, 2008; Thomson and Scott, 1991), and for being too biological, scientific or placing too much emphasis on physiological changes (Holland et al., 1998; Measor, Tiffin and Miller, 2000; Allen, 2005). While sex education is predominantly about the reproductive body, it rarely focuses on bodily sensations and experiences, and the body is often presented as desexualised and divorced from sensuality. For example, British textbooks rarely use photographs of naked men or women and genitalia are represented in medical-style diagrams giving cross sections of the body (Lewis and Knijn, 2003). They seldom mention female sexual arousal or pleasure (Lewis and Knijn, 2003), and identification and explanation of the clitoris is often missing from diagrams of sexual organs (Reiss, 1998; Diorio and Munro, 2000).

In her groundbreaking ethnographic research, Michelle Fine (1988) identified a 'missing discourse of desire' in sex education, where a focus on risk (particularly the risks of teenage pregnancy, or contracting HIV/ AIDS or STIs) comes at the expense of a focus on the pleasurable or fun aspects of sex. This 'missing discourse of desire' has been found to characterise sex education in a range of differing policy and political contexts, including New Zealand (Allen, 2007), Australia (Hillier, Harrison and Bowditch, 1999), United Kingdom (Measor, Tiffin and Miller, 2000), Canada (Connell, 2005), and Ireland (Keily, 2005), although The Netherlands appears to be a rare exception in offering comprehensive sex education which routinely addresses topics of pleasure and desire (see Ferguson, Vanwesenbeeck and Knijn, 2008). These absences are important since sex education is a route for the cultural transmission of sexual values and norms to young people (Bay-Cheng, 2001; Haywood, 1996). A 'missing discourse of desire' which positions young women as the potential victims of male sexual aggression, is identified as problematic because it fails to address them as sexual subjects and undermines the development of the kind of sexual agency needed to negotiate safe, pleasurable and consensual sex (Allen, 2005, 2007; Fine, 1988; Holland et al., 1998; Fine and McClelland, 2006). Researchers have suggested that such limited education may explain why many young women appear to have little experience of exploring their own bodies and are unprepared for the physical realities of their first sexual experiences (Thomson and Scott, 1991). Young women often lack an accurate vocabulary for describing sexual practices or anatomy – particularly their own genitals (Hirst, 2008), and are more likely to describe their experiences of first intercourse as characterised by guilt, embarrassment, sadness, boredom, pain, fear or regret rather than pleasure and excitement (Holland et al., 1998; Higgins et al., 2010; Thompson, 1996; Wight et al., 2008). Fine's work prompted a small but growing body of work exploring the role of desire in adolescent female sexuality (Tolman, 1994, 2005), and the links between desire and sexual agency (Horne and Zimmer-Gembeck, 2005). This work argues strongly that ownership of *embodied* desire is foundational for developing a sense of sexual entitlement that enables young women to both assert and protect their sexual interests. These theorists see sexual subjectivity and agency as embedded in a particular kind of embodied presence, as stemming from an embodied desire or a connection with one's own body and bodily experiences (Tolman, 1999, 2002, 2006; Bay-Cheng, 2003). Internalising the norms of femininity and sex education, which deprioritise desire and embodied pleasure, Tolman describes how young women become distanced from their bodies: has distanced or disconnected young women from their bodies:

> ... in the process of girls learning to look at, rather than experience, themselves, to know themselves from the perspective of men, thereby losing touch with their own bodily feelings and desires. (Tolman, 1994: 325)

Many have called for a more positive approach to understanding young people's sexuality, which includes a focus pleasure and desire to redress this imbalance (Allen, 2007; Burns and Torre, 2005; Jackson and Wetherell, 2010; Tolman, Striepe and Harman, 2003; Horne and Zimmer-Gembeck, 2005). A focus on sexual pleasure is seen as a move towards acknowledging women's sexual subjectivity and affording 'personal empowerment and pleasurable entitlement to young women' (Allen, 2007: 252).

Magazines, and increasingly the internet, offer alternative sources of information about sexuality alongside other media formats such as television, film, music videos and video games. Magazines aimed at young women have a substantial readership and are valued by them as an important resource for learning about sexuality and sexual health issues (Currie, 2001; Kehily, 1999), and are often perceived to be a reliable and important source of information. Feminist analyses of lifestyle magazines (including those presented here) have persistently shown that this 'information' is infused with dominant ideologies concerning sex and sexuality, which generate different kinds of sexual subjectivities for women to negotiate. Women's magazines are permeated with sexual and gender-role stereotypes in which the primary goal should be to attract and please a male partner, both sexually and otherwise (Duran and Prusank, 1997; Durham, 1996, 1998). However, traditional messages which position women as sexual objects who are sexually active in the service of men, who must not be too overtly sexual, or who demonstrate their sexual desirability without showing desire, have been increasingly overshadowed by the contemporary postfeminist sensibility which emphasises women's sexual agency and empowerment as sexually adventurous, 'up for it' subjects (Gill, 2009). But these analyses of media representations of sex have rarely focused specifically on orgasm, seldom pay attention to the sexual body and rarely explore representations of embodied sexual sensation. This is the objective of this chapter. Here, we concentrate not on training and disciplining the body for orgasmic excellence (see Chapter 5), but on 'teaching' women about embodied sensation. In other words, we examine embodied pedagogy about sensory and sensate sexual embodiment.

This chapter draws on an analysis of both *Cosmopolitan* magazine and *DearCupid* – a web-based discussion forum which describes itself as 'an online agony aunt service, aimed mainly at answering questions on relationships, dating and sex'. This site was sampled as part of a larger study exploring the provision of sex education on the internet in which websites were sampled by entering the question 'what is an orgasm?' into a popular search engine. This question format reflects the way that young people seek information on the internet (Noar et al., 2006; Smith et al., 2000), and because this mirrors the 'agony aunt' or advice columns which are familiar in teen magazines or radio programmes (Jackson, 2005). However, unlike traditional advice columns in magazines, the advice provided on the internet forum is given by other (lay) members of the forum – others users with no particular claim to expertise other than their own experience. Analysis of reading practices has shown that although these columns may variously be read to criticise, ridicule or mock those who seek advice (Kehily, 1999), problem pages may also be read as a privileged site of 'truth' and as addressing 'actual problems that girls might encounter' (Currie, 2001: 265). The analysis of both *Cosmopolitan* magazine and the *DearCupid* site focused on identifying the ways in which they represented the felt experience of orgasm. Three key themes are discussed below: 'You'll know when you have an orgasm ...' which deals with the indeterminacy of the orgasmic experience; 'It feels AMAZING!!!' which explores the ways in which orgasmic experience is described, and 'Do you feel like you have to pee?' which examines debates about the significance of a specific bodily sensation.

You'll know when you have an orgasm...

The opening quotes with which we started this chapter were prompted by questions about the indeterminacy of orgasmic sensation. The first was 'not sure' if she was 'reaching orgasm' and wanted to know what an orgasm feels like in order to be able to compare this to her own experience. The second wanted to know whether a specific bodily experience (feeling 'like you have to pee') indicated that she was 'about to have an orgasm'. As noted at the outset, these questions both evoke an uncertainty about the presence or absence of orgasm, and raise questions about the status of bodily experience as a way of addressing this uncertainty. As we have seen throughout this book, orgasmic uncertainty is troubling. Here, orgasmic ambiguity is marked as troubling through its inclusion in a 'problem' page – it is troubling to the individual and perhaps to other readers who may share this experience. Elsewhere, the magazine reports that the experience of uncertainty is common – 'Nearly two-thirds of women say there have been times when they thought they were having an orgasm, but weren't totally sure' (*Cosmopolitan* 41). One response to the sense of ambiguity or indeterminacy evoked by these questions is to assert that orgasm is *definitively* knowable through recourse to an authentic embodied experience. Forum respondents advise that the intensity of feeling and sensation makes orgasm unmistakeable – 'When you have an orgasm, trust me, YOU'LL KNOW!', 'Believe me when I say that YOU WILL KNOW when you have an orgasm!' or 'As for an orgasm, when you have one youll know! there will be no doubt' (*DearCupid*). Orgasmic experience is constructed as unmistakably distinct, but also as only really knowable through direct, embodied experience:

> Honestly. When you have an orgasm, you will know it. Until that moment you will wonder what they feel like. Then you will know. It's really that simple. (*DearCupid*)

These responses mirror the calls of some feminist researchers who advocate that girls should 'listen when their bodies speak' (Tolman, 1994: 339), and suggest that bodily experience offers a route to the authentic or real.

Uncertainty itself is reworked as evidence that an orgasm has *not* occurred; that the bodily sensations experienced could *not* possibly be a sign of orgasmic experience. For example, the magazine's expert advises that: 'Chances are, if you're not sure whether you've reached the big O, you probably haven't because the feeling is so distinct, it's unlikely you'd confuse it with anything else' (*Cosmopolitan* 14). Yet at the same time asserts that orgasm is unambiguously knowable – 'if you have to use the word *think*, it ain't happening' (emphasis in original). Uncertainty is dismissed as evidence *in itself* that orgasm definitely has not occurred. Similar assertions were evident in the discussion on the internet forum: 'The fact that you don't know if you've had an orgasm means that you most likely didn't have one', 'if you have to question weather [sic] you had one or not. then most likely you didn't have an orgasm', or 'if you think you might've had one then you didn't because if you did you wouldn't need to ask'. Like the hyperbolic accounts in the magazine's editorial narrative, first person accounts describe orgasm as instantly recognisable because of its distinctive intensity:

> When i did get my 1st orgasm I began to breathe really heavily I didn't even realise this as I was enjoying the feeling so much I at that time felt happy and there was a feeling going through my hole body like no other feeling. It was AMAZING!!! (*DearCupid*)

Orgasm was routinely described in the forum posts as 'amazing', 'the most intense feeling in the world', 'like the earth is shaking!', 'the most amazing thing ever', 'sensational' or 'an incredible feeling'. In short, orgasmic experience is unmistakably good. These responses confirm a cultural investment in the certainty of orgasmic experience that we have seen echoed elsewhere in the fascination with the elusiveness of female orgasm, and in anxieties about differentiating real orgasms from fake orgasms. The orgasmic imperative requires the definitive presence of orgasm, and here this presence is known through the body. The body is seen as offering unmediated access to orgasmic experience.

A tingling sensation from your head to your toes...

> It's as if you can't breathe for a few moments, a tingling sensation from your head to your toes.

> An orgasm feels like a wave that starts in your shoulder and moves towards the tips of your toes. you may want to bend like a bow, stop breathing and close your eyes.

> It feels like you are getting tickled so hard you can't take it. Then you finally feel warm and tingly and then your vagina muscles CONTRACT. (*DearCupid*)

Against this backdrop of orgasmic indeterminacy and uncertainty, magazines like *Cosmopolitan* typically draw on two different kinds of knowledge to educate women about how they can interpret whether or not bodily signs and sensations are indicative of orgasm. The first is to offer 'expert' advice based on scientific accounts of orgasmic experience to provide a list of bodily signs, changes and responses associated with orgasm for young women to watch out for:

> ... there are some general tip-offs, such as contractions in your vagina, pelvic lifting or thrusting, curling of the toes or fingers, heavy, rapid breathing and moaning, followed by a sense of euphoria. (*Cosmopolitan* 14)

Providing a recognised checklist of orgasmic experience (much like the ones offered in response to questions about 'faking' orgasm – see Chapter 6) offers information *about* the body, but it offers little in the way of understanding what an orgasm *feels* like beyond a 'sense of euphoria'. Indeed, the shortcomings of these checklists are noted, as orgasm is simultaneously constructed as unique and individual, something which is 'different for everyone':

> While the physical process is the same for everyone, the actual orgasmic experience varies from woman to woman. In fact, every orgasm is unique, even your own. (*Cosmopolitan* 14)

A second approach is to offer first-person narratives of orgasmic experience – descriptions purportedly offered by 'ordinary' women, using ordinary language, about the felt sensation of experiencing an orgasm. *Cosmopolitan* asked 'real women to describe the moment when they're 100 percent sure they're climaxing and how they know it's the real deal', and presented a range of different responses from individual women:

> Everything starts to tighten and my breathing gets faster and more difficult. Then all of a sudden, there are waves of pleasure going through my whole body. It's so intense that sometimes all my muscles just kinda stop working. (*Cosmopolitan* 41)

Similarly, many of the respondents on the *DearCupid* site gave descriptions of their own orgasmic experience as a way of answering the initial post. Respondents described feeling 'hot and cold, tingly and very shivery', 'my whole body shakes and I get tingly feelings in my vagina and legs', 'my left leg gets shooting hot tingles, my lower body tenses, the area just under my clit gets really hot', or 'I feel flushed and warm my knees buckle and go numb'. These women (older and younger) had no problem giving detailed descriptions of their sexual desire and pleasure, which were embedded in bodily sensations. Such descriptions are rarely available in more formal educational settings which focus primarily on reproduction and they offer an account of sexual embodiment which both names body parts routinely excluded from sex education (the clitoris) and shifts away from a purely genital focus for sensation. The emphasis on orgasm as a unique and individual experience, which will be felt differently through the body of each woman, provides a context in which the sharing of individual experience becomes meaningful. Individual descriptions can be offered up as a point of reference for women – something to compare their own experiences to – in order to help them decide whether or not their own experience is an orgasmic one. If orgasm 'is different for every single woman on the planet' (*DearCupid*), it is ultimately knowable only through one's own unique bodily experience.

Do you feel like you have to pee?

The discussion on the *DearCupid* site was characterised in part by an attempt to answer the question posed about whether a particular embodied sensation – feeling 'like you need to pee' – is, or is not, indicative of orgasm. This provides an interesting counterpoint to the discussion posed by 'experts' about whether, for example, anal contractions or vaginal temperature offer definitive physical signs of arousal and orgasm since it focuses specifically on the felt experience of women. In other words, it starts not from scientific observations of physiological changes in women's bodies assisted by the use of observational technologies. Instead, it offers a phenomenological focus on women's attempts to make sense of their felt experiences. Interestingly then, the discussion prompted by the initial question showed considerable disagreement about whether feeling 'like you need to pee' is a sign of orgasmic experience. Some were adamant that 'feeling like you need to pee' *is* indicative of orgasm:

> babe you had an orgasm cause ive had it loads nd thats just what it feels like x well done babe.

> yeah u feel like u have to pee that was an orgasm :)

Others were just as adamant that 'you did not have an orgasm', or 'sorry hun that wasn't an orgasm':

> You did not have an orgasm. Feeling like you have to pee just means you're really turned on and being pleasured, but haven't hit orgasm. An orgasm feels like this: All of your muscles get tense and then just let go and it is the most incredible thing you'll ever feel.

A small number of responses showed that other young women also found these sensations confusing, difficult to make sense of, or were unsure about whether these feelings were pleasurable or uncomfortable. Some advised the advice seeker that the feeling of needing to urinate might indicate that she would 'squirt' or ejaculate with her orgasm, others that she might just be experiencing pressure against her bladder, or that this meant her g-spot was being touched in some way. As in the extract above, some respondents argued that the advice-seeker was 'close' to orgasm and just needed to continue a little longer to experience orgasm, or offered congratulations that an orgasm had been experienced. Offering such encouragement can serve to unsettle dominant discourses about girls' sexuality by anchoring sexual pleasure with certainty to the bodies and subjectivities of young women (Frith, 2013b), perhaps especially when the certainty and uncertainty of orgasmic experience is contested. Despite claims that orgasm is distinctive and knowable through bodily experience, exactly what this experience is remains obscure – especially when considering whether specific bodily sensations are, or are not, signs of orgasm. The point here is not whether this advice is right or wrong – even if this were a judgement which could be made – but rather that 'knowing' bodily sensations involves a process of interpretation which is, or can be, mediated by advice and information from others. In other words, this is an interpersonal rather than (or as well as) an intrapersonal process of interpretation.

Conclusions

This chapter speaks to the uncertainty of orgasmic experience and the body as a source of orgasmic certainty. While the certainty of male orgasm is assured – or so the story goes – through a visible ejaculation, female orgasm is less certain. Indeed, women themselves are uncertain about whether felt sensations 'really are' an orgasm or not. This uncertainty opens up the possibility of exploring how bodily sensations become knowable, and to question accounts of bodily experience which rest on notions of authentic or pre-social embodiment. One area in which debates about the felt sensation of pleasure – including orgasm – have been played out is in feminist theorising about the bodies of adolescent girls and young women. Some feminist theorists have identified the absence of embodied desire and pleasure from school-based sex education as both failing to engage young people, and as perpetuating ideas about female sexuality which keep young women disconnected from their bodies and distant from a fully agentic sexual subjectivity. These writers have drawn a connection between sexual agency, subjectivity and embodiment. One suggestion has been to infuse sex education with a 'discourse of erotics' (Allen, 2004) through which young women could be more thoroughly engaged with pleasure and desire.

Through informal pedagogy in magazines and web-based advice columns, young people can access accounts of lived experience in ways not usually available through sex education. Young people can pose questions about bodily sensation and retrieve varied descriptions of orgasmic sensations and detailed advice with which to make sense of their own embodiment. In sharp contrast to interview data in which young women find it difficult to talk about their own embodied desire, or are reluctant to name their genitals (Tolman, 2005), 'real life' accounts from 'ordinary' women are bursting with sensations, bodily feelings and 'taboo' topics such as female ejaculation. While this may reflect the openness of those who contribute to online settings, it may also reflect the perceived anonymity and relative safety of the internet as a space for divulging personal, private, or socially transgressive information (Muise, 2011; Flowers-Coulson et al., 2000). Although perhaps far from the kind of 'pleasurable pedagogy' imagined by feminist writers (Allen, 2007), it may open up a space for young people (and others) to discuss, share and make sense of the physical sensations they experience. According to Allen (2001) young people employ a hierarchical ranking of sexuality knowledge in which knowledge gained from secondary sources (such as sexuality education, television, books, friends, the internet) is seen as inferior to information derived from personal sexual experience. This reflects a distinction between 'being knowledgeable about' or having an intellectual grasp of sexuality activity, and being 'knowledgeable of' sexuality through practical personal experience. Moreover, young people further distinguish between different types of secondary sources – between the 'official' clinical, scientific and morally sanctioned knowledge about sexual dangers (such as STIs, HIV, and unplanned pregnancies), and what they see as the more valuable knowledge which describes the 'lived experience' of sexual activity including emotional and bodily feelings about sexual desire and pleasure. If this kind of information is highly valued, yet often ignored in school sex education, then educators miss the opportunity to engage young people in learning about sexuality in a way that speaks to their own interests, motivations and concerns. Although some young people think that sexual pleasure is not something which can be learned in schools and is only something which can be learned through personal experience (Allen, 2007), perhaps these second-hand descriptions of what it feels like to experience orgasm could provide a useful bridge between 'formal' knowledge and young people's own lived experience. At the very least, they might provide a language for discussing pleasure. Yet, what these accounts share in common, is a representation of orgasm as ultimately knowable through recourse to bodily experience.

I noted earlier than some feminist theorists have offered up a model of female sexuality underpinned by 'embodied desire' as a framework for healthy sexuality, which would foster a sexual subjectivity marked by agency and empowerment. Lamb (2010) identifies this model of embodied pleasure and desire as a response to the objectification of women, an antidote to women's sexual victimisation and abuse, and a counter to stereotypes of women's sexual passivity. However, she also identifies a number of problems with this model including the idea that girls must aspire to be superwomen with an unrealistic model of sexuality to which few, if any, adult women could aspire:

> She ought to learn about, understand, and identify desires, feel sexual feelings in her genitals, use full reasoning ability in making choices, be uninfluenced by romance narratives and beauty ideals from TV, books, or movies, pursue her own pleasure as much or even more than her partner's, and exist always as a subject and never as an object. She can not be passive, and must be an agent; she ought to know both how to consent and how to refuse sex; and perhaps more importantly, unambivalently know if she wants to consent or refuse. (Lamb, 2010: 299)

Of particular concern here is the naturalising of desire and pleasure in these accounts, in which authentic 'embodied' sexuality is contrasted with a false or fake performance sexuality, which is enacted to meet the requirements of oppressive social norms. Embodied sexuality is depicted as flowing forth from bodily experience in a way that is untarnished by patriarchal demands or attempts to adapt to damaging feminine norms and standards. Desire is seen as subverting or sitting beneath attempts to control or channel it in particular ways. In a context in which girls have been distanced from desire, or where desire and agency are repackaged in ways which suit commercial interests (as evident in the figure of the postfeminist 'sexual adventurer'), the pre-social naturally desirous girl who 'listens when her body speaks' is presented as authentically embodied. Such an opposition is in stark contrast to Jackson and Scott's attempts to re-socialise the body. Jackson and Scott (2007) draw on Howard Becker's (1963) study of marijuana users to illustrate the ways in which the interpretation of bodily experiences is subject to social processes. Becker (1963) argued that although it is necessary for users to use marijuana 'properly' in order to get high, this in itself is not enough. They must also learn to relate their physical sensations to the drug, but also to perceive these sensations as comparable to the experiences of other users. As one of Becker's respondents said 'I heard little remarks that were made by other people. Somebody said, "my legs are rubbery", I was very attentively listening to all these cues for what I was supposed to feel like'. Jackson and Scott argue that this three stage process – learning to use the drug, learning to perceive its effects, and learning to define them as pleasurable – all apply to the process of learning to orgasm. In this case, then, it might mean learning to be sexually stimulated, perceiving the effects of this stimulation (feeling like you need to pee), and learning to define these effects as pleasurable (was it an orgasm or not?). In this sense, then, this internet forum provides an opportunity for young people (and old) to explore this process of learning how to make sense of physical sensations and define them as sexual or not, and pleasurable or not. Such detailed instruction about the body and bodily sensation highlight the social embeddedness of orgasmic sensation. Orgasm holds an ambiguous position as being constructed as both a 'natural' and normal bodily reflex to stimulation, and as something which needs to be learned, mastered, and improved upon. Orgasms don't 'just happen'. We have to work to make orgasms happen (Chapter 5), and we have to learn how to interpret physical sensations as orgasmic and/or pleasurable. Magazines, self-help books and internet forums offer informal embodied pedagogy through which people acquire the cultural competency to experience orgasm and to know their experience to be orgasm.

There is a tension between discourses which position orgasm as unmistakably knowable (since the feeling is unmissable and unique) and a discourse which positions orgasm as uncertain and not easily distinguishable from other sensations. Any uncertainty is positioned as evidence that orgasm is not occurring – orgasm is marked by certainty.

For example, the indeterminacy of orgasm is positioned as a feature of (some) women's subjective experience – that is, through positioning this as a question and uncertainty which requires further (expert?) knowledge. In sum, by offering descriptions of embodied, felt, experiences of orgasm and by discussing whether particular sensations are (or are not) indicative of orgasm, offer informal educational sources the kind of information which is missing from school-based sex education but which young people say they would like more knowledge about. Such discussions refer specifically to parts of the female anatomy which may be routinely talked about in girls' magazines but which are routinely absent from sex education materials.

8
The Climax: Conclusions and Reflections

Orgasm is a not 'just' a bodily experience; it is laden with meaning and sits at the intersection of competing discourses about health/ill-health, femininity/masculinity, science/experience, rationality/emotionality, empowerment/repression, and care of the self/care of the other. This book has concerned itself with the discursive construction of orgasm and the meanings given to orgasm in contemporary heterosex. As such, this book could be accused of reifying orgasm, of privileging orgasm above other forms of sexual desire and pleasure and of buying into the very 'orgasmic imperative' I seek to describe. It is true that I have not sought to topple orgasm from its exalted status as the pinnacle of sexual success. Instead, I have chosen to interrogate and expose the meanings of orgasm, and the ways in which discourses of orgasm reproduce particular versions of masculinity, femininity and heterosexuality. I chose to focus on orgasm with a critical awareness of its status, and a healthy scepticism of the idea that this is the 'natural' place of orgasm.

This book has concerned itself with orgasm as a culturally meaningful 'event' in contemporary heterosex; an event which is experienced in and through the body in ways which are necessarily mediated through social discourse. In particular, the book has addressed four key themes:

1. An 'orgasmic imperative' which frames a narrow, goal-oriented view of sex and propels individuals towards orgasm as the natural and most desirable end-point of sex and is a key discourse which structures individuals' understanding and experience of contemporary heterosex.
2. The construction of orgasmic certainty for men and orgasmic uncertainty for women provides a differential context within which the orgasmic imperative takes effect.

3. The orgasmic imperative, coupled with postfeminism and hegemonic masculinity, creates different entitlements and obligations
   for men and women – especially in the context of monogamous
   relationships.
4. The body is a contested site for knowing the orgasmic body. Objective
   scientific knowledge gained through observation and measurement is
   contrasted with subjective, unique experience of the body knowable
   only to the individual. I argue that sensate experience of the body is
   necessarily social.

I briefly summarise these four areas before outlining some of the (many)
omissions from the book and indicating some of the key questions that
need to be asked about the cultural entity that is orgasm.

Orgasmic imperative

Orgasm in and of itself is inherently neither 'good' nor 'bad', but I have
argued that a set of discourses converge to create an 'orgasmic imperative' (see also Potts, 2000a) in which having, or not having, an orgasm is
not simply a neutral matter of choice. When orgasm is positioned as the
most appropriate, expected and desirable outcome of sexual activity and
even as offering spiritual or transcendental enlightenment, the 'orgasmic
imperative' compels individuals towards orgasmic sex as a goal. The
presence or *absence* of orgasm is worked up as symbolic of the intimacy
or compatibility of a couple, the ability of an individual to function or
perform their sexuality in a prescribed way, and as indicative of one's
status in gender power relations. The coupling of the orgasmic imperative with neoliberal drives for self-improvement positions pursuing the
'ultimate orgasm' is adopted as the most appropriate attitude to adopt
towards sex. Scientific expertise and popular discourse converge in a
version of the repressive hypothesis which sees a proliferation of knowledge and talk about orgasm as a project of enlightenment which propels
individuals towards sexual self-actualisation. The three different frames
(introduced in Chapter 1) through which knowledge about orgasm
is produced all position orgasm as the most healthy, pleasurable and
desirable outcome of sexual activity and even as offering spiritual or
transcendental enlightenment. As Foucault (1978) argues, power and
knowledge are intimately entangled such that mechanisms of power
produce different types of knowledge (including narratives of orgasmic
experience, measurements of bodily changes in orgasm, counting how
often individuals orgasm, etc.), which in turn reinforces the exercise

of power – the institutional power of biomedicine and also the subtler form of disciplinary power.

Orgasmic uncertainty

While both men and women are subject to the 'orgasmic imperative', they are differently positioned by discourses of certainty/uncertainty. I have demonstrated that female orgasm is subject to 'constructed uncertainty' – the *presence* of female orgasm is continually in doubt, tentative or unreliable and always potentially absent. This tapestry of uncertainty is woven from many different threads which appeared throughout the book: the possibility of a 'fake' rather than 'authentically experienced' orgasm, and the idea that this is commonplace; the widely reported 'orgasm gap' between men and women where women are less likely to orgasm than men; the representation of women's bodies and sexual responses as more complex than men's; the idea that women's sexuality is 'slower' while men's is more urgent and immediate; and, uncertainty about whether women's orgasm can be 'read-off' from the body. This fragility is troubling, both for lovers who are keen to have orgasm confirm the normality of their sexual functioning or to prove their love-making skills, and for the successful maintenance of heterosexuality as a natural and proper institutional arrangement. At the same time, this fragility diverts the trouble of heterosexuality onto the bodies of women. Positioning women's orgasm as suspect, mysterious, complex, elusive and unreliable perpetuates sustained attention to the 'problem' of female orgasm in ways which obscure the role of gender ideologies in creatively *producing* these mysteries. The increasing proliferation of cultural chatter – in both formal scientific debate and informal pedagogical texts – which offer the promise of certitude through the creation and dissemination of 'expert' knowledge, simultaneously subject the female body to more intense forms of surveillance and governance.

At the same time, and in contrast, male orgasm is subject to 'constructed certitude' (Beck, 1997: 61) in which the ideology of hegemonic masculinity is creatively maintained by displacing ambiguity or complexity. Thus, male orgasm is marked as self-evidently unproblematic and uninteresting. Throughout this book we have noted the relative silence of scientific and social scientific work on men, orgasm and ejaculation. This under-theorisation of male heterosexualities, especially as this relates to the sexuality of adult men, is typically attributed to three key issues (Richardson, 2010; Bertone and Camoletto, 2009). First, the positioning of male (hetero)sexuality as natural, biologically driven and pre-given. Second, masculinity is the invisible side of the gender binary and the norm against which female sexuality is judged. Finally, critical analyses of heterosexuality have come primarily from feminist scholars where the emphasis has been on the regulatory effects of heterosexuality on *women*. While the certainty of male orgasm is assured – or so the story goes – through a visible ejaculation, female orgasm is less certain. While research has explored the normative disciplinary effects of heterosexuality and hegemonic masculinity on men, especially in the context of 'erectile dysfunction', the complexity of men's sensate embodied experience of sex remains invisible (see below). This certitude sustains the myth that women are 'the problem' in heterosex, and that it is the mysterious and elusive nature of female orgasm that prevents the ethic of reciprocity or the mutual exchange of orgasm to be realised in full.

Entitlement and obligation

I have demonstrated that the orgasmic imperative is heavily gendered, resulting in different responsibilities and obligations for men and women to work on themselves (and each other) to achieve orgasmic success. Postfeminism and hegemonic masculinity give male and female orgasm very different meanings and significance in heterosex which, despite the ethic of reciprocity, maintains essentialist notions of gender and secures gender inequality.

Against a historical backdrop of constructed uncertainty about the presence of female orgasm, the *absence* of female orgasm has shifted from being depicted as expected and 'natural' to being unnatural and dysfunctional. The precariousness of female orgasm, and shifting gender relations which have produced an ethic of reciprocity, make the presence of orgasm a requirement for the success of the relationship (read heterosexuality) and for the production of a postfeminist sexual subjectivity. The establishment – at least superficially – of women's entitlement to orgasm, as inscribed in the ethic of reciprocity, means that women are compelled to demonstrate orgasm as 'proof' of their empowerment and sexual autonomy. More than this, neoliberal drives for self-improvement, propel women towards the ultimate orgasmic experience attained through hard work and dedication to improving sexual skills. Rather than relying on men to awaken their sexuality, women are positioned as 'taking control' of their orgasm, choosing to enhance their own pleasure, and actively seeking to develop their own sexual expertise. Women are called upon to take responsibility for knowing their bodies and their own individual and unique sexual responses. A woman's ability to orgasm is taken to signify her sexual self-determination, her active and agentic approach to securing her own pleasure, and her status as a modern, liberated woman. Moreover, women are expected to use this newly-acquired knowledge and expertise to 'teach' male partners how to turn them on and bring them to orgasm. Feminist messages about sexual autonomy and bodily self-determination are appropriated for an individualistic, neoliberal goal of orgasm. Not only does this belie the unequal gender power relations within which women have to negotiate sexual pleasure and safety, it also places responsibility for sexual success, and sexual failure, squarely on women's shoulders. Moreover, women's entitlement to orgasm is as precarious as its uncertain presence. This raises some questions. Under what conditions are women able to assert this entitlement? When is this entitlement taken for granted? and When is it contested? In the context of committed relationships women's entitlement to orgasm is overshadowed by their responsibility to care and protect their male partners.

The compulsory nature of heterosexuality, and the constructed certitude around male orgasm, positions men as having a physical need for sex, as having desires which need to be met, and as seeking *more* sex rather than *better* sex. Reflecting this focus, men's magazines advise readers to operate strategically to secure more frequent sex. Almost as an afterthought, given that men's pleasure is depicted as guaranteed, advice about how to secure a more intense orgasm is of secondary importance. Evidence that a substantial proportion of men report faking orgasm (Muehlenhard and Shippee, 2010) is rarely taken as evidence of a widespread 'problem' with male sexuality or men's roles in sexual conduct. Admittedly, men may not fake orgasms for the same reasons as women, and their orgasm signals the end of intercourse in a way that a woman's does not (Muehlenhard and Shippee, 2010), but this practice does say something about how the orgasmic imperative operates on men. Yet, many young women respond with astonishment to the idea that men might fake orgasm – as if it were both not possible and very improbable. This inconvenient truth has failed to make it into the cultural imagination since it sits in contradiction to the popular depiction of men as sexually inexhaustible, as constantly seeking more frequent and more adventurous sex, and whose orgasm is present and irrefutable. For men, for whom the presence of orgasm is rarely in question, sexual success is measured not by the quality of his own orgasm, but by his ability to 'give' a spectacular, unforgettable orgasm to his partner. This is presented as a strategic move to secure access to an endless supply of sex, gain a reputation as a 'good lover', and demonstrate his superiority to other men. Men have always been positioned at active, agentic and as in control of their own sexuality (even if, at times, this is also constructed as uncontrollable and animalistic). Men's success at delivering this orgasm is fraught with difficulty since women's bodies are depicted as complicated and their orgasms elusive, mysterious or hard work. Sex is presented as a competitive domain, and developing sexpertise and mastery of the mysterious female are key to competitive success. The *presence* of women's orgasm is central to affirmation of men's masculinity, and its *absence* is a threat to masculinity – something which is not lost on women themselves.

In different ways, then, men and women are invited to develop a technical mastery of their own and each other's bodies, and to produce and deliver orgasms to themselves and each other. Heteronormative assumptions about 'natural' differences in male and female sexuality, including the timing of sexual responses, men's greater desire for sex, women's need for intimacy and so on, are obstacles to be overcome or worked around through the development of sexual skills, techniques and knowledge. Failure to deliver an appropriate orgasm at the right time, in the right context, or in a recognisable way is, at best, a failure to meet the gendered norms of sexual performance, and at worst evidence of a dysfunctional sexuality. Moreover, the ethic of reciprocity in intimate committed relationships, means that 'giving' an orgasm is also positioned as an act of care. While neoliberalism positions sexual actors as largely motivated by self-interest, this is tempered by the requirements of monogamous relationships for reciprocity and (uneven) responsibilities to love and care for each other. An ethic of equality or reciprocity structures contemporary heterosexual relationships. This does not mean that heterosexual relationships *are* equal or reciprocal, but the idea that they *should* be is important. This extends to the idea that sex should involve a mutual exchange of orgasms where both partners 'have' an orgasm. These responsibilities press more heavily in the context of committed relationships, but are not felt equally. Since men are seen as actively producing their own and their partner's orgasm (rendering invisible the work that women do to 'give' men an orgasm), and because female orgasm is constructed as more mysterious, elusive and difficult, a man who 'gives' an orgasm is marked as particularly caring. A bit like doing the housework, this obligation is freely chosen and presented as men 'going the extra mile' rather than an absolute requirement; as something that 'good guys' will do as a show of affection, care or love. Women's love and care in 'giving' orgasms to men is not afforded the same status. While women 'protect' men by not being too demanding and managing sexual encounters so that men do not have to work too hard, or are rewarded for their efforts, and putting men's pleasure first, this labour is naturalised and minimised. In contrast, the labour that men are required to invest in, in 'giving' an orgasm to their partner, is recognised explicitly as an (optional) act of love and care.

Body and embodiment

As an event which is constructed as happening in and through the body, this book has explored the different ways in which the body is conceptualised in various regimes of knowledge. I have considered the tensions between the biomedical view of the body as an organic system or machine which either functions or malfunctions, the body as a project to be worked on which is integral to the construction of self-identity, and the sensate body which is felt and experienced. This book has had a particular focus on the body but has hinted at experiences of embodiment. Focusing on representations of the body and orgasmic experience in cultural texts is useful for identifying cultural stories about body projects. This book has highlighted the pedagogical focus of these texts which 'teach' women (and men) about bodies. While this is presented as an enlightened and empowering approach, Foucault (1978) teaches us to be cautious about accepting this story at face value. What is being offered is a technical mastery of the body.

In pursuing 'objective truths' and identifying clinical norms, the biomedical and behavioural frames serves to create and perpetuate new standards against which the sexual body and its performance can be judged, measured and deemed deficient. Neoliberal drives for self-improvement place obligations on men and women to work on their sexual selves to achieve the 'ultimate' orgasm and deliver an appropriate gender performance in line with these 'scientific' standards. I have highlighted the ways in which individuals are impelled to work on the 'sexy body' and to acquire 'technologies of sexiness' or the skills and techniques necessary to demonstrate sexual expertise. I argue that working on the 'sexy body' involves much more than transforming the surface of the body into something which is read as (hetero)sexually attractive. Capitalising on the corporeal body requires a working on and working over of the musculature, hormonal, and neurochemical mechanisms of the body through exercise, diet, and an accumulation of atomistic tricks and tips for enhancing sexual experience and expertise. The project of the body means transforming the body into something which is 'known' and can be subjugated to the will of the actor/owner. It is not enough to mould and manipulate the body – it needs to be mastered. The 'sexy body' is subject to intense rational control, self-examination, measurement and improvement. If biomedical and behavioural research is driven by a will to know the body through observation and measurement, lifestyle magazines and other popular discourse is driven by a will to teach the body, to offer a detailed and explicit 'pedagogy of the body' with specific instruction on bodily techniques, anatomy, fit and functioning. This expert tuition prompts a genitally focused, mechanistic approach to sex and to the body, and invites a different rational, calculating subject who wishes to capitalise on sexual success by harnessing their bodily capital.

Expert knowledge of the body is often pitted against (lay) subjective knowledge of the body gained through experiential means. At times, this experiential knowledge is dismissed as inaccurate and unhelpful as individuals' ability to report on their own bodily experiences is seen as muddied by their own expectations, fears and responses to societal norms. Science claims to be able to find the 'truth' about sexual bodies, which is independent from these societal influences. At other times, embodied experience is offered up as a 'pure' experience, which is in itself authentic and arising in an unmediated and 'natural' way from the body. This tension is also reflected in feminist theorising about the body, and Jackson and Scott (2007) offer an alternative model for understanding bodily experience as socially mediated. This is addressed particularly in Chapter 7 where I explore women's uncertainty about whether felt sensations 'really are' an orgasm or not. This uncertainty opens up the possibility of exploring how bodily sensations become knowable, and to question accounts of bodily experience which rest on notions of authentic or pre-social embodiment. I argue that these sensations must be made meaningful through a process of socially mediated interpretation. One of the pedagogical functions of lifestyle magazines and the informal sex education offered by the internet is to offer a framework within which women can make sense of bodily sensation and experiences. 'Knowing' that one has experienced an orgasm requires knowledge of what an orgasm is and what is 'should' feel like. Ironically, despite considerable uncertainty and ambiguity about the felt sensations of orgasm, orgasm itself is constructed as instantly knowable and recognisable. Bodily knowledge is never unmediated but only recognisable through cultural discourse.

Orgasmic omissions

This book has been heavily influenced by media representations of orgasm – especially those presented by *Cosmopolitan*, *Men's Health* and other lifestyle magazines – and by biomedical and scientific academic research about orgasm. This is not the only or even the most popular source of cultural chatter about sexuality and orgasm in particular. But they do offer a relatively convenient way of sampling at least some of the ways that orgasm is given meaning in society. This inevitably gives rise to a number of important omissions since the dominant or public discourse often fails to address issues of difference, not least since it seeks to offer certitude through exclusion. In this final section, I outline three such omissions (although I am sure there are many more) and consider the issues that they raise for a thorough theorisation of orgasm.

Orgasmic divisions

Popular media and mainstream scientific/sexological literature share in common a presumption of a sexual actor who is typically white, middle-class, able-bodied, cisgendered and engaged in monogamous relationships in which penis-in-vagina sex is normative. This does not, of course, mean that those who do not, or cannot, or do not want to, fit this norm operate entirely outside of its influence. I have focused particularly on the *gendered* construction of orgasm – looking at the differences in the way in which orgasmic experience is constructed for men and women. This is at the expense of a wide range of other social divisions which structure orgasmic experience, and a close examination of the differences between women or between men. Little sustained attention is given to exploring how discourses around orgasm shape sexual relationships between lesbians and gay men or to the social ordering of relationships within heterosexuality along the lines of race, class, ability, ethnicity, age, or other social divisions or those who engage in 'kinky' or non-normative sex. Some quantitative studies have highlighted intriguing patterns in orgasmic frequency but often lack any explanatory power. I give a brief discussion of the social patterning of orgasm according to sexual orientation and social class as a provocative illustrations.

There is a limited literature that looks at the distribution of orgasm across populations who identify as lesbian or gay. A recent internet survey of singles in the US found that although the occurrence of orgasm did not differentiate between gay and heterosexual men, lesbian women were much more likely than hetero- or bi-sexual women to have experienced orgasm with a familiar partner (Garcia et al., 2014). The Australian Study of Health and Relationships showed similar findings, with more women reporting orgasm in their last sexual encounter with a woman compared to that with a man, but also that fewer men reported that they had an orgasm when their last sexual encounter was with another man (Grulich et al., 2003). Again, these figures reveal little about the meaning of orgasm for lesbians and gay men, and in line with the orgasmic imperative, imply that orgasm is an appropriate or useful measure of sexual satisfaction. There is some evidence the orgasmic imperative structures the sexuality of (some) lesbian women. For example, there is evidence that lesbian women fake orgasm for many of the same reasons as heterosexual women – although not perhaps to the same extent (Fahs, 2011), and discourses around 'giving' or 'taking' orgasms structure some lesbians' experience of sex (Bolsø, 2001). Similarly, in his interviews with young gay men in Australia, Ridge (2004: 267) found that many men 'talked as though there were tacit "contracts" between them and their sexual partners that required them to complete sex to orgasm, even if they changed their mind during sex'. Moreover, the meaning of orgasm may be one of the ways in which various sexual identities are differentiated and performed. For example, what is often taken as one of the defining characteristics of the 'Stone Butch' identity is a deep investment in masculinity, and that sexual pleasure is attained by giving, not necessarily receiving orgasm. Indeed, some Stone Butches report that they do not need to experience orgasm in their bodies at all, and that giving pleasure evokes a transcendental experience which is satisfying in itself (Maltz, 1998). Similarly, the meaning of orgasm – and ejaculation in particular – is creatively reworked in gay subcultures (see discussion of embodiment below). It is perhaps not surprising that gay cultures form norms for sexual practices in relation to (even if this is a resistance to) dominant constructions of sex and the place of orgasm within this. Attention to the detail of how local situated meanings are constructed in specific contexts. Might help us to move towards not only more detailed accounts of homosexual cultures, but towards more nuanced and differentiated accounts of heterosexuali*ties*.

Sexology and sexual science has had very little to say about the way in which heterosexuality is structured by social class (Jackson, 2011). The research that has been conducted is typically limited to the large-scale quantitative surveys which, like the figures about gender, may tell us that a 'gap' exists, but provides little insight into why or how this difference comes about or how to make sense of it. Kinsey's (1948/1998) early research, for example, found that sexual activity differed greatly between men of varied socioeconomic backgrounds, but relatively little difference among women – working-class women masturbated less, experienced earlier sexual intercourse and had a narrower range of sexual activities than middle-class women. Nearly 50 years later, the US *National Health and Lifestyle Survey* reported again that more highly educated people tended to have a broader repertoire of sexual activities (Laumann et al., 1994).

Similarly, recent analysis of the *Australian Study of Health and Relationships* found that at their last sexual encounter, while most men (94.8%) and women (68.9%) experienced orgasm, a woman was *more likely* to have reached orgasm if she had completed post-secondary education, had a higher household income, and had a managerial/professional occupation (Richters et al., 2006). These same factors had no bearing on men's likelihood of experiencing orgasm. The associations between orgasm and demographic characteristics suggest a social class effect. Research on the relationship between (hetero)sexual practices and class remains largely atheoretical, but two secondary analyses of the *National Health and Social Life Survey* (NHSLS) data have linked these patterns in orgasm to social power. Gonzales and Rolison (2005) theorised that dominated groups would have less access to sexual capital and would therefore engage in more behavioural self-surveillance and be more restrictive of their sexuality (Gonzales and Rolison, 2005). Looking at the intersection of race and class, they found that Black women are more likely to report a lack of interest in sex, having un-pleasurable sex, as well as an inability to orgasm, in the past year. White women and Black men also reported more negative sexual experiences than White men. Similarly, Fahs and Swank (2011) explored whether membership of privileged or stigmatised social statuses enhanced or inhibited women's sexual satisfaction. Lower status women (women of colour, working-class women, younger women, less-educated women, women who worked full-time) reported both the lowest levels of satisfaction and the highest frequency of sexual activity. These figures suggest that class privilege (and its intersection with other forms of disadvantage and stigmatisation) is played out in the social patterning of orgasm and other sexual practices, but it tells us little about how pleasures are constructed and differentiated or how class positions and sexualities might be mutually constituted in the doing of sex.

Orgasm provides an interesting focus for such an analysis, which would lend itself to a consideration of both material and symbolic analyses of class and how this impacts on sexual practises, intimacies and subjectivities. If women's greater entitlement to orgasm is a gain of feminism (even as this is problematic), then it raises the question of whether all women have gained *equally* from this. The material advantages of class might create more opportunities to engage in sex as a recreational activity, with the greater availability of time and effort to create the romance said to be essential to women's arousal. Sexual practices have been shown to vary depending on the vagaries of domestic economic life and the household division of labour (Elliot and Umberson, 2008; Kornrich, Brines and Leupp, 2012).

In their insightful ethnographic study of 'hooking up' on American college campuses, Hamilton and Armstrong (2009) draw attention to the conflicting intersections of classed and gendered rules for sexual conduct in the context of neoliberal drives for self-improvement through education. Gender norms require that young women avoid non-romantic, casual sex in favour of a committed relationship, while middle-class norms suggest that women should delay relationships while pursuing educational goals. Hook-ups offer opportunities for sexual activity in a way which better fits the demands of educational aspirations for self-betterment. These examples draw our attention to the ways in which, by focusing on sex in isolation, we miss the opportunity to explore the ways in which sex forms part of the mundane stuff of everyday life – even as it, and orgasm in particular, is often heralded as an escape from 'real life' or a transcendental vacation from normal responsibilities. If the mutual exchange or 'gift' of orgasms can be considered part of the heterosexual contract, to what extent can the exchange of orgasm be swapped for other 'household chores' such as childcare or housework, and are these prioritised differently in households occupying different class positions? How might economic conditions impact on expectations about what is fair, reasonable or expected in the sex work of orgasm?

Yet, there is also room for more cultural or symbolic analyses of class and sexuality since taste, style and consumption practices are put to service in the drawing and policing of class boundaries. The increasing commercialisation of sex, for example, has meant that markets need to proliferate and become more nuanced, including the more explicit marketing of sex-related products to the female consumer. Attwood (2005a) argues convincingly that women are addressed as sexual consumers through a discourse of pleasure, which is sutured to existing discourses of fashion, consumerism, bodily pleasure and sexuality in ways which are mediated by class. Notions of taste are negotiated in relation to gender and class norms such that products are characterised as downmarket and shoddy or upmarket, feminine and classy. The traditional stigmatisation of working class women as excessively sexual, has meant that upmarket or 'classy' products such as lingerie are typically marketed as '*not about sex*' to maintain middle-class respectability (Storr, 2003: 201). Skeggs' (1997, 2005) discussion of working-class young women's sexualised appearance as managed by them in the context of stigmatisation by others, rested on a contrast between working-class glamour and middle-class respectability. She demonstrated how class is used to draw boundaries around the acceptability and respectability of sexual conduct. Paul Johnson's (2008) work on the eroticisation of class difference, largely through the figure of the Chav, in gay culture is another interesting example. He argues that chav masculinity, which is largely devalued, is transformed into a desirable commodity used to market varied goods and services to gay men through the sexualisation and eroticisation of lack. Johnson's concern is with how the commodification of the figure of the Chav functions as an object of both desire and disgust for those with the symbolic power to consume it, and so reproduces a *general* symbolic economy of class distinctions. Such work tells us about the relationships between class and sexual sensibilities, about the ways in which the pleasures of classed bodies are differentiated, but we know little about how and if these translate into differentiated sexual practices, experiences and the embodied negotiations. How do classed variants of masculinity and femininity impact on the scripts for the mutual exchange of orgasm? How might class impact on our understanding of 'tasteful' and 'disgusting' sexual bodies or practices and how might this open up or close down orgasmic possibilities?

Men and embodiment

The 'constructed certitude' attributed to men's bodies and sexual responses, the depiction of men's orgasmic experiences as simple and straightforward, has forestalled a more thorough investigation of men's embodied experience. The idea that there is nothing to say about men's experience, reinforces the message that men should not be too interested in their own bodies or sensate experience. The relationship between an erect penis, ejaculation and orgasm is often not distinguished in men's accounts of their sexuality, and researchers rarely think to ask men about these different aspects of their sexual experience. All three are tightly bound together in accounts of masculinity. It is only when one or other of these aspects is disrupted in some way that the meaning and experience of each comes into focus. Ejaculation as the visible embodiment of men's pleasure, for example, has a central role in claiming certainty of men's orgasm. Yet, orgasm and ejaculation are not the same. We have little understanding of how the reification of ejaculation – especially as this is visually represented and made iconic in pornography – impacts on men's experience and understanding of their own ejaculation. Men who no longer ejaculate experience this as a loss. Although the complete loss or lessening of ejaculate is a common consequence of treatments for prostate cancer, patients often report the continued ability to experience the sensations of orgasm (see Koeman et al., 1996). Yet, interviews with men about the impact of prostate cancer on their experience of masculinity and sexuality found that although orgasms were attainable by many men, the absence of ejaculation lessened their intensity and pleasure:

> You can deal with the impotence, [but] the fact that you can't ejacu-late any more – you see, I miss that. I really miss that! Because, that's almost, you think of that with sex. If you use a pump, you don't have the same good sensation, you still have the feeling of an orgasm, but it's not as intense. (Fergus, Gray and Fitch, 2002: 311–312)

It would be a mistake to interpret this lessening of 'intensity' as a purely physical sensation – a change in the firing of neurons and receptors – as if this were separate from the meaning of ejaculation. The embodied meaning of ejaculation is little understood – perhaps particularly as this relates to men in heterosexual sex. Visual representations of ejaculation have an important role here. Men's ejaculation onto women's bodies rather than into their vaginas or anuses, and the ubiquitous facial 'cum shot', is eroticised in heterosexual pornography, yet we know little about the meaning attributed to this or how men and women negotiate these cultural scripts in the context of their own relationships. Recent research among gay male sexual communities has begun to explore the symbolic meaning of ejaculation as signalling 1) the completion of sexual activity, and 2) sexual power, strength, virility and masculinity (Reynolds, 2007). In particular, the eroticisation of semen/ejaculation in barebacking (intentional unprotected anal sex), snowballing (ejaculating into a partners mouth and then erotically kissing) and feltching (ejacu-lating into the rectum then sucking it out with the mouth), performs an important symbolic role in the sexual experience of some gay men (Parsons and Grov, 2012). Similarly, female ejaculation is identified as playing a symbolic role in queer/lesbian porn which signifies more than the visible veracity of female orgasm or the culmination of the action, it is 'conflated with and becomes an integral part of an identity political project aiming at representing – providing visibility for – real lesbians and trans persons' (Ryberg, 2008: 73). These examples point to the rich symbolic meaning of orgasm, and ejaculate in gay sexual cultures; a parallel analysis of heterosexual cultures would be illuminating.

Meaning making

What is offered in this book is a rather broad-sweep look at the ways key discourses structure the meaning of orgasm, and has given some hints about how this may impact on the experience of individuals as they try to make sense of their experiences. But, the book has, by necessity, focused rather more on the meaning than on the experience, since in-depth studies of orgasmic experience which focus on how people make sense of these experiences are few and far between. I have drawn on empirical research wherever possible to illuminate this (in particular the work of Braun et al., Fahs, Roberts, Nicolson and Burr, Lavie, Potts, etc. have been extremely helpful). However, the question of how the orgasmic imperative inserts itself into the subjectivities of individuals and shapes the ways in which they negotiate, manage and experience their sexual selves – alone and together – is perhaps most urgently in need of attention. This means paying attention to the inter-personal contexts in which the meanings of orgasm are negotiated and contested.

Our understanding of the construction of orgasmic certitude and uncertainty, would be strengthened by an in-depth examination of the ways in which these uncertainties are taken on, rejected or worked out in the moment-by-moment negotiation of sex during sexual encoun-ters. 'Constructed certitude' creates as many anxieties as it assuages, but what happens when individuals come together as imperfectly fash-ioned and uniquely fleshy, embodied selves? There are hints that these cultural stories shape individuals' expectations and responses to each other's bodies – for example when men wonder about how they can tell whether their girlfriend has had an orgasm, when they question why their partner isn't making as much noise as they think she should, or why her genitals don't look or feel like the article described. The certainty offered by cultural texts is that all bodies are the same and can and should respond in the same way. So, how do individuals, couples or partners make sense of bodies which do or don't live up to expecta-tions? Under what circumstances, and following what meaning-making processes, are bodies interpreted as faulty, lovers as unsuitable or clumsy, partners as repressed or unadventurous, an ejaculation as occurring too soon, or an orgasm as fake?

Although the dominant 'orgasmic imperative' discourse presents orgasm as synonymous with pleasure, focus on the situated nature of orgasm might enable a deconstruction of the idea that orgasm is neces-sarily positive or enjoyable. An orgasm in itself is not inherently 'good' and can be experienced as troubling or unpleasant if it occurs in the 'wrong' context or with the 'wrong' person – such as orgasm that occurs in the course of sexual abuse or rape. Indeed 'making' a woman (or man) orgasm can be an expression of domination which can be playful or exploitative depending on the context. Groth and Burgess (1980) note that a major strategy used by some men who sexually assault or rape other men is to get the victim to ejaculate, which they argue may symbolise the offender's ultimate and complete control, may confirm their fantasy that the victim actually wanted the assault, or may bewilder the victim and discourage the victim from reporting the assault. For example, when male US sex tourists to Mexico delight in 'making' the sex worker orgasm, not least because it provides an opportunity to brag about this to other men (Katsulis, 2010). Enjoyment of porn is, for some, dependent on reading the porn stars' orgasms as 'real', especially when this is accompanied by an understanding of porn production as being potentially exploitative (Parvez, 2006; Frith, 2014). The construction of mutuality and reciprocity is central to the eroticisation of paid sex – at least in some contexts – even when such exchanges are far from egalitarian and do not reflect the experience of sex workers themselves. Likewise, the experience of some women whose partners try to 'force' them to orgasm as a recognition of their own skill and a job well done, or out of a concern that they are satisfied, or to ensure that sex is reciprocal, can be far from pleasurable (Fahs, 2011; Lavie-Ajayi, 2005). Discourses of mutuality and reciprocity can be put to service in even the most unequal of settings (Braun, Gavey, and McPhillips, 2003). The question then is, how does power structure the experience of orgasm and under what circumstances is orgasm experienced as pleasurable, or not?

Appendices

Appendix 1   Table of *Cosmopolitan* Articles

The online version of the popular women's magazine *Cosmopolitan* (*Cosmopolitan.Com*) was searched using the keyword 'orgasm' in the site's own search mechanism on 19 October 2012. The search yielded 287 hits, of which the first 50 were sampled for analysis and were assigned a number. Six hits were discarded since the content of these pages did not focus on sexuality or orgasm (for example, one site focused on consumer products for men). The remaining 44 hits were subjected to thematic analysis focusing solely on the textual aspects of the pages – that is, disregarding all images, ribbons, advertising, etc.

No.	Title	URL Address
01	Why are my orgasms more intense during masturbation?	http://www.cosmopolitan.com/sex-love/advice/intense-masturbation?click=main_sr
02	I've been faking my orgasms	http://www.cosmopolitan.com/sex-love/advice/faking-orgasms?click=main_sr
03	Is it true that men can have multiple orgasms?	http://www.cosmopolitan.com/sex-love/advice/men-multiple-orgasms?click=main_sr
04	How do I 'fess up that I've been faking my orgasms?	http://www.cosmopolitan.com/sex-love/advice/fess-up-to-faking-orgasms?click=main_sr
05	'I have orgasms all day long'	http://www.cosmopolitan.com/advice/health/what-is-pgad?click=main_sr
06	Have orgasms more easily	http://www.cosmopolitan.com/sex-love/tips-moves/how-to-have-an-orgasm?click=main_sr
07	How to have multiple orgasms	http://www.cosmopolitan.com/sex-love/tips-moves/Orgasms-Unlimited?click=main_sr
08	My guy rarely orgasms	http://www.cosmopolitan.com/sex-love/advice/my-guy-rarely-orgasms?click=main_sr
09	I told him that I'd been faking my orgasms	http://www.cosmopolitan.com/sex-love/advice/told-him-im-faking-orgasms?click=main_sr

Continued

163

No.	Title	URL Address
10	The orgasm: Everything you need to know	http://www.cosmopolitan.com/sex-love/advice/orgasm?click=main_sr
11	Your orgasm – guaranteed!	http://www.cosmopolitan.com/sex-love/tips-moves/your-orgasm-guaranteed?click=main_sr
12	Multiple O's: Why one orgasm is never enough	http://www.cosmopolitan.com/sex-love/tips-moves/multiple-O?click=main_sr
13	I masturbate regularly, yet I never orgasm. What am I doing wrong?	http://www.cosmopolitan.com/sex-love/advice/masturbation-no-orgasm?click=main_sr
14	How do I know if I'm having an orgasm?	http://www.cosmopolitan.com/sex-love/advice/carnal-counselor-having-an-orgasm?click=main_sr
15	Can a woman feel when her man has an orgasm?	http://www.cosmopolitan.com/sex-love/advice/woman-feel-man-orgasm?click=main_sr
16	Sexual Health: Sometimes I pee a little when I have an orgasm! How can I stop?	http://www.cosmopolitan.com/sex-love/sexual-health/pee-when-orgasm?click=main_sr
17	Can guys tell when a girl is having an orgasm?	http://www.cosmopolitan.com/sex-love/advice/guys-tell-when-girl-orgasm?click=main_sr
18	Can men orgasm without ejaculating?	http://www.cosmopolitan.com/sex-love/advice/orgasm-no-ejaculating?click=main_sr
20	Give him the best orgasm ever	http://www.cosmopolitan.com/sex-love/tips-moves/give-him-the-best-orgasm?click=main_sr#slide-1
21	What's the trick to being multiorgasmic?	http://www.cosmopolitan.com/sex-love/advice/trick-to-multiorgasmic?click=main_sr
22	Cosmo's better sex workout	http://www.cosmopolitan.com/sex-love/tips-moves/Cosmos-Better-Sex-Workout?click=main_sr
24	How to Have an Orgasm Every. Single. Time.	http://www.cosmopolitan.com/sex-love/tips-moves/orgasm-tips-for-women?click=main_sr#slide-1
25	The biology behind her orgasm	http://www.cosmopolitan.com/cosmo-for-guys/sex-dating/biology-of-her-orgasm?click=main_sr
26	Three things that get in the way of your orgasm	http://www.cosmopolitan.com/sex-love/tips-moves/things-that-get-in-the-way-of-your-orgasm?click=main_sr

Continued

No.	Title	URL Address
27	Sex positions that help you orgasm	http://www.cosmopolitan.com/sex-love/tips-moves/sex-positions-that-help-women-orgasm?click=main_sr#slide-1
28	How to have a 15-minute female orgasm	http://www.cosmopolitan.com/sex-love/tips-moves/fifteen-minute-orgasm-four-hour-body-book?click=main_sr
29	Reasons you don't have an orgasm	http://www.cosmopolitan.com/sex-love/tips-moves/Reasons-You-Dont-Have-an-Orgasm?click=main_sr
30	Were you an 'orgasm virgin'?	http://www.cosmopolitan.com/forums-freebies/appear-in/orgasm-virgin?click=main_sr
32	The blended orgasm	http://www.cosmopolitan.com/sex-love/tips-moves/blended-orgasm?click=main_sr
33	Turn him into the orgasm whisperer	http://www.cosmopolitan.com/sex-love/tips-moves/turn-him-into-the-orgasm-whisperer-0809?click=main_sr
34	Have you ever faked an orgasm?	http://www.cosmopolitan.com/forums-freebies/appear-in/faked-orgasm?click=main_sr
36	How to climax together	http://www.cosmopolitan.com/sex-love/tips-moves/simultaneous-orgasm-0507?click=main_sr
37	'50 Great Things to do with your Breasts?	http://www.cosmopolitan.com/sex-love/advice/things-to-do-with-breasts?click=main_sr
38	It's 7 am. Do you know where your orgasm is?	http://www.cosmopolitan.com/sex-love/tips-moves/how-to-have-morning-sex?click=main_sr
39	Why bad sex is shortening your life	http://www.cosmopolitan.com/sex-love/tips-moves/orgasm-news?click=main_sr
40	25 sex tips you didn't know	http://www.cosmopolitan.com/sex-love/tips-moves/hottest-sex-tips-ever?click=main_sr#slide-1
41	'What the big O feels like for me'	http://www.cosmopolitan.com/sex-love/tips-moves/what-an-orgasm-feels-like?click=main_sr#slide-1
42	5 pleasure-maxing positions	http://www.cosmopolitan.com/sex-love/tips-moves/5-pleasure-poses?click=main_sr
43	The figure eight	http://www.cosmopolitan.com/sex-love/positions/the-figure-eight-sex-position?click=main_sr

Continued

No.	Title	URL Address
44	The 15 hottest sex articles of 2012	http://www.cosmopolitan.com/sex-love/tips-moves/top-cosmo-sex-tips-stories-2011?click=main_sr
45	The cosmo sex challenge: 77 positions in 77 Days	http://www.cosmopolitan.com/sex-love/great-sex-ideas/77-positions-day-sixty-one?click=main_sr
46	'The crazy way I faked it'	http://www.cosmopolitan.com/sex-love/tips-moves/the-craziest-way-i-faked-it?click=main_sr
48	Take your climax to the max	http://www.cosmopolitan.com/sex-love/tips-moves/climax-to-max?click=main_sr
49	'I need to masturbate during sex'	http://www.cosmopolitan.com/sex-love/tips-moves/masturbate-during-sex?click=main_sr

Appendix 2   Table of *Men's Health* Articles

The online version of the popular men's magazine *Men's Health* (Men's Health.co.uk) was searched using the keyword 'orgasm' in the site's own search mechanism on 2 December 2013. The search yielded 128 hits, of which the first 50 were sampled for analysis and were assigned a number. No hits were discarded from the analysis. All 50 hits were subjected to thematic analysis focusing solely on the textual aspects of the pages – that is, disregarding all images, ribbons, advertising, etc.

No	Title	URL Address
1	Are you good in bed?	http://www.menshealth.co.uk/sex/better/are-you-good-in-bed-428773?click=main_sr
2	Get a bigger penis	http://www.menshealth.co.uk/sex/your-penis/get-a-bigger-penis-9245?click=main_sr
3	How to improve your sex life	http://www.menshealth.co.uk/sex/better/how-to-improve-your-orgasm?click=main_sr
4	Give her an orgasm in 15 minutes	http://www.menshealth.co.uk/sex/better/Give-her-an-orgasm-in-15-minutes?click=main_sr

Continued

No	Title	URL Address
5	100 days of sex	http://www.menshealth.co.uk/sex/mens-health-dating/100-days-of-sex?click=main_sr
6	Improve your foreplay technique	http://www.menshealth.co.uk/sex/better/improve-your-foreplay-technique?click=main_sr
7	24 hour seductions skills	http://www.menshealth.co.uk/sex/please-woman/24-hour-seduction-skills?click=main_sr
8	How sex can save your life	http://www.menshealth.co.uk/sex/better/how-sex-can-save-your-life-281599?click=main_sr
9	Train hard to stay harder	http://www.menshealth.co.uk/sex/build-bedroom-stamina-at-gym?click=main_sr
10	10 ways to upgrade your sex life	http://www.menshealth.co.uk/sex/better/10-ways-improve-your-sex-life?click=main_sr
11	Give her a 30-minute orgasm	http://www.menshealth.co.uk/sex/better/give-her-a-30-minute-orgasm-438481?click=main_sr
12	Improve your sex life with yoga	http://www.menshealth.co.uk/sex/better/improve-your-sex-life-yoga-409300?click=main_sr
13	How to hit her G-spot	http://www.menshealth.co.uk/sex/better/how-to-hit-her-g-spot-364584?click=main_sr
14	Guarantee her more orgasms	http://www.menshealth.co.uk/sex/better/guarantee-her-more-orgasms-323364?click=main_sr
15	The MH pleasure-enhancer: Orgasm	http://www.menshealth.co.uk/sex/better/the-imhi-pleasure-enhancer-orgasm-445830?click=main_sr
16	The orgasm GPS	http://www.menshealth.co.uk/sex/better/the-orgasm-gps-312338?click=main_sr
17	Make her orgasm every time	http://www.menshealth.co.uk/sex/better/make-her-orgasm-every-time-83325?click=main_sr
18	Can an orgasm last all day?	http://www.menshealth.co.uk/sex/better/can-an-orgasm-last-all-day?click=main_sr
19	Nought to quickie in 300 seconds	http://www.menshealth.co.uk/sex/better/nought-to-quickie-in-300-seconds-536980?click=main_sr

Continued

No	Title	URL Address
20	3 ways to guarantee all night sex	http://www.menshealth.co.uk/sex/better/3-ways-to-guarantee-all-night-sex-348984?click=main_sr
21	Have your hottest sex ever this winter	http://www.menshealth.co.uk/sex/better/have-your-hottest-sex-ever-this-winter-379088?click=main_sr
22	The story of ohhhhh!	http://www.menshealth.co.uk/sex/better/the-story-of-ohhhhh-281590?click=main_sr
23	New Years sex resolutions	http://www.menshealth.co.uk/sex/better/new-years-sex-resolutions-264972?click=main_sr
24	Spot the map	http://www.menshealth.co.uk/sex/better/spot-the-map-210666?click=main_sr
25	Is she faking it?	http://www.menshealth.co.uk/sex/better/is-she-faking-it-337698?click=main_sr
26	Are you ill-cliterate?	http://www.menshealth.co.uk/sex/better/are-you-ill-cliterate-419634?click=main_sr
27	Legal high #2: Orgasmic bliss	http://www.menshealth.co.uk/sex/better/legal-high-improve-your-orgasm?click=main_sr
28	Al frisko	http://www.menshealth.co.uk/sex/better/al-frisko-334675?click=main_sr
29	A guide to her vagina	http://www.menshealth.co.uk/sex/better/a-guide-to-her-vagina-20252?click=main_sr
30	Oral success	http://www.menshealth.co.uk/sex/better/mh-masterclass-oral-sex-26889?click=main_sr
31	Did she come?	http://www.menshealth.co.uk/sex/please-woman/did-she-come-9979?click=main_sr
32	The great outdoors	http://www.menshealth.co.uk/sex/better/the-great-outdoors-223368?click=main_sr
33.	Reboot your relationship	http://www.menshealth.co.uk/sex/better/reboot-your-relationship-425630?click=main_sr
34	How to be a better lover	http://www.menshealth.co.uk/sex/better/how-to-be-a-better-lover-407630?click=main_sr
35	The MH pleasure enhancer: Arousal	http://www.menshealth.co.uk/sex/better/the-imhi-pleasure-enhancer-arousal-445804?click=main_sr

Continued

No	Title	URL Address
36	The MH pleasure enhancer: Priming	http://www.menshealth.co.uk/sex/better/the-imhi-pleasure-enhancer-priming-445810?click=main_sr
37	The MH pleasure enhancer: Enlightenment	http://www.menshealth.co.uk/sex/better/the-imhi-pleasure-enhancer-enlightenment-445823?click=main_sr
38	The MH pleasure enhancer: Instinct	http://www.menshealth.co.uk/sex/better/the-imhi-pleasure-enhancer-instinct-445813?click=main_sr
39	The MH pleasure enhancer: Touch	http://www.menshealth.co.uk/sex/better/the-imhi-pleasure-enhancer-touch-445819?click=main_sr
40	Tune into her subconscious desires	http://www.menshealth.co.uk/sex/please-woman/tune-into-her-subconscious-desires-532576?click=main_sr
41	The MH pleasure enhancer: Flirting	http://www.menshealth.co.uk/sex/better/the-imhi-pleasure-enhancer-flirting?click=main_sr
42	Moregasms	http://www.menshealth.co.uk/sex/please-woman/moregasms-9731?click=main_sr
43	Supercharge your sex life	http://www.menshealth.co.uk/sex/better/supercharge-your-sex-drive-364591?click=main_sr
44	Take her for a ride	http://www.menshealth.co.uk/sex/better/take-her-for-a-ride-10133?click=main_sr
45	Sizzling sex	http://www.menshealth.co.uk/sex/better/sizzling-sex-239913?click=main_sr
46	Get your morning sex	http://www.menshealth.co.uk/sex/more/get-your-morning-sex-89173?click=main_sr
47	Exercise for sex	http://www.menshealth.co.uk/sex/better/exercise-for-sex-9483?click=main_sr
48	Fantastic first time sex	http://www.menshealth.co.uk/sex/better/fantastic-first-time-sex-340208?click=main_sr
49	Get her in the mood	http://www.menshealth.co.uk/sex/better/get-her-in-the-mood-345237?click=main_sr
50	Raise your energy levels	http://www.menshealth.co.uk/sex/better/raise-your-game-140609?click=main_sr

Notes

2 The Orgasmic Imperative

1. This book draws heavily on two analyses of popular lifestyle magazines – *Cosmopolitan* and *Men's Health*. Examples from the magazines will be used throughout the book and these are cited by the magazine title and a number which has been assigned to each article used in the analysis. A list of the articles can be found in Appendix 1 (*Cosmopolitan*) and Appendix 2 (*Men's Health*).

3 Coming Together: The Timing of Orgasm

1. Davies, A. (2013) Have great sex...even when you don't have an orgasm. *Women's Health*, 18 June 2013. Available at: http://www.womenshealthmag.com/sex-and-relationships/orgasms. Accessed 2 November 2014.
2. Prigg, M. (2014) Researchers say women have 'more varied' orgasms than men – but males have more of them. *Daily Mail*, 18 August 2014.Available at: http://www.dailymail.co.uk/sciencetech/article-2728267/Women-really-unpredictable-bed-Researchers-say-females-varied-responses-men-orgasm-85-time-familiar-partner.html #ixzz3D5olzHEZ. Accessed 2 November 2014.
3. This study also reported that lesbian women are more likely to orgasm than heterosexual women and this aspect of the study was also heavily reported in the media.
4. Available at: http://www.everydayhealth.com/sexual-health-pictures/dr-laura-berman-top-10-female-orgasm-myths.aspx#01. Accessed 1 November 2014.
5. Davies, M. (2014) The vaginal orgasm doesn't exist – it's the clitoris that holds the key to female pleasure, study claims. *Daily Mail*, 7 October 2014. Available at: http://www.dailymail.co.uk/health/article-2783791/The-vaginal-orgasm-doesn-t-exist-s-clitoris-holds-key-female-pleasure-study-claims.html. Accessed 2 November 2014.
6. Buchanan, R.T. (2014) Vaginal orgasms are a 'myth', claim researchers. *The Independent*, 8 October 2014. Available at: http://www.independent.co.uk/life-style/health-and-families/vaginal-orgasms-are-a-myth-claim-researchers-9781706.html. Accessed 2 November 2014.
7. Leake, J. (2010) Scan reveals secrets of female orgasm. *The Sunday Times*, 7 November 2010. Available at: http://www.thesundaytimes.co.uk/sto/news/uk_news/Health/article439933.ece. Accessed 1 November 2014.
8. Mei Lan, S. (2014) Scientists reveal mystery behind the female orgasm: When having sex its all about distance not size. *The Mirror*, 21 February 2014. Available at: http://www.mirror.co.uk/news/world-news/how-make-woman-orgasm-scientists-3170447. Accessed 1 November 2014.
9. These women were a mixture of heterosexual, bisexual and lesbian and LGBT and queer-identified men in the study also talked about using a partner's expectations as a benchmark for their own level of sexual satisfaction.

10. Available at: http://www.sharecare.com/health/sex-and-relationships/emotion-related-womans-sexual-arousal. Accessed 13 October 2014.

4 Coming Together: The Timing of Orgasm

1. Kennedy, S. (2014) Orgasm 411: Have a wegasm tonight. *Women's Health*, 14 March 2014. Available at: http://www.womenshealthmag.com/sex-and-relationships/wegasm. Accessed 14 October 2014.
2. Delvin, D. (2010) Simultaneous orgasm. *NetDoctor*, 2 February 2010. Available at: http://www.netdoctor.co.uk/sex-and-relationships/simultaneous-orgasm.htm. Accessed 14 October 2014.
3. Anonymous (n.d.) How to come together. *Cosmopolitan*. Available at: http://www.cosmopolitan.co.uk/love-sex/sex/tips/g2538/how-to-come-together-orgasms-sex-love-relationships/?slide=4. Accessed 2 November 2014.
4. Anonymous (2005) How can I delay his climax? *Cosmopolitan*, 1 August 2005. Available at: http://www.cosmopolitan.com/sex-love/advice/a285/delay-his-climax/. Accessed 2 November 2014.
5. Available at: http://www.bondara.co.uk/stud-d-lay-cream. Accessed 18 September 2012.

5 Orgasmic Labour: Training the Body for Orgasmic Success

1. NHS is a reference to the UK's National Health Service.

6 Performing Orgasm: Blurring the 'Real' and the 'Fake'

1. Dold, K. (2011) Never fake an orgasm again. *Women's Health*. Available at: http://www.womenshealthmag.com/sex-and-relationships/fake-orgasm. Accessed 5 November 2013.
2. Leigh, J. Signs she's faking it. AskMen.Com. Available at: http://uk.askmen.com/dating/vanessa_150/152_love_secrets.html. Accessed 5 November 2013.
3. Morton, D. (n.d.) Is she faking it? *Men's Health*. Available at: http://www.menshealth.co.uk/sex/better/is-she-faking-it-337698. Accessed 5 November 2013.
4. Morris, M. (2013) Let's stop faking our orgasms. *Cosmopolitan*. Available at: http://www.cosmopolitan.com/celebrity/news/women-fake-orgasms. Accessed 28 October 2013.

7 Embodying Orgasmic Sensation

1. Original grammar and spelling for the extracts from *DearCupid* has been kept throughout the chapter.

References

Abramson, P.R. and Mechanic, M.B. (1983) Sex and the media: Three decades of best-selling books and major motion pictures. *Archives of Sexual Behavior*, 12(3): 185–206.

Adam, B.D. (2005) Constructing the neoliberal sexual actor: Responsibility and care of the self in the discourse of barebackers. *Culture, Health & Sexuality*, 7(4): 333–346.

Adams, A.E., Haynes, S.N. and Brayer, M.A. (1985) Cognitive distraction in female sexual arousal. *Psychophysiology*, 22(6): 689–696.

Alexander, S.M. (2003) Stylish hard bodies: Branded masculinity in Men's Health magazine. *Sociological Perspective*, 46(4): 535–554.

Allen, L. (2001) Closing sex education's knowledge/practice gap: The re-conceptualisation of young people's sexual knowledge, *Sex Education*, 1(2): 109–122.

Allen, L. (2004) Beyond the birds and the bees: Constituting a discourse of erotics in sexuality education. *Gender and Education*, 16(2): 151–167.

Allen, L. (2005) *Sexual subjects: Young people, sexuality and education*. Houndmills: Palgrave.

Allen, L. (2007) 'Pleasurable pedagogy': Young people's ideas about teaching 'pleasure' in sexuality education. *Twenty-first Century Society: Journal of the Academy of Social Sciences*, 2(3): 249–264.

Allen, L. (2008) 'They think you shouldn't be having sex anyway': Young people's suggestions for improving sexuality education content. *Sexualities*, 11(5): 573–594.

Althof, S.E. (2006) Prevalence, characteristics and implications of premature ejaculation/rapid ejaculation. *The Journal of Urology*, 175: 842–848.

American Psychiatric Association (2000) *Diagnostic and statistical manual of mental disorders*. Washington, DC: American Psychiatric Association.

Angel, K. (2012) Contested psychiatric ontology and feminist critique: 'Female Sexual Dysfunction' and the Diagnostic and Statistical Manual. *History of the Human Sciences*, 25(4): 3–24.

Armstrong, E.A., England, P. and Fogarty, A.C.K. (2012) Accounting for women's orgasm and sexual enjoyment in college hookups and relationships. *American Sociological Review*, 77(3): 435–462.

Attwood, F. (2005a) Fashion and passion: Marketing sex to women. *Sexualities*, 8(4): 392–406.

Attwood, F. (2005b) 'Tits and ass and porn and fighting': Male heterosexuality in magazines for men. *International Journal of Cultural Studies*, 8: 83–100.

Bancroft, J. (2002) The medicalization of female sexual dysfunction: The need for caution. *Archives of Sexual Behavior*, 31(5): 451–455.

Bancroft, J., Scott, J.S. and McCabe, J. (2011) Sexual well-being: A comparison of US Black and White women in heterosexual relationships. *Archives of Sexual Behavior*, 40(4): 725–740.

Bartky, S.L. (1990) *Femininity and domination: Studies in the phenomenology of oppression*. New York: Routledge.

Basson, R. (2000) The female sexual response: A different model. *Journal of Sex & Marital Therapy*, 26(1): 51–65.

Baumeister, R.F., Catanese, K.R. and Vohs, K.D. (2001) Is there a gender difference in strength of sex drive? *Personality and Social Psychology Review*, 5: 242–273.

Bay-Cheng, L.Y. (2001) SexEd. com: Values and norms in web-based sexuality education. *Journal of Sex Research*, 38(3): 241–251.

Bay-Cheng, L.Y. (2003) The trouble of teen sex: The construction of adolescent sexuality through school-based sexuality education. *Sex Education: Sexuality, Society and Learning*, 3(1): 61–74.

Bay-Cheng, L.Y., Livingston, J.A. and Fava, N.M. (2011) Adolescent girls' assessment and management of sexual risks: Insights from focus group research. *Youth & Society*, 43(3): 1167–1193.

Bechtel, S. and Stains, L.R. and the editors of Men's Health Books (1996) *Sex: A man's guide*. Roedale Press Inc. Available at: http://www.cosmopolitan.com/sex-love/tips-moves/how-to-have-an-orgasm?click=main_sr. Accessed 29 October 2012.

Beck, U. (1997) *The reinvention of politics: Rethinking modernity in the global social order*. Cambridge, UK: Polity.

Becker, H. (1963) Outsiders: *Studies in the sociology of deviance*. New York: Free Press.

Benwell, B. (2002) Is there anything 'new' about these Lads? The textual and visual construction of masculinity in men's magazines. In L. Litosseliti and J. Sunderland (eds) *Gender Identity and Discourse Analysis*. Amsterdam/Philadelphia: John Benjamins Press.

Benwell, B. (2004) Ironic discourse: Evasive masculinity in men's lifestyle magazines. *Men and Masculinities*, 7: 3–21.

Benwell, B. (2007) New sexism? Readers' responses to the use of irony in men's magazines. *Journalism Studies*, 8(4): 539–549.

Bernstein, B. (2001) From pedagogies to knowledges. In A. Morias, I. Neves, B. Davies and H. Daniels (eds) *Towards a sociology of pedagogy: The contribution of Basil Bernstein to research*. New York: Peter Lang.

Bernstein, E. (2007) Sex work for the middle classes. *Sexualities*, 10(4): 473–488.

Bertone, C. and Camoletto, R.F. (2009) Beyond the sex machine? Sexual practices and masculinity in adult men's heterosexual accounts. *Journal of Gender Studies*, 18(4): 369–386.

Birke, L. (1999) *Feminism and the biological body*. Edinburgh: Edinburgh University Press.

Bolsø, A. (2001) When women take: Lesbians reworking concepts of sexuality. *Sexualities*, 4(4): 455–473.

Boni, F. (2002) Framing media masculinities: Men's lifestyle magazines and the biopolitics of the male body. *European Journal of Communication*, 17(4): 465–478.

Bordo, S. (2003) *Unbearable weight: Feminism, Western culture, and the body*. Berkeley: University of California Press.

Bourdieu, P. (1984) *Distinction: A social critique of the judgement of taste*. Harvard: Harvard University Press.

Braun, V., Gavey. N. and McPhillips, K. (2003) The 'fair deal'? Unpacking accounts of reciprocity in heterosex. *Sexualities*, 6(2): 237–261.

Brewis, J. and Linstead, S. (2000) *Sex, work and sex work: Eroticizing organizations*. London: Routledge.

Brody, S. (2006) Penile–vaginal intercourse is better: evidence trumps ideology. *Sexual and Relationship Therapy*, 21(4): 393–403.

Brody, S. (2007a) Intercourse orgasm consistency, concordance of women's genital and subjective sexual arousal, and erotic stimulus presentation sequence. *Journal of Sex & Marital Therapy*, 33(1): 31–39.

Brody, S. (2007b) Vaginal orgasm is associated with better psychological function. *Sexual and Relationship Therapy*, 22(2): 173–191.

Brody, S. and Weiss, P. (2011) Simultaneous penile–vaginal intercourse orgasm is associated with satisfaction (sexual, life, partnership and mental health). *The Journal of Sexual Medicine*, 8(3): 734–741.

Brody, S., Laan, E. and van Lunsen, R.H.W. (2003) Concordance between women's physiological and subjective sexual arousal is associated with consistency of orgasm during intercourse but not other sexual behavior. *Journal of Sex and Marital Therapy*, 29: 15–23.

Brown, W. (2003) Neoliberalism and the end of liberal democracy. *Theory and Event*, 7(1): 15–18.

Bullock, C.M. and Beckson, M. (2011) Male victims of sexual assault: Phenomenology, psychology, physiology. *Journal of American Academy of Psychiatry and Law*, 39: 197–205.

Burkett, M. and Hamilton, K. (2012) Postfeminist sexual agency: Young women's negotiations of sexual consent. *Sexualities*, 15(7): 815–833.

Burns, A. and Torre, M.E. (2005) IV. Revolutionary sexualities. *Feminism & Psychology*, 15(1): 21–26.

Buss, D.M. and Schmitt, D.P. (1993) Sexual strategies theory: An evolutionary perspective on human mating. *Psychological Review*, 100(2): 204–232.

Byers, E.S. (1996) How well does the traditional sexual script explain sexual coercion? Review of a program of research. *Journal of Psychology & Human Sexuality*, 8(1–2): 7–25.

Byers, E.S. and Grenier, G. (2003) Premature or rapid ejaculation: Heterosexual couples' perceptions of men's ejaculatory behaviour. *Archives of Sexual Behavior*, 32(3): 261–270.

Cacchioni, T. (2007) Heterosexuality and 'the labour of love': A contribution to recent debates on female sexual dysfunction. *Sexualities*, 10(3): 299–320.

Califia, P. (1979) Lesbian sexuality. *Journal of Homosexuality*, 4(3): 255–266.

Carpenter, L.M., Nathanson, C.A. and Kim, Y.J. (2009) Physical women, emotional men: Gender and sexual satisfaction in midlife. *Archives of Sexual Behavior*, 38: 87–107.

Carrellas, B. (2007) *Urban tantra: Sacred sex for the Twenty-first Century*. Celestial Arts.

Carroll, J.A., Volk, K.D. and Hyde, J.S. (1985) Differences between males and females in motives for engaging in sexual intercourse. *Archives of Sexual Behavior*, 14(2): 131–139.

Chia, M., Chia, M., Abrams, D. and Abrams, R.C. (2001) *The multi-orgasmic couple*. Thorsons.

Chivers, M.L., Seto, M.C., Lalumière, M.L., Laan, E. and Grimbos, T. (2010) Agreement of self-reported and genital measures of sexual arousal in men and women: A meta-analysis. *Archives of Sexual Behavior*, 39: 5–56.

Clark, D. (1991) Constituting the marital world: A qualitative perspective. In D. Clark (ed.) *Marriage, domestic life and social change: Writings for Jacqueline Burgoyne* (pp. 117–139). London: Routledge.

Clifford, R.E. (1978) Subjective sexual experience in college women. *Archives of Sexual Behavior*, 7: 183–197.

Colson, M.H. (2010) Female orgasm: Myths, facts and controversies. *Sexologies*, 19(1): 8–14.

Colson, M.H., Lemaire, A., Pinton, P., Hamidi, K. and Klein, P. (2006) Couples' sexual Dysfunction: Sexual Behaviors and Mental Perception, Satisfaction and Expectations of Sex Life in Men and Women in France, *The Journal of Sexual Medicine*, 3(1): 121–131.

Conley, T.D., Moors, A.C., Matsick, J.L., Ziegler, A. and Valentine, B.A. (2011) Women, men, and the bedroom: Methodological and conceptual insights that narrow, reframe, and eliminate gender differences in sexuality. *Current Directions in Psychological Science*, 20(5): 296–300.

Connell, E. (2005) Desire as interruption: Young women, sexuality and education in Ontario, Canada. *Sex Education*, 5(3): 253–268.

Connell, E. and Hunt, A. (2006) Sexual ideology and sexual physiology in the discourses of sex advice literature. *The Canadian Journal of Human Sexuality*, 15(1): 23–45.

Connell, R.W. (1987) *Gender and power*. Sydney, Australia: Allen and Unwin.

Cooper, E.B., Fenigstein, A. and Fauber, R.L. (2014) The faking orgasm scale for women: Psychometric properties. *Archives of Sexual Behavior*, 43: 423–435.

Corbiel, A. (2012) *The simultaneous O: A couples guide to achieving the ultimate climax*. Berkeley, CA: Amorata Press. Available at: http://www.amazon.co.uk/Simultaneous-O-Editors-Amorata-Press/dp/1612430589/ref=sr_1_41?s=books&ie=UTF8&qid=1355764554&sr=1–41. Accessed 17 December 2012.

Crawford, C.S. (2012) 'You don't need a body to feel a body': phantom limb syndrome and corporeal transgression. *Sociology of Health and Illness*, 35(3): 434–448.

Currie, D. (2001) Dear Abby Advice pages as a site for the operation of power. *Feminist Theory*, 2(3): 259–281.

Darling, C.A. and Davidson, J.K. (1986) Enhancing relationships: Understanding the feminine mystique of pretending orgasm. *Journal of Sex and Marital Therapy*, 12: 182–196.

Dekker, A. and Schmidt, G. (2002) Patterns of masturbatory behaviour: Changes between the sixties and the nineties. *Journal of Psychology and Human Sexuality*, 14: 35–48.

Densmore, D. (1973) Independence from the sexual revolution. In A. Koedt, E. Levine and A. Rapone (eds) *Radical Feminism*. New York: Quadrangle Books.

Diorio, J.A. and Munro, J.A. (2000) Doing harm in the name of protection: Menstruation as a topic for sex education. *Gender and Education*, 12(3): 347–365.

Duncombe, J. and Marsden, D. (1993) Love and intimacy: The gender division of emotion and 'emotion work': A neglected aspect of sociological discussion of heterosexual relationships. *Sociology*, 27(2): 221–241.

Duncombe, J. and Marsden, D. (1995) 'Workaholics' and 'whingeing women': Emotion and 'emotion work'. *Sociology*, 27: 150–169.

Duncombe, J. and Marsden, D. (1996) Whose orgasm is this anyway? Sex work in long-term couple relationships. In J. Weeks and J. Holland (eds) *Sexual Cultures*. Basingstoke: MacMillan.

Dunn, K.M., Croft, P.R. and Hackett, G.I. (1998) Sexual problems: A study of the prevalence and need for health care in the general population. *Family Practice*, 15(6): 519–524.

Duran, R.L. and Prusank, D.T. (1997) Relational themes in men's and women's popular non-fiction magazine articles. *Journal of Personal and Social Relationships*, 14(2): 165–189.

Durham, M.G. (1996) The taming of the shrew: Women's magazines and the regulation of desire. *Journal of Communication Inquiry*, 20(1): 18–31.

Durham, M.G. (1998) Dilemmas of desire: Representations of adolescent sexuality in two teen magazines. *Youth & Society*, 29(3): 369–389.

Dworkin, A. (1987) *Intercourse*. New York: Basic Books.

Edwards, T. (1997) *Men in the mirror: Men's fashion, masculinity and consumer society*. London: Cassell.

Edwards, T. (2003) Sex, booze and fags: Masculinity, style and men's magazines. *The Sociological Review*, 51(S1): 132–146.

Edwards, J.N. and Booth, A. (1994) Sexuality, marriage and well-being: The middle years. In A. S. Rossi (ed.) *Sexuality across the life course*. Chicago: The University of Chicago Press.

Eichel, E.W., Eichel, J.D. and Kule, S. (1988) The technique of coital alignment and its relation to female orgasmic response and simultaneous orgasm. *Journal of Sex & Marital Therapy*, 14(2): 129–141.

Elliott, S. and Umberson, D. (2008) The performance of desire: Gender and sexual negotiation in long term marriages. *Journal of Marriage and the Family*, 70: 391–406.

Emslie, C., Ridge, D., Ziebland, S. and Hunt, K. (2006) Men's accounts of depression: Reconstructing or resisting hegemonic masculinity? *Social Science & Medicine*, 62(9): 2246–2257.

Erickson, R.J. (2005) Why emotion work matters: Sex, gender and the division of household labor. *Journal of Marriage and the Family*, 67(2): 337–351.

Fahs, B. (2011) *Performing sex: The making and unmaking of women's erotic lives*. Albany: SUNY Press.

Fahs, B. and Swank, E. (2011) Social identities as predictors of women's sexual satisfaction and sexual activity. *Archives of Sexual Behavior*, 40(5): 903–914.

Farvid, P. and Braun, V. (2006) 'Most of us guys are raring to go anytime, anyplace, anywhere': Male and female sexuality in *Cleo* and *Cosmo*. *Sex Roles*, 55(5–6): 295–310.

Farvid, P. and Braun, V. (2014) The 'sassy woman' and the 'performing man': Heterosexual casual sex advice and the (re)constitution of gendered subjectivities. *Feminist Media Studies*, 14(1): 118–134.

Fergus, K.D., Gray, R.E. and Fitch, M.I. (2002) Sexual dysfunction and the preservation of manhood: Experiences of men with prostate cancer. *Journal of Health Psychology*, 7(3): 303–316.

Ferguson, R.M., Vanwesenbeeck, I. and Knijn, T. (2008) A matter of facts…and more: An exploratory analysis of the content of sexuality education in The Netherlands. *Sex Education*, 8(1): 93–106.

Finch, J. and Summerfield, P. (1991) Social reconstruction and the emergence of companionate marriage, 1945–59. In D. Clark (ed.) *Marriage, Domestic Life and Social Change: Writings for Jacqueline Burgoyne* (pp. 6–27). London: Routledge.

Fine, M. (1988) Sexuality, schooling, and adolescent females: The missing discourse of desire. *Harvard Educational Review*, 58(1): 29–54.

Fine, M. and McClelland, S.I. (2006) Sexuality education and desire: Still missing after all these years. *Harvard Educational Review*, 76(3): 279–338.

Flood, M. (2008) Men, sex, and homosociality: How bonds between men shape their sexual relations with women. *Men and Masculinities*, 10(3): 339–359.

Flowers-Coulson, P.A., Kushner, M.A. and Bankowski, S. (2000) The information is out there but is anyone getting it? Adolescent misconceptions about sexuality education and reproductive health and the use of the internet to get answers. *Journal of Sex Education and Therapy*, 25(2–3): 178–188.

Foucault, M. (1973) *The birth of the clinic: An archaeology of medical perception.* London: Routledge.

Foucault, M. (1978) *The history of sexuality, volume 1: An introduction* (R. Hurley, Trans.). New York: Vintage.

Freud, S. (1905) *Three essays on the theory of sexuality.* Standard edition of the complete works of Sigmund Freud (J. Strachey, ed. and trans.) (pp. 73–109). London: Hogarth Press.

Frith, H. (2013a) Accounting for orgasmic absence: Responses to 'missing' orgasms in heterosexual sex using the story completion method. *Psychology & Sexuality*, 4(3): 310–322.

Frith, H. (2013b) 'CONGRATS!! You had an orgasm': Constructing orgasm on an internet discussion board. *Feminism & Psychology*, 23(2): 252–260.

Frith, H. (2013c) Labouring on orgasms: embodiment, efficiency, entitlement and obligations in heterosex. *Culture, Health and Sexuality: An International Journal for Research, Intervention and Care*, 15(4): 494–510.

Frith, H. (2014) Visualising the 'real' and the 'fake': Emotion work and the representation of orgasm in pornography and everyday sexual interactions. *Journal of Gender Studies*. Available at: http://www.tandfonline.com/doi/abs/10.1080/0 9589236.2014.950556#.VFugnctyYcA

Fugl-Meyer, K.S., Öberg, K., Lundberg, P.O., Lewin, B. and Fugl-Meyer, A. (2006) On orgasm, sexual techniques, and erotic perceptions in 18- to 74-year-old Swedish women. *Journal of Sexual Medicine*, 3: 56–68.

Garcia, J.R., Lloyd, E.A., Wallen, K. and Fisher, H.E. (2014) Variation in orgasm occurrence by sexual orientation in a sample of U.S. singles. *Journal of Sexual Medicine*, 11: 2645–2652.

Gavey, N. (1989) Feminist poststructuralism and discourse analysis: Contributions to feminist psychology. *Psychology of Women Quarterly*, 13(4): 459–475.

Gavey, N. (1992) Technologies and effects of heterosexual coercion. *Feminism & Psychology*, 2(3): 325–351.

Gavey, N. (2012) Beyond 'empowerment'? Sexuality in a sexist world. *Sex Roles*, 66(11–12): 718–724.

Gavey, N., McPhillips, K. and Braun, V. (1999) Interruptus coitus: Heterosexuals accounting for intercourse. *Sexualities*, 2(1): 35–68.

Gerhard, J. (2000) Revisiting 'the myth of the vaginal orgasm': The female orgasm in American sexual thought and second wave feminism. *Feminist Studies*, 26(2): 449–476.

Giddens, A. (1991) *Modernity and self-identity: Self and society in the late modern age.* Cambridge: Polity.

Giddens, A. (1992) *The transformation of intimacy: Sexuality, love and eroticism in modern societies.* Cambridge: Polity.

Gilfoyle, J., Wilson, J. and Brown (1992) Sex, organs and audiotape: A discourse analytic approach to talking about heterosexual sex and relationships. *Feminism & Psychology*, 2(2): 209–230.

Gill, R. (2007) Postfeminist media culture: Elements of a sensibility. *European Journal of Cultural Studies*, 10(2): 147–166.

Gill, R. (2008) Empowerment/sexism: Figuring female sexual agency in contemporary advertising. *Feminism & Psychology*, 18(1): 35–60.

Gill, R. (2009) Mediated intimacy and postfeminism: A discourse analytic examination of sex and relationships advice in a women's magazine. *Discourse & Communication*, 3(4): 345–369.

Gill, R. and Scharff, C. (eds) (2011) *New femininities: Postfeminism, neoliberalism, and subjectivity*. Palgrave Macmillan.

Gonzales, A.M. and Rolison, G. (2005) Social oppression and attitudes toward sexual practices. *Journal of Black Studies*, 35(6): 715–729.

Gordon, M. (1971) From an unfortunate necessity to a cult of mutual orgasm: Sex in American marital education literature, 1830–1940. In J.M. Henslin (ed.) *The sociology of sex: An introductory reader* (pp. 53–77). New York: Appleton-Century-Crofts.

Gotell, L. (2008) Rethinking affirmative consent in Canadian sexual assault law: Neoliberal sexual subjects and risky women. *Akron Law Review*, 41: 865–898.

Grace, V., Potts, A., Gavey, N. and Vares, T. (2006) The discursive condition of Viagra. *Sexualities*, 9(3): 295–314.

Graham, C.A. (2010) The DSM diagnostic criteria for female orgasmic disorder. *Archives of Sexual Behavior*, 39: 256–270.

Graham, C.A. and Bancroft, J. (2006) Assessing the prevalence of female sexual dysfunction with surveys: What is feasible? In I. Goldstein, C.M. Meston, S.R. Davis and A.M. Traish (eds) *Women's sexual function and dysfunction: Study, diagnosis and treatment* (pp. 52–60). Abingdon, Oxon: Taylor & Francis.

Gray, J. (1992) *Men are from Mars, Women are from Venus*. New York: Harper Collins.

Gray, J. (1995) *Mars and Venus in the bedroom: A guide to lasting romance and passion*. New York: Harper Collins.

Greer, G. (1971) *The Female Eunuch*. London: Paladin.

Groth, N. and Burgess, A.W. (1980) Male rape: Offenders and victims. *American Journal of Psychiatry*, 137(7): 806–810.

Grulich, A.E., de Visser, E.O., Smith, A.M.A., Rissel, C.E. and Richters, J. (2003) Sex in Australia: Homosexual experience and recent homosexual encounters. *Australian and New Zealand Journal of Public Health*, 27(2): 155–163.

Gupta, K. and Cacchioni, T. (2013) Sexual improvement as if your health depends on it: An analysis of contemporary sex manuals. *Feminism & Psychology*, 23(4): 442–458.

Haavio-Mannila, E. and Kontula, O. (1997) Correlates of increased sexual satisfaction. *Archives of Sexual Behavior*, 26(4): 399–419.

Hamilton, L. and Armstrong, E.A. (2009) Gendered sexuality in young adulthood: Double binds and flawed options. *Gender & Society*, 23(5): 589–616.

Haning, R.V., O'Keefe, S.L., Randall, E.J., Kommor, M.J., Baker, E. and Wilson, R. (2007) Intimacy, orgasm likelihood, and conflict predict sexual satisfaction in heterosexual male and female respondents. *Journal of Sex & Marital Therapy*, 33: 93–113.

Haning, R.V., O'Keefe, S.L., Beard, K.W., Randall, E.J., Kommer, M.J. and Stroebel, S.S. (2008) Empathetic sexual responses in heterosexual women and men. *Sexual and Relationship Therapy*, 23(4): 325–344.

Harris, J.M., Cherkas, L.F., Kato, B.S., Heiman, J.R. and Spector, T.D. (2008) Normal variations in personality are associated with coital orgasmic infrequency in heterosexual women: A population based study. *Journal of Sexual Medicine*, 5: 1177–1183.

Hartman, W.E. and Fithian, M.A. (1994) Physiological response patterns of 751 research volunteers. Paper presented at the Society for the Scientific Study of Sexuality, Western Region Conference, San Diego, April 1994.

Hartmann, U., Schedlowski, M. and Kruger, T.H.C. (2005) Cognitive and partner-related factors in rapid ejaculation: Differences between dysfunctional and functional men. *World Journal of Urology*, 23: 93–101.

Harvey, L. and Gill, R. (2011) Spicing it up: Sexual entrepreneurs and the sex inspectors. In R. Gill and C. Scharff (eds) *New Femininities: Postfeminism, Neoliberalism and Subjectivity*. Basingstoke: Palgrave.

Hayfield, N. and Clarke, V. (2012) 'I'd be just as happy with a cup of tea': Women's accounts of sex and affection in long-term heterosexual relationships. *Women's Studies International Forum*, 35(2): 67–74.

Haywood, C. (1996) Sex education policy and the regulation of young people's sexual practice. *Educational Review*, 48: 121–129.

Hebson, G., Earnshaw, J. and Marchington, L. (2007) Too emotional to be capable? The changing nature of emotion work in definitions of 'capable teaching'. *Journal of Education Policy*, 22(6): 675–694.

Heiman, J. and LoPiccolo, L. (1976) *Becoming orgasmic: A sexual growth program for women*. Englewood Cliffs, New Jersey: Prentice Hall.

Herbenick, D. and Fortenberry, J.D. (2011) Exercise-induced orgasm and pleasure among women. *Sexual and Relationship Therapy*, 26(4): 373–388.

Herbenick, D., Reece, M., Schick, V., Sanders, S.A., Dodge, B. and Fortenberry, J.D. (2010) An event-level analysis of the sexual characteristics and composition among adults ages 18 to 59: Results from a national probability sample in the United States. *Journal of Sexual Medicine*, 7(suppl 5): 346–361.

Higgins, J.A., Trussell, J., Moore. N.B. and Davidson, J.K. (2010) Virginity lost, satisfaction gained? Physiological and psychological sexual satisfaction at heterosexual debut. *Journal of Sex Research*, 47(4): 384–394.

Hillier, L., Harrison, L. and Bowditch, K. (1999) 'Never ending love' and 'blowing your load': The meanings of sex to rural youth. *Sexualities*, 2(1): 69–88.

Hines, T.M. (2001) The G-spot: A modern gynecological myth. *American Journal of Obstetrics and Gynecology*, 185(2): 359–362.

Hirst, J. (2008) Developing sexual competence? Exploring strategies for the provision of effective sexualities and relationships education. *Sex Education*, 8(4): 399–413.

Hite, S. (1976) *The Hite Report: A nationwide survey of female sexuality*. London: Bloomsbury.

Hochschild, A.R. (1979) Emotion work, feeling rules and social structure. *American Journal of Sociology*, 85(3): 551–575.

Hochschild, A.R. (1983) *The managed heart*. Berkeley: University of California Press.

Hochschild, A.R. (1989) *The second shift: Working parents and the revolution at home* (with Anne Machung). New York: Viking Penguin.

Hockey, J., Meah, A. and Robinson, V. (2007) *Mundane heterosexualities: From theory to practices*. New York: Palgrave Macmillan.

Holland, J., Ramazanoglu, C., Scott, R., Sharpe, S. and Thompson, R. (1998) *The male in the head: Young people, heterosexuality and power.* London: Tufnell Press.

Hollway, W. (1984) Women's power in heterosexual sex. *Women's Studies International Forum*, 7(1): 63–68.

Hoppe, T. (2011) Circuits of power, circuits of pleasure: Sexual scripting in gay men's bottom narratives. *Sexualities*, 14(2): 193–217.

Horne, S. and Zimmer-Gembeck, M.J. (2005) Female sexual subjectivity and well-being: Comparing late adolescents with different sexual experiences, *Sexuality Research and Social Policy*, 2(3): 25–55.

Hurlbert, D.F., Apt, C. And Rebehl, S.M. (1993) Key variables to understanding female sexual satisfaction: An examination of women in nondistressed marriages. *Journal of Sex & Marital Therapy*, 19(2): 154-165.

Inglis, D. and Holmes, M. (2000) Toiletry time: Defecation, temporal strategies and dilemmas of modernity. *Time and Society*, 9(2/3): 223–245.

Ingraham, C. (2002) 'Heterosexuality: It's just not natural!'. In S. Seidman and D. Richardson (eds) *Handbook of Gay and Lesbian Studies*. London: Sage Publications.

Jackson, P., Stevenson, N., and Brooks, K. (2001) *Making sense of men's magazines.* Oxford and Malden: Polity.

Jackson, S. (2005) 'I'm 15 and desperate for sex': 'Doing' and 'undoing' desire in letters to a teenage magazine. *Feminism and Psychology*, 15(3): 295–313.

Jackson, S. (2011) Heterosexual hierarchies: A commentary on class and sexuality. *Sexualities*, 14(1): 12–20.

Jackson, S. and Scott, S. (1997) Gut reactions to matters of the heart: Reflections on rationality, irrationality and sexuality. *Sociological Review*, 45(4): 551–575.

Jackson, S. and Scott, S. (2001) Embodying orgasm: Gendered power relations and sexual pleasure. In E. Kaschak and L. Tiefer (eds) *A new view of women's sexual problems*. London: Haworth Press.

Jackson, S. and Scott, S. (2007) Faking it like a woman? Towards an interpretive theorization of sexual pleasure. *Body & Society*, 13(2): 95–116.

Jackson, S. and Wetherell, A. (2010) The (im)possibilities of feminist school based sexuality education. *Feminism & Psychology*, 20: 166–185.

Jackson, S.M. and Cram, F. (2003) Disrupting the sexual double standard: Young women's talk about heterosexuality. *British Journal of Social Psychology*, 42(1): 113–127.

Jagose, A. (2010) Counterfeit pleasures: Fake orgasm and queer agency. *Textual Practice*, 24(3): 517–539.

James, N. (1992) Care = organisation + physical labour = emotional labour. *Sociology of Health and Illness*, 14: 488–509.

Jamieson, L. (1999) Intimacy transformed? A critical look at the 'pure relationship'. *Sociology*, 33(3): 477–494.

Jannini, E.A., Whipple, B., Kingsberg, S.A., Buisson, O., Foldès, P. and Vardi, Y. (2010) Who's afraid of the G-spot? *Journal of Sexual Medicine*, 7: 25–34.

Janus, S.S. and Janus, C.L. (1993) *The Janus report on sexual behavior*. New York: John Wiley & Sons.

Johnson, A.M., Wadsworth, J., Wellings, K. and Field, J. (1994) *Sexual attitudes and lifestyles*. Blackwell Scientific: Oxford.

Johnson, M. (2010) 'Just getting off': The inseparability of ejaculation and hegemonic masculinity. *Journal of Men's Studies*, 18(3): 238–248.

Johnson, P. (2008) 'Rude boys': The homosexual eroticization of class. *Sociology*, 41(1): 65–82.

Jones, G.E. (1995) Constitutional and physiological factors in heartbeat perception. In D. Vaitl and R. Schandry (eds) *From the heart to the brain: The psychophysiology of circulation-brain interaction* (pp. 173–192). Frankfurt/Main: Peter Lang.

Kaighobadi, F., Shackelton, T.K. and Weekes-Shackelton, V.A. (2012) Do women pretend orgasm to retain a mate? *Archives of Sexual Behavior*, 41(5): 1121–1125.

Kaplan, H.S. (1977) Hypoactive sexual desire. *Journal of Sex and Marital Therapy*, 3(1): 3–9.

Kaplan, H.S. (1995) *The sexual desire disorders: Dysfunctional regulation of sexual motivation*. New York: Brunner/Routledge.

Katsulis, Y. (2010) 'Living like a king': Conspicuous consumption, virtual communities, and the social construction of paid sexual encounters by US sex tourists. *Men and Masculinities*, 13(2): 210–230.

Kehily, M.J. (1999) More sugar? Teenage magazines, gender displays and sexual learning. *European Journal of Cultural Studies*, 2(1): 65–89.

Keily, E. (2005) Where is the discourse of desire? Deconstructing the Irish Relationships and Sexuality Education (RSE) resource materials. *Irish Educational Studies*, 24(2–3): 253–266.

Kilchevsky, A., Vardi, Y., Lowenstein, L. and Gruenwald, I. (2012) Is the female G-spot truly a distinct anatomic entity? *The Journal of Sexual Medicine*, 9(3): 719–726.

Kimmel, M.S. (199) Masculinity as homophobia: Fear, shame, and silence in the construction of gender identity. In H. Brod and M. Kaufman (eds) *Theorizing masculinities*. London: SAGE.

King, M., Holt, V. and Nazareth, I. (2007) Women's views of their sexual difficulties: Agreement and disagreement with clinical diagnoses. *Archives of Sexual Behavior*, 36: 281–288.

Kinsey, A., Pomeroy, W., Martin, C. and Gebhard, P. (1948/1998) *Sexual behavior in the human male*. Philadelphia: W.B. Saunders; Bloomington, Indiana: Indiana University Press.

Kinsey, A., Pomeroy, W., Martin, C. and Gebhard, P. (1953) *Sexual behavior in the human female*. Philadelphia: Saunders.

Kitzinger, C. and Wilkinson, S. (1993) *Heterosexuality: A feminism & psychology reader*. London: SAGE.

Koedt, A. (1974) The myth of the vaginal orgasm. In The Radical Therapist Collective (eds) *The Radical Therapist* (pp. 133–142). Harmondsworth: Pelican.

Koeman, M., van Driel, M.F., Schultz, W.C.M.W. and Mensink, H.J.A. (1996) Orgasm after radical prostatectomy. *British Journal of Urology*, 77(6): 861–864.

Komisaruk, B.R. and Whipple, B. (2011) Non-genital orgasms. *Sexual and Relationship Therapy*, 26(4): 356–372.

Komisaruk, B.R., Beyer-Flores, C. and Whipple, B. (2006) *The science of orgasm*. Baltimore: John Hopkins University Press.

Kornrich, S., Brines, J. and Leupp, K. (2012) Egalitarianism, housework, and sexual frequency in marriage. *American Sociological Review*, 78(1) 26–50.

Krassas, N., Blauwkamp, J., and Wesselink, P. (2003) 'Master your Johnson': Sexual rhetoric in Maxim and Stuff magazines. *Sexuality & Culture*, 7(3): 98–119.

Laan, E. and Everaerd, W. (1995) Determinants of female sexual arousal: Psychophysiological theory and data. *Annual Review of Sex Research*, 6: 32–76.

Laan, E. and Janssen, E. (2007) How do men and women feel? Determinants of subjective experience of sexual arousal. *The Psychophysiology of Sex*, 278–290.

Laan, E. and Rellini, A.H. (2011) Can we treat anorgasmia in women? The challenge to experiencing pleasure. *Sexual and Relationship Therapy*, 26(4): 329–341.

Laan, E., Everaerd, W., van Aanhold, M. and Rebel, M. (1993) Performance demand and sexual arousal in women. *Behavior Research and Therapy*, 31, 25–35.

Laipson, P. (1996) 'Kiss without shame, for she desires it': Sexual foreplay in American marital advice literature, 1900–1925. *Journal of Social History*, 29(3): 507–525.

Lamb, S. (2010) Feminist ideals for a healthy female adolescent sexuality: A critique. *Sex Roles*, 62(5–6): 294–306.

Laqueur, T. (1986) Orgasm, generation and the politics of reproductive biology. *Representations*, 14: 1–41.

Laqueur, T.W. (2009) Sexuality and the transformation of culture: The longue duree. *Sexualities*, 12(4): 418–436.

Laumann, E.O., Paik, A., and Rosen, R.C. (1999) Sexual dysfunction in the United States: Prevalence and predictors. *Journal of the American Medical Association*, 6: 537–544.

Laumann, E.O., Gagnon, J.H., Michael, R.T. and Michaels, S. (1994) *The social organization of sexuality: Sexual practices in the United States*. Chicago: University of Chicago Press.

Laumann, E.O., Nicolosi, A., Glasser, D.B., Paik, A., Gingell, C., Moreira, E. and Wang, T. for the GSSAB Investigators' Group (2005) Sexual problems among women and men aged 40–80 y: Prevalence and correlates identified in the Global Study of Sexual Attitudes and Behaviors. *International Journal of Impotence Research*, 17: 39–57.

Lavie, M. and Willig, C. (2005) 'I don't feel like melting butter': An interpretative phenomenological analysis of the experience of 'Inorgasmia'. *Psychology & Health*, 20(1): 115–128.

Lavie-Ajayi, M. (2005) 'Because all real women do': The construction and deconstruction of 'female orgasmic disorder'. *Sexualities, Evolution & Gender*, 7(1): 57–72.

Lavie-Ajayi, M. and Joffe, H. (2009) Social representations of female orgasm. *Journal of Health Psychology*, 14(1): 98–107.

Levin, R.J. (2003) The G-spot – reality or illusion? *Sexual and Relationship Therapy*, 18(1): 117–119.

Levin, R.J. (2004) An orgasm is…who defines what an orgasm is? *Sexual and Relationship Therapy*, 19(1): 101–107.

Levin, R.J. (2011) The human female orgasm: A critical evaluation of its proposed reproductive functions. *Sexual and Relationship Therapy*, 26(4): 301–314.

Levin, R.J. (2012) The deadly pleasures of the clitoris and the condom – a rebuttal of Brody, Costa and Hess (2012). *Sexual and Relationship Therapy*, 27(3): 272–295.

Levin, R.J. and van Berlo, W. (2004) Sexual arousal and orgasm in subjects who experience forced or non-consensual sexual stimulation – a review. *Journal of Clinical Forensic Medicine*, 11: 82–88.

Levin, R.J. and Wagner, G. (1985) Heart rate changes and subjective intensity of orgasm in women. *International Research Communications System – Medical Science*, 13: 885–886.

Lewis, J. and Knijn, T. (2003) Sex Education materials in The Netherlands and in England and Wales: A comparison of content, use and teaching practice. *Oxford Review of Education*, 29(1): 113–150.

Lloyd, E.A. (2005) *The case of female orgasm: Bias in the science of evolution*. Harvard, MA: Harvard University Press.

Loe, M. (2001) Fixing broken masculinity: Viagra as a technology for the production of gender and sexuality. *Sexuality and Culture*, 5(3): 97–125.

Loe, M. (2004) *The rise of Viagra: How the little blue pill changed sex in America*. New York: New York University Press.

Lorentzen, J. (2007) Masculinities and the phenomenology of men's orgasms. *Men and Masculinities*, 10(1): 71–84.

Lousada, M. and Angel, S. (2011) Tantric orgasm: Beyond Masters and Johnson. *Sexual and Relationship Therapy*, 26(4): 389–402.

Lydon, S. (1970) *The politics of orgasm*. New York: Vintage Books.

Mace, D. R. (1948) *Marriage counselling*. Oxford, England: J. & A. Churchill.

Machin, D. and Thornborrow, J. (2003) Branding and discourse: The case of Cosmopolitan. *Discourse & Society*, 14(4): 453–471.

Mah, K. and Binik, Y.M. (2001) The nature of human orgasm: A critical review of major trends. *Clinical Psychology Review*, 21: 823–856.

Mah, K. and Binik, Y.M. (2002) Do all orgasms feel alike? Evaluating a two-dimensional model of the orgasm experience across gender and sexual context. *Journal of Sex Research*, 39(2): 104–113.

Mah, K. and Binik, Y.M. (2005) Are orgasms in the mind or the body: Psychosocial versus physiological correlates of orgasmic pleasure and satisfaction. *Journal of Sex and Marital Therapy*, 31: 187–200.

Maltz, R. (1998) Real butch: The performance/performativity of male impersonation. *Journal of Gender Studies*, 7(3): 273–286.

Marcus, B.S. (2011) Changes in a woman's sexual experience and expectations following the introduction of electric vibrator assistance. *Journal of Sexual Medicine*, 8(12): 3398–3406.

Marshall, B.L. (2002) 'Hard science': Gendered constructions of sexual dysfunction in the 'Viagra-Age.' *Sexualities*, 5(2): 131–158.

Masters, W.H. and Johnson, V.E. (1966) *Human sexual response*. Boston: Little Brown and Company.

Masters, W.H. and Johnson, V.E. (1970) *Human sexual inadequacy*. Boston: Little and Brown.

McCarthy, B.W. and Metz, M.E. (2008) The 'good-enough sex' model: A case illustration. *Sexual and Relationship Therapy*, 23(3): 227–234.

McClelland, S.I. (2010) Intimate justice: A critical analysis of sexual satisfaction. *Social and Personality Psychology Compass*, 4: 663–680.

McClelland, S.I. (2011) Who is the 'self' in self reports of sexual satisfaction? Research and policy implications. *Sexuality Research and Social Policy*, 8(4): 304–320.

McClelland, S.I. (2013) 'What do you mean when you say that you are sexually satisfied?' A mixed methods study. *Feminism & Psychology*, 24(1): 74–96.

McNulty, J.K. and Fisher, T.D. (2008) Gender differences in response to sexual expectancies and changes in sexual frequency: A short-term longitudinal study of sexual satisfaction in newly married couples. *Archives of Sexual Behavior*, 37(2): 229–240.

Measor, L., Tiffin, C. and Miller, K. (2000) *Young people's views on sex education: Education, attitudes and behaviour.* London: Routledge/Falmer.

Ménard, A.D. and Kleinplatz, P.J. (2008) Twenty-one moves guaranteed to make his thighs go up in flames: Depictions of 'great sex' in popular magazines. *Sexuality and Culture*, 12(1): 1–20.

Mercer, C.H., Fenton, K.A., Johnson, A.M., Wellings, K., Macdowall, W., McManus, S., Nanchahal, K. and Erens, B. (2003) Sexual function problems and help seeking behaviour in Britain: National probability sample survey. *British Medical Journal*, 327(7412): 426–427.

Meston, C.M. and Buss, D.M. (2007) Why humans have sex. *Archives of Sexual Behavior*, 36: 477–507.

Meston, C.M. and Levin, R.J. (2005) Female orgasm dysfunction. In R. Balon and R.T. Segraves (eds) *Handbook of sexual dysfunction* (pp. 193–214). Florida: Taylor & Francis Group.

Meston, C.M., Trapnell, P.D. and Gorzalka, B.B. (1998) Ethnic, gender, and length of residency influences on sexual knowledge and attitudes. *Journal of Sex Research*, 35(2): 176–182.

Meston, C.M., Hull, E., Levin, R.J. and Sipski, M. (2004a) Disorders of orgasm in women. *Journal of Sexual Medicine*, 1(1): 66–68.

Meston, C.M., Levin, R.J., Sipski, M.L., Hull, E.M. and Heiman, J.R. (2004b) Women's orgasm. *Annual Review of Sex Research*, 15(1): 173–257.

Mialon, H.M. (2011) The economics of faking ecstasy. *Economic Inquiry*, 50(1): 277–285.

Michael, R.T., Gagnon, J. H., Laumann, E. O. and Kolata, G. B. (1994). *Sex in America: A definitive survey.* New York: Little, Brown and Company.

Minnotte, K.L., Stevens, D.P., Minnotte, M.C. and Kiger, G. (2007) Emotion-work performance among dual-earner couples: Testing four theoretical perspectives. *Journal of Family Issues*, 28(6): 773–793.

Mirone, V., Imbimbo, C., Bortolotti, A., Di Cintio, E., Colli, E., Landoni, M., Lavezzari, M. and Parazzini, F. (2002) Cigarette smoking as risk factor for erectile dysfunction: Results from an Italian epidemiological study. *European Urology*, 41, 294–297.

Mooney-Somers, J. and Ussher, J. (2010) Sex as commodity: Single and part-nered men's subjectification as heterosexual men. *Men and Masculinities*, 12(3): 353–373.

Moore, L.J. and Clarke, A.E. (1995) Clitoral conventions and transgressions: Graphic representations in anatomy textbooks, c. 1900–1991. *Feminist Studies*, 21: 255–301.

Moran, C. and Lee, C. (2011) On his terms: Representations of sexuality in women's magazines and the implications for negotiating safe sex. *Psychology & Sexuality*, 2(2): 159–180.

Mort, F. (1996) *Cultures of consumption: Masculinities and social space in late Twentieth-Century Britain.* London: Routledge.

Moynihan, R. (2003) The making of a disease: Female sexual dysfunction. *British Medical Journal*, 326: 45–47.

Muehlenhard, C.L. and Peterson, Z.D. (2005) III. Wanting and not wanting sex: The missing discourse of ambivalence. *Feminism & Psychology*, 15(1): 15–20.

Muehlenhard, C.L. and Shippee, S.K. (2010) Men's and women's reports of pretending orgasm. *Journal of Sex Research*, 47(6): 552–567.

Muise, A. (2011) Women's sex blogs: Challenging dominant discourses of hetero-sexual desire. *Feminism & Psychology*, 21(3): 411–419.

Mulhall, H., King, R., Glina, S. and Hvidsten, K. (2008) Importance of and satisfaction with sex among men and women worldwide: Results of the global better sex survey. *Journal of Sexual Medicine*, 5: 788–795.

Neuhaus, J. (2000) The importance of being orgasmic: Sexuality, gender, and marital sex manuals in the United States, 1920–1963. *Journal of the History of Sexuality*, 9(4): 447–473.

Nicolson, P. and Burr, J. (2003) What is 'normal' about women's (hetero)sexual desire and orgasm? A report of an in-depth interview study. *Social Science & Medicine*, 57: 1735–1745.

Nixon, S. (1996) *Hard looks: Masculinities, spectatorship and contemporary consumption*. London: University College London.

Noar, S.M., Clark, A., Cole, C. and Lustria, M.L.A. (2006) Review of interactive safer sex web sites: Practice and potential. *Health Communication*, 20(3): 233–241.

Öberg, K. and Sjogren F.M.K. (2005) On Swedish women's distressing sexual dysfunctions: some concomitant conditions and life satisfaction. *Journal of Sexual Medicine*, 2: 169–180.

Ogden, G. (2001) Spiritual passion and compassion in late-life sexual relationships. *Electronic Journal of Human Sexuality*, 4, 14 August 2001. Available at: http://mail.ejhs.org/volume4/Ogden.htm.

Oliver, M.B and Hyde, J.S. (1993) Gender differences in sexuality: A meta-analysis. *Psychological Bulletin*, 114(1): 21–59.

Opperman, E., Braun, V. and Clarke, V. (2013) 'It feels so good it almost hurts': Young adults' experiences of orgasm and sexual pleasure. *Journal of Sex Research*, 51(5): 503–515.

Osborn, M., Hawton, K. and Gath, D. (1988) Sexual dysfunction among middle aged women in the community. *British Medical Journal*, 296(6627): 959–962.

Parsons, J.T. and Grov, C. (2012) Gay male identities, desires and sexual behaviors. In C.J. Patterson and A.R. D'Augelli (eds) *Handbook of psychology and sexual orientation*. Oxford: Oxford University Press.

Parvez, Z.F. (2006) The labor of pleasure: How perceptions of emotional labor impact women's enjoyment of pornography. *Gender & Society*, 20(5): 605–631.

Patrick, D.L., Althof, S.E., Pryor, J.L., Rosen, R., Rowland, D.L., Ho, K.F., McNulty, P., Rothman, M. and Jamieson, C. (2005) Premature ejaculation: An observational study of men and their partners. *Journal of Sexual Medicine*, 2(3): 358–367.

Pennebaker, J.W. and Roberts, T.A. (1992) Towards a his and hers theory of emotion: Gender differences in visceral perception. *Journal of Social and Clinical Psychology*, 11, 199–212.

Peplau, L.A. (2003) Human sexuality: How do men and women differ? *Current Directions in Psychological Science*, 12(2): 37–40.

Petersen, J.L. and Hyde, J.S. (2010) A meta-analytic review of research on gender differences in sexuality, 1993–2007. *Psychological Bulletin*, 136(1): 21–38.

Philippsohn, S. and Hartmann, U. (2009) Determinants of Sexual Satisfaction in a Sample of German Women. *Journal of Sexual Medicine*, 6(4): 1001–1010.

Plummer, K. (2003) Queers, bodies and postmodern sexualities: A note on revisiting the 'sexual' in symbolic interactionism. *Qualitative Sociology*, 26(4): 515–530.

Polsky, A. (2002) Biomedical sciences and popular culture: Mutually constitutive, not oppositional. *Journal of Medical Humanities*, 23(3–4): 167–169.

Porst, H., Montorsi, F., Rosen, R.C., Gaynor, L., Grupe, S. and Alexander, J. (2007) The Premature Ejaculation Prevalence and Attitudes (PEPA) survey: Prevalence, comorbidities and professional help-seeking. *European Urology*, 51: 816–824.

Potts, A. (2000a) Coming, coming gone: A feminist deconstruction of heterosexual orgasm. *Sexualities*, 3(1): 55–76.

Potts, A. (2000b) 'The essence of the hard on': Hegemonic masculinity and the cultural construction of 'erectile dysfunction'. *Men and Masculinities*, 3(1): 85–103.

Potts, A. (2002) *The science/fiction of sex: Feminist deconstruction and the vocabularies of heterosex*. London: Routledge.

Potts, A., Grace, V., Gavey, N. and Vares, T. (2004) 'Viagra stories': Challenging 'erectile dysfunction'. *Social Science and Medicine*, 59: 489–499.

Potts, A., Grace, V.M., Vares, T. and Gavey, N. (2006) 'Sex for life'? Men's counter stories on 'erectile dysfunction', male sexuality and ageing. *Sociology of Health & Illness*, 28(3): 306–329.

Prause, N. (2011) The human female orgasm: Critical evaluations of proposed psychological sequelae. *Sexual and Relationship Therapy*, 26(4): 315–328.

Prause, N. (2012) A response to Brody, Costa and Hess (2012): theoretical, statistical and construct problems perpetuated in the study of female orgasm. *Sexual and Relationship Therapy*, 27(3): 260–271.

Puppo, V. and Gruenwald, I. (2012) Does the G-spot exist? A review of the current literature. *International Urogynecology Journal*, 23: 1665–1669.

Puppo, V. and Puppo, G. (2014) Anatomy of sex: Revision of the new anatomical terms used for the clitoris and female sexuality by sexologists. *Clinical Anatomy*. Available at: http://onlinelibrary.wiley.com/doi/10.1002/ca.22471/abstract?deniedAccessCustomisedMessage=&userIsAuthenticated=false. Accessed 5 November 2014.

Radner, H. (2008) Compulsory Sexuality and the Desiring Woman. *Sexualities*, 11(1-2): 94–100.

Ramsdale, D.A. and Gentry, C.W. (2004) *Red hot tantra: Erotic secrets of red tantra for intimate soul-to-soul sex and ecstatic, enlightened orgasms*. Gloucester, MA: Fair Winds Press.

Reiss, M. (1998) The representation of human sexuality in some science books for 14–16 year olds. *Research in Science and Technological Education*, 16(2): 137–149.

Renshaw, D.C. (2007) Women's reactions to partner's ejaculation problems. *Comprehensive Therapy*, 33(2): 94–98.

Revicki, D., Howard, K., Hanlon, J., Mannix, S., Greene, A. and Rothman, M. (2008) Characterizing the burden of premature ejaculation from a patient and partner perspective: A multi-country qualitative analysis. *Health and Quality of Life Outcomes*, 6: 33–42.

Reynolds, E. (2007) 'Pass the cream, hold the butter': Meaning of HIV positive semen for 'bugchasers' and 'giftgivers'. *Anthropology and Medicine*, 14: 259–266.

Rich, A. (1980) Compulsory heterosexuality and lesbian existence. *Signs, Women: Sex and Sexuality*, 5(4): 631–660.

Richards, M.P.M. and Elliott, B.J. (1991) Sex and marriage in the 1960s and 1970s. In D. Clark (ed.) *Marriage, domestic life and social change: Writings for Jacqueline Burgoyne* (pp. 28–46). London: Routledge.

Richardson, D. (1996) *Theorising heterosexuality: Telling it straight*. Buckingham: Open University Press.

Richardson, D. (2004) *Tantric orgasm for women*. Rochester, Vermont: Destiny Books.

Richardson, D. (2010) Youth masculinities: Compelling male heterosexuality. *British Journal of Sociology*, 61(4): 737–756.

Richters, J., de Visser, R., Rissel, C. and Smith, A. (2006) Sexual practices at last heterosexual encounter and occurrence of orgasm in a national survey. *Journal of Sex Research*, 43(3): 217–226.

Ridge, D.T. (2004) 'It was an incredible thrill': The social meanings and dynamics of younger gay men's experiences of barebacking in Melbourne. *Sexualities*, 7(3): 259–279.

Riskin, M., Banker-Riskin, A. and Grandinetti, B. (1997) *Simultaneous orgasm and other joys of intimacy*. California: Hunter House Inc.

Roberts, C., Kippax, S., Waldby, C. and Crawford, J. (1995) Faking it: The story of 'Ohh!'. *Women's Studies International Forum*, 18(5/6): 523–532.

Rogers, A. (2005) Chaos to control: Men's magazines and the mastery of intimacy. *Men and Masculinities*, 8(2): 175–194.

Rosen, R.C. and Althof, S. (2008) Impact of premature ejaculation: The psychological, quality of life and sexual relationship consequences. *Journal of Sexual Medicine*, 5(6): 1296–1307.

Rosen, R.C., McMahon, C.G., Niederberger, C., Broderick, G.A., Jamieson, C. and Gagnon, D.D. (2007) Correlates to the clinical diagnosis of premature ejaculation: Results from a large observational study of men and their partners. *Journal of Urology*, 177: 1059–1064.

Rowland, D., van Diest, S., Incrocci, L. and Koos Slob, A. (2005) Psychosexual factors that differentiate men with inhibited ejaculation from men with no dysfunction or another sexual dysfunction. *Journal of Sexual Medicine*, 2: 383–389.

Ryberg, I. (2008) Maximizing visibility. *Film International*, 6(6): 72–79.

Sakheim, D.K., Barlow, D.H., Beck, J.G. and Abrahamson, D.J. (1984) The effect of an increased awareness of erectile cues on sexual arousal. *Behavior Research and Therapy*, 22, 151–158.

Sanders, T. (2005) 'It's just acting': Sex workers' strategies for capitalizing on sexuality. *Gender, Work and Organization*, 12(4): 319–342.

Schaefer, L.C. (1973) *Women and sex: Sexual experiences and reactions of a group of thirty women as told to a female psychotherapist*. New York: Pantheon.

Schneider, V., Cockcroft, K. and Hook, D. (2008) The fallible phallus: A discourse analysis of male sexuality in a South African men's interest magazine. *South African Journal of Psychology*, 38(1): 136–151.

Schreurs, K.M.G. (1993) Sexuality in lesbian couples: The importance of gender. *Annual Review of Sex Research*, 4(1): 49–66.

Seal, D.W. and Ehrhardt, A.A. (2003) Masculinity and urban men: Perceived scripts for courtship, romantic, and sexual interactions with women. *Culture, Health & Sexuality*, 5(4): 295–319.

Seery, B.L. and Crowley, M.S. (2000) Women's emotion work in the family: Relationship management and the process of building father–child relationships. *Journal of Family Issues*, 21(1): 100–127.

Seidler, V.J. (1997) *Man enough: Embodying masculinities*. London: SAGE.

Seidman, S. (2009) Critique of compulsory heterosexuality. *Sexuality Research & Social Policy*, 6(1): 18–28.

Shifren, J. L., Monz, B. U., Russo, P. A., Segreti, A. and Johannes, C. B. (2008) Sexual Problems and Distress in United States Women: Prevalence and Correlates. *Obstetrics & Gynecology*, 112(5): 970–978

Shilling, C. (2005) *The body in culture and society*. London: SAGE Publications.

Simonds, W. (2002) 'Watching the clock: Keeping time during pregnancy, birth, and postpartum experiences', *Social Science & Medicine*, 55(4): 559–570.

Simons, J.S. and Carey, M.P. (2001) Prevalence of sexual dysfunctions: Results from a decade of research. *Archives of Sexual Behavior*, 30(2): 177–219.

Skeggs, B. (2005) The making of class and gender through visualizing moral subject formation. *Sociology*, 39(5): 965–982.

Skeggs, S. (1997) *Formations of class and gender: Becoming respectable*. London: SAGE.

Smith, M., Gertz, E., Alvarez, S. and Lurie, P. (2000) The content and accessibility of sex education information on the internet. *Health Education & Behaviour*, 27(6): 684–694.

Sprecher, S. (2002) Sexual satisfaction in premarital relationships: Associations with satisfaction, love, commitment, and stability. Journal of Sex Research, 39(3): 190–196.

Steggall, M.J. and Pryce, A. (2006) Premature ejaculation: Defining sex in the absence of context. *Journal of Men's Health and Gender*, 3(1): 25–32.

Stibbe, A. (2004) Health and the social construction of masculinity in Men's Health magazine. *Men and Masculinities*, 7(1): 31–51.

Storr, M. (2003) *Latex and lingerie: Shopping for pleasure at Ann Summers parties*. Oxford and New York: Berg.

Symonds, T., Roblin, D., Hart, K. and Althof, S. (2003) How does premature ejaculation impact a man's life? *Journal of Sex and Marital Therapy*, 29(5): 361–370.

Tasker, Y. and Negra, D. (eds) (2007) *Interrogating postfeminism: Gender and the politics of popular culture*. Duke University Press.

Taylor, L.D. (2005) All for him: Articles about sex in American lad magazines. *Sex Roles*, 52: 153–163.

Terry, G. and Braun, V. (2009) 'When I was a bastard': constructions of maturity in men's accounts of masculinity. *Journal of Gender Studies*, 18(2): 165–178.

Thomson, R. and Scott, S. (1991) Learning about sex: Young women and the social construction of sexual identity. *Women, Risk and Aids Project* (Paper 4). London: Tufnell Press.

Thompson, S. (1996) *Going all the way: Teenage girls' tales of sex, romance, and pregnancy*. London: Macmillan.

Tiefer, L. (1991) Historical, scientific, clinical and feminist criticisms of 'The Human Sexual Response Cycle' model. *Annual Review of Sex Research*, 2(1): 1–23.

Tiefer, L. (1994) The medicalization of impotence: Normalizing phallocentrism. *Gender & Society*, 8(3): 363–377.

Tiefer, L. (1995) *Sex is not a natural act and other essays. Psychology, gender, and theory*. Boulder, CO, US: Westview Press.

Tiefer, L. (1996) The medicalization of sexuality: Conceptual, normative, and professional issues. *Annual Review of Sex Research*, 7(1): 252–282.

Tiefer, L. (2001) A new view of women's sexual problems: Why new? Why now? *Journal of Sex Research*, 38, 89–96.

Tiefer, L., Hall, M. and Tavris, C. (2002) Beyond dysfunction: A new view of women's sexual problems. *Journal of Sex & Marital Therapy*, 28(S1): 225–232.

Tolman, D. L. (1999). Femininity as a barrier to positive sexual health for adolescent girls. *Journal of the American Medical Women's Association*, 54, 133–138.

Tolman, D. L. (2002). *Dilemmas of desire: Teenage girls and sexuality*. Cambridge, MA: Harvard University Press.

Tolman, D.L. (2005) I. Found(ing) discourses of desire: Unfettering female adolescent sexuality. *Feminism & Psychology*, 15(1): 5–9.

Tolman, D.L. (1994) Doing desire: Adolescent girls' struggles for/with sexuality. *Gender and Society*, 8: 324–342.

Tolman, D. L. (2006) In a different position: Conceptualizing female adolescent sexuality development within compulsory heterosexuality, New Directions for Child and Adolescent Development, 112: 71–89.

Tolman, D.L., Striepe, M.I. and Harmon, T. (2003) Gender matters: Constructing a model of adolescent sexual health. *Journal of Sex Research*, 40(1): 4–12.

Trice-Black, S. (2010) Perceptions of women's sexuality within the context of motherhood. *The Family Journal*, 18(2): 154–162.

Tyler, M. (2004) Managing between the sheets: Lifestyle magazines and the management of sexuality in everyday life. *Sexualities*, 7(1): 81–106.

Vance, C.S. (ed.) (1984) *Pleasure and danger: Exploring female sexuality*. New York: Routledge and Kegan Paul.

van Netten, J.J., Georgiadis, J.R., Nieuwenburg, A. and Kortekaas, R. (2008) 8–13 Hz fluctuations in rectal pressure are an objective marker of clitorally-induced orgasm in women. *Archives of Sexual Behavior*, 37: 279–285.

Wade, J. (2000) Mapping the courses of heavenly bodies: The varieties of transcendent sexual experience. *The Journal of Transpersonal Psychology*, 32(2): 103–122.

Waite, L. J. and Joyner, K. (2001) Emotional Satisfaction and Physical Pleasure in Sexual Unions: Time Horizon, Sexual Behavior, and Sexual Exclusivity. *Journal of Marriage and Family*, 63(1): 247–264.

Waldinger, M.D. (2003) Towards evidence-based drug treatment research on premature ejaculation: A critical evaluation of methodology. *International Journal of Impotence Research*, 15: 309–313.

Waldinger, M.D. and Schweitzer, D.H. (2006) Changing paradigms from a historical DSM-III and DSM-IV view toward an evidence-based definition of premature ejaculation. Part 1- Validity of DSM-IV-TR. *Journal of Sexual Medicine*, 3: 682–692.

Waldinger, M.D., Hengeveld, M.W., Zwinderman, A.H. and Olivier, B. (1998) An empirical operationalization study of DSM-IV diagnostic criteria for premature ejaculation. *International Journal of Psychiatry and Clinical Practice*, 2: 287–293.

Warr, D.J. (2001) The importance of love and understanding: Speculation on romance in safe sex health promotion. *Women's Studies International Forum*, 24(2): 241–252.

Waskul, A.P.D. and Vannini, P. (2012) Introduction: The body in symbolic interactionism. In P. Vannini and A.P.D. Waskul (eds) *Body/embodiment: Symbolic interaction and the sociology of the body*. Hampshire: Ashgate.

Waterman, C. K. and Chiauzzi, E. J. (1982) "http://www.tandfonline.com/doi/abs/10.1080/00224498209551145 The role of orgasm in male and female sexual enjoyment. *Journal of Sex Research*, 18(2):146–159.

Weedon, C. (1987) *Feminist practice and poststructuralist theory*. Oxford: Basil Blackwell.

Weiderman, M.W. (1997) Pretending orgasm during sexual intercourse: Correlates in a sample of young adult women. *Journal of Sex and Marital Therapy*, 23: 131–135.

Westheimer, R. (2011) *Sex for dummies*. London: John Wiley and Sons.

Wichroski, M.A. (1994) The secretary: Invisible labor in the work world of women. *Human Organisation*, 53: 233–41.

Wight, D., Parkes, A., Strange, V., Allen, E., Bonell, C. and Henderson, M. (2008) The quality of young people's heterosexual relationships: A longitudinal analysis of characteristics shaping subjective experience. *Perspectives on Sexual and Reproductive Health*, 40(4): 226–237.

Wilkins, K.M. and Warnock, J.K. (2009) Sexual dysfunction in older women. *Primary Psychiatry*, 16(3): 59–65.

Wincze, J.P. and Barlow, D.H. (1996) *Enhancing sexuality: A problem solving approach*. Oxford: Oxford University Press.

Witting, K., Santtila, P., Varjonen, M., Jern, P., Johansson, A., Von Der Pahlen, B. and Sandnabba, K. (2008) Couples' sexual dysfunctions: Female sexual dysfunction, sexual distress, and compatibility with partner. *Journal of Sexual Medicine*, 5(11): 2587–2599.

World Health Organization (1992) *The ICD-10 Classification of Mental and Behavioural Disorders: clinical descriptions and diagnostic criteria for research*. Geneva: World Health Organization.

Young, M., Denny, G., Luquis, R. and Young, T. (1998) Correlates of sexual satisfaction in marriage. *Canadian Journal of Human Sexuality*, 7(2): 115–127.

Zapf, D. (2002) Emotion work and psychological well-being: A review of the literature and some conceptual considerations. *Human Resource Management Review*, 12(2): 237–268.

Zilbergeld, B. (1983) *The new male sexuality: The truth about men, sex and pleasure*. New York: Bantam Books.

Index

Printed in Great Britain
by Amazon